IMAGES OF IMPERIAL RULE

Images of Imperial Rule

HUGH RIDLEY

CROOM HELM
London & Canberra
ST.MARTINS PRESS
New York

© 1983 Hugh Ridley
Croom Helm Ltd, Provident House, Burrell Row,
Beckenham, Kent BR3 1AT

British Library Cataloguing in Publication Data

Ridley, Hugh
    Images of Imperial Rule.
    1. Colonies in literature 2. Literature,
    Modern—19th century—History and criticism
    I. Title
    809'.93353   PN56.C63
    ISBN 0—7099—2244—2

Library of Congress Cataloging in Publication Data

Ridley, Hugh.
    Images of imperial rule.

    Bibliography: p.
    Includes index.
    1. Colonies in literature. 2. English literature——
History and criticism. 3. French literature——History
and criticism. 4. German literature——History and
criticism. I. Title.
PN56.C63R5   1983   809.3'9358   82—25547
ISBN 0—312—40926—5

Printed and bound in Great Britain by
Biddles Ltd, Guildford and King's Lynn

TABLE OF CONTENTS

For Jenny

Preface

This book attempts to give a picture of the literature which was produced in France, Britain and Germany describing and praising the achievements of the colonial expansion of the late nineteenth century. In covering three literatures and three historical backgrounds it crosses many of the barriers between academic subjects which it was once fashionable to regard as artificial but which are real enough to trip up those who try to cross. In straying outside the confines of German literature, I have been indebted to the advice and help of Krishnan Kumar, Clive Wake and Christine Bolt, all of them former colleagues at the University of Kent. They speak more eloquently through their own works than through mine, but my debt to them is very real.

My particular thanks are also due to the German Academic Exchange Service and to the Faculty of Humanities at the University of Kent for financial assistance in undertaking the research on which this book is based.

I am indebted to Peggy Windle and Helen Gallagher for their skills with a typewriter, and especially to Nuala Clarke for her virtuoso performance on a word-processor and for her unfailing patience with a less well programmed author.

Sections of this book appeared in different form in German Life and Letters, Journal of European Studies and Revue de la littérature comparée. I am grateful for permission to reproduce this material. The extensive quotations from the work of Pierre Mille are reproduced by kind permission of Editions Calmann-Levy, Paris.

University College Dublin

INTRODUCTION: ROBINSON CRUSOE AND THE READING OF COLONIAL LITERATURE

As a young man Alexander conquered India
All by himself?
Caesar defeated the Gauls.
Didn't he take his cook with him?

Bertolt Brecht

This book is a study of the considerable body of fiction which portrayed European colonial activity during the years of 'New Imperialism', roughly in the period 1870-1914. As the European powers divided the world between themselves and scrambled over Africa, so their writers went with them, recording in fiction as well as as in historical narrative the events and issues of the colonial expansion. The literature which they left behind them is the subject of this book.

Fifty years ago the terms 'colonial literature' or 'literature of empire' would have been sufficient to define the field of our interest. Certainly in France and Germany the terms 'colonial novel' and 'colonial literature' were regarded as self-explanatory, and when writers applied them to their own works they were consciously fitting in to a defined genre. Even in English some critics have kept such phrases in currency, but with the rapid shift of taste which has consigned so much of the fiction to oblivion, above all with the shifting attitudes towards the whole imperial episode in European history, the terms have lost something of their clarity and some approach at a definition is therefore required.

Our subject is the literature in French, English and German which took its themes from the colonial conquest and settlement of the period of 'New Imperiliasm'. It is a historically limited genre. The writers we study, although not necessarily resident permanently in the colonies, regarded the activity of colonization itself as a proper and sufficient topic for literature. They focussed on the landscape, peoples and problems of the colonies, found among the soldiers, colonial administrators and settlers their central characters, and wove their plots from the fighting and farming, governing and socializing of the white colonists.

These writers inherited from the Realist novel of the nineteenth century an interest in the impact of history upon ordinary people, on Caesar's cook and Alexander's soldiers, rather than on the few great figures of the period who took decisions and played the glamorous roles in history. Like the Realists, colonial novelists portrayed the lives of ordinary people, the typical and day-to-day experiences of the many rather than only the exceptional lives of the few. They shared in a general assent to colonial conquest, even though the overall purposes of colonial expansion were seldom in the foreground of their work, which was concerned with the individual perspective, the personal benefits of colonial life to particular individuals.

The themes and preoccupations which I suggest as defining the colonial genre are found across a variety of literary forms, and on many different literary levels. Colonial literature, so defined, includes writers of the sophistication of Kipling and the more popular figures such as Henty and Maud Diver. A glance into publishers' lists at the turn of the century will show what a considerable middle-ground, in terms of quality, within the literary scene was given over to colonial themes, quite apart from the almost distinct sub-genre of the Anglo-Indian novel. The same variety can be found within French and German colonial literature, although the peaks seldom reach as high. The advantages of defining colonial literature in this broad fashion is that it preserves the distinction which both French and German writers were most conscious of, that between colonial and exotic writing, and enables them to be treated as related but separate genres. Even with this boundary the field is large enough, and one might find upward of fifty writers in each language contributing to the genre throughout the years in question. Of these I have tried simply to concentrate on those works which were taken as canonical by the earlier histories of colonial literature using critera of an often very diverse kind, sometimes aesthetic quality, sometimes 'representativeness', sometimes geographical completeness, and which focussed in an exemplary way on the issues which concern us: notably questions of the self-understanding of white colonial society, race-relations, and the political legacy of colonialism in Europe. These are, of course, historically specific questions, not general literary ones.

There have been other studies of colonial literature, and English criticism still contains regular and often excellent offerings to the imperial muse, notably of course to Kipling. In drawing the attention of English-speaking readers to the colonial fiction of France and Germany, I hope to place English writing in a wider context and to suggest a homogeneity in the various national traditions of colonial literature which goes beyond mere flag-waving. I hope to suggest similarities of a more interesting kind, bridging the often enormous gaps which exist between both the scale and nature of the various colonial territories in which these works were set.

It will be clear that this book is about the mentality and behaviour of the whites, and that the colonized peoples are not prominently discussed. Recent historians have emphasized the active involvement of the colonized peoples, the much despised 'Natives', as the shapers of race-relations and the makers of their own history. I welcome this emphasis, and it is out of respect for it that I treat colonial literature as an exclusively European phenomenon with next to nothing worthwhile to say about other races and cultures. No more than antisemitic literature can be used as a handbook to Jewish culture should colonial literature be treated as a source-book on the Third World.

Little previous criticism of colonial literature has attempted to see its subject historically, as a reflection of the European mind. Much of it has tended to overemphasize general aesthetic criteria, or - where it expressed criticism - historically unspecific moral dilemmas. Benita Parry's excellent study of the Anglo-Indian novel, however, successfully unites both colonial and European perspectives and I gladly follow her example, drawing also on O. Mannoni's brilliant study of the colonial encounter, Prospero and Caliban (1956). While the psychological insights of the work have been taken up by historians and students of race-relations, Mannoni's work has been little used by literary critics.(1) We base our reading of colonial literature on the text which Mannoni suggests as its starting-point, Defoe's Robinson Crusoe.

I

A man defies his father and leaves home in an aimless search for adventure. He begins a seafaring life and makes the early acquaintance of shipwreck and disaster. Untutored by experience, he is finally shipwrecked alone upon an uninhabited island where he spends twenty-eight years, the majority in total solitude. Released from the island by the arrival of an European ship, the man returns to Europe, leaving behind him a small settlement to cultivate the island according to the precepts he lays down. Such, as everyone knows, is the story of Crusoe, a story beloved of every generation since its publication in 1715, championed by Goethe and Rousseau among others and translated and pirated countless times into every major world language, giving a name in literary history to a veritable landslide of 'imaginary voyages'.

A historian of literature would not choose Crusoe's island as the starting-point for a literary journey to the colonies. More than one hundred and fifty years separate Defoe's masterpiece from the heyday of European colonial fiction. Still greater differences of scale divide Crusoe's modest settlement from the vast expanses of the European empires. Yet Mannoni sees in Crusoe the archetype of the colonial personality and in his island an anticipation of the essence of nineteenth-century imperialism. Above all in Crusoe's view of Friday, his belated companion in solitude, Mannoni sees the forerunner of future colonial views of the 'Native', and in their relationship an early account of the colonial race-contact which was to come. By following his argument as it impinges on the reading of literature (his observations are too well known to need repeating in toto) we may formulate an approach suitable to the reading of colonial fiction.

Robinson Crusoe is regarded by literary historians today as a work of Realism, standing 'at the fountain-head of the English realist novel' .(2) Mannoni, however, is anxious to show Defoe's novel to be entirely a work of the imagination. The technical processes of life which Crusoe has to learn are, it is true, realistically described. Crusoe solves the problems of pottery, house-building and so forth in an empirical and realistic manner. In comparison with many of Defoe's predecessors and imitators in the 'imaginary journey' or narrative of shipwreck, Defoe's approach seems positively documentary. He claims the narrative to be 'a true history of fact' without any 'appearance of fiction' in it. Few of his contemporaries could make the same claim. Yet Mannoni argues that the whole foundation of the novel is non-realistic. The external world of the island, the development of the plot, the very peopling of the island with events and other human beings are based, Mannoni shows, not on the author's observation of reality but on the externalizing of a private vision; or, to be more specific, on the working out by Defoe of 'a massive misanthropic neurosis'.(3) The landscape and its few inhabitants are transplanted from an inner drama within the author's soul.

Nowhere is this link more evident than in the pathological fear which grips Crusoe on his island, for he is frightened not of solitude but of other men. When, eventually and reluctantly, Defoe introduces other men to the island, they fall into distinct and extreme categories. There are bestial cannibals and gentle slaves, extreme examples of hostility and subservience like Kipling's 'half devil, half child' nearly two centuries later. Crusoe never looks for a relationship, either with Friday or with the subsequent arrivals on his island. Fawning and grovelling acknowledgement of his own superiority is what Crusoe seeks in the imaginary world of his island, and nothing in Defoe's handling of the plot implies that the author takes a different view of personal relations. Those who deny Crusoe due acknowledgement are consigned to the outer pale of savagery. Such is the world peopled via the neurosis of the misanthrope and paranoic, and in such a standpoint Mannoni sees a model for the exploration of the colonial mind.

In a striking image Mannoni compares the colonial to a deep-sea fish. In its normal habitat the fish is compact, adapted to survive the pressures of the sea-floor; when lifted out into the atmosphere, however, the fish expands, deforms and even explodes, since its body no longer has the external restraints to withstand the pressures inbuilt into its frame. That is to say, by analogy, 'that the personality of the colonial is made up, not of characteristics acquired during and through experience of the colonies, but of traits(...)already in existence in a latent and repressed form in the European psyche, traits which the colonial experience has simply brought to the surface and made manifest'.(4) The change of pressure is the change from Europe to the freedom and lack of constraint in the colonies. For Mannoni, therefore, the 'colonial experience' is a product of the white mind alone.(5) Friday and Crusoe have no actual relationship, no more do the colonial and the 'Native' in the colonial understanding of the colonial encounter: their meeting is the encounter of the European imagination with supposed equivalents in reality on which it has projected its trauma. The essentials of the colonial encounter are pre-formed within the European psyche, pre-recorded in the deep waters of European life and waiting merely for actual faces and landscape to take up pre-ordained roles.(6) Crusoe's island, like the fictional representations of European colonies which succeed it, is peopled with figures which lay already within the traveller's mind; the journey across the world, the shipwrecks and the strange adventures lead - although the protagonist by no means realizes this - back to Europe and to the European self.

Robinson Crusoe stands in direct descent from the great voyages of discovery of the sixteenth and seventeenth centuries, yet shows, like the whole genre of the imaginary journey, how readily the exploration of new worlds became a pretext for the demonstration of the qualities of the old. In their innumerable national variants, the Crusoe stories revealed how little interest lay in the newness of the worlds to be discovered and how much in the innate character of the discoverer, which the action of the book was designed to reveal. Hence the emphasis on the different national heroes of the stories: the Saxon, Swiss, German Robinson Crusoe, to name but a few.(7) The authors took their tastes and values overseas and saw the outside world merely as a parade ground for their own national characteristics.

Crusoe's island helps to show colonial fiction as imaginative literature, rather than as documentary evidence of actual colonial conditions. Raymond Lebel, in a major study of French colonial writing to which we return in a later chapter, sees the first cousin of colonial fiction far sooner in the text-book, the work of information, than in imaginative literature. Not only does his approach diminish the links with literary traditions already existing in the nineteenth century - Lebel was criticized in his own day by French colonial novelists for neglecting their links with the exotic tradition (8) - , but it greatly exaggerates the realism of colonial fiction, just as early accounts of America were taken too realistically by early immigrants, with disastrous results. Mannoni frees us from such narrow criteria and encourages us to see the realism of colonial fiction (the fact that places and events are described in documentary style) as superficial. The significant experience, Mannoni shows us, lies behind the narrative, is seldom made explicit in the action, and the narrative itself is therefore less than realistic.

II

We have so far discussed Mannoni's analysis in its unhistorical perspective. The argument has seemed purely personal, claiming the novel to result from a 'misanthropic neurosis' peculiar to Defoe himself. Mannoni tentatively extended this perspective when he defined the real colonial as a person 'impelled by infantile complexes which were not properly resolved in adolescence' (9), but while such insights are no doubt valuable in individual cases, they are hardly likely to be useful in helping us to place colonial literature against its historical background.

There are, broadly speaking, two ways in which the historical situation and typicality of a writer can be introduced into Mannoni's argument. The first, suggested by Mannoni himself in his account of Crusoe, is to argue that the enthusiastic reception of the book proved the novel's theme and situation to be generally applicable, and that the individual neurosis from which the novel started was characteristic of the age as well as of Defoe. 'When his dream was published...', Mannoni remarks of the meteoric success of Defoe's novel, 'all Europe realized that it had been dreaming it' (10). Mannoni extends his picture of the typicalness of Defoe's neurosis by arguing that the late eighteenth century expressed, through the twin phenomena of the 'Noble Savage' and the Terror, a contradiction similar in subject and cause to that demonstrated in <u>Robinson Crusoe</u>. The second method is not used directly by Mannoni, but is implicit in his argument and was most notably applied to <u>Robinson Crusoe</u> by Ian Watt. It is this method of historical reading which I wish to apply to colonial fiction, and which can be demonstrated here on the model of Crusoe's island.

Mannoni suggested that Crusoe peopled his island with embodiments of his own fears, and that this resulted in a tendency to see social relations on the island in extremes. The juxtaposition of cannibal and gentle slave, Caliban and Ariel, is however far from being the only such fundamental contradiction within the novel. Crusoe's actions are, for instance, motivated by on the one hand an extreme utilitarianism and on the other by a no less extreme spirituality. He sees Friday merely as a means to fulfil his own personality, never asking his actual name but blithely assuming that Friday exists and is worthy of a name only within his relationship to Crusoe. At the same time the entire action of the novel is inspired by the belief in the pre-eminence of the individual and his destiny. Crusoe comes to see the hand of providence directing the universe for the sole purpose of his own moral education. When all the members of Crusoe's ship drown in the shipwreck from which he is saved, their deaths and his survival merely serve to convince him of the importance Providence attached to his spiritual journey.

We see at work a double form of historicity here. Crusoe's world reflects its age both in the virtues which it parades and in the shortcomings and blindspots which it contains. The island is a microcosm of its age in what it trusts and in what it fears, both its light and shade come from constellations that shine in Europe, rather than on the island itself. Ian Watt has examined the novel in its relationship to the burgeoning capitalism of the early eighteenth century, and shown how it both consciously demonstrates the virtues on which capitalism grew - the dignity of the economic value of labour - and unconsciously operates as a 'monitory image' of the failures of that age.

Such a reading of the text does not 'blame' Defoe for those attitudes which, with hindsight, are recognized as a limited and even at times reprehensible. Part of his ability as a writer was that of assimilating the pressures and attitudes of his age, and making manifest in fiction factors in his society of which it was itself scarcely aware.

To take another example, still more relevant to the historical examination of colonial fiction: when Crusoe sets himself up as 'governor' of the island, he obviously seeks to escape from the class-system of Europe within which his father had directed him to so precise a station ('the middle state, or what might be called the upper station of low life'). Crusoe's exercise of his sovereign power shows, however, that the European class-system is very much with him still and conditions his own approach to the organisation of his tiny society. If, as Arnold Hauser remarked, Crusoe is 'the classical representative of the middle class' then this is because of the failings and fears of which he is unaware just as much as because of the positive values he proudly exhibits.(11)

These fears are particularly revealing in Robinson Crusoe and its successors as well as in colonial fiction. They are not simply personal, but can reveal what are felt to be the weak-spots of society and of man as part of society. We watch while Crusoe hews civilization from raw nature, to see where is he least confident; what most threatens the human status of the life he leads? Defoe's novel anticipates and dramatizes the debate comparing the state of nature and the blessings of society which was to dominate the age of Rousseau. Its plot is a commentary on this issue, and its outcome argues that man can preserve his nobility when deprived of the trappings of civilization. (The question will be relevant to that colonial fiction which spoke of the civilizing mission of the European powers in an age already tired of civilization and its discontents.) The hesitations, uncertainties and joints in the fabric of Defoe's plot give the clue to the tensions which lies underneath.

Defoe fudges the issue. He permits Crusoe to rescue from the shipwreck all the paraphernalia of civilization, in particular the tools with which he can work. Defoe allows Crusoe to take so much with him because, as Watt argues, he was anxious to prove that the division of labour which he saw spreading through his own society had not spoilt the universality of homo faber. Defoe wanted his hero to embody in his own person all the skills of civilization and to maintain them in the face of nature: his obvious-anxiety in supplying this proof suggests his doubts that a fragmenting society could be subsumed in the individuality and skills of one man.

Half a century later Rousseau compounded the confusion when, in those famous pages in Emile which commend Robinson Crusoe as his pupil's sole reading, he speaks of Crusoe as being

7

'deprived of the help of his fellows and of the instruments of various skills' (12). He wanted to read into Crusoe's story a triumphant demonstration of the superiority of natural over civilized man, a kind of manual for natural living. Rousseau showed his own historical situation as he picked on what later readers would criticize in Defoe and insisted on that 'monitory image' of absolute individualism as the positive gain of Crusoe's experience. His dismissed as 'padding' everything in the book but Crusoe's island life, and saw even the arrival of Friday, the novel's first step towards the portrayal of man in society, as a diminution of the story's interest. Once again the Utopia of Crusoe's island can be seen as dream and nightmare, and both its light and shade are historically informative.

III

With Rousseau, of course, we have reached much closer to the literature of the nineteenth century which was to shape colonial literature itself, and in particular that literature of travel which formed the exotic tradition. Before we turn to this in its own right, it is worth suggesting the way in which post-Rousseau Crusoe stories can be read in the light of Mannoni's approach and the fresh light which such a reading may shed upon European society. We restrict this brief examination to four celebrated versions of the genre.

J.H. Campe's Junior Robinson Crusoe (1795) was the most strongly Rousseauist of these variants,* based entirely on the aims Rousseau had set out in Emile, although he was at pains to point out the illogicality of Crusoe being given all the tools of civilization. He felt that Rousseau had cheated. Campe's Robinson is shipwrecked therefore with only the clothes on his back. He has to make stone axes and ropes out of lianas, he hunts with bow and arrow. He is even reduced to the pre-civilization state of lacking fire. Robinson overcomes all these problems by means of his intelligence. His achievement is natural, in that he has no tools to help him, yet it is inaccessible to uncivilized man. Friday,

---

*Also one of the most abidingly popular works of the late eighteenth century. Translated into twenty languages from the original German (including, ironically, a translation into English), Campe's work had gone through well over one hundred editions by 1900. Elke Liebs gives a fascinating account of another Crusoe story at the end of the eighteenth century which had attempted to explore the revolutionary aspects of Rousseauism through the medium of Defoe's novel (Die pädagogische Insel, Stuttgart 1977, p. 95ff, discussing J.C. Wezel's Robinson Krusoe). Wezels's book was elbowed out by the more conservative Campe's success.

with the 'weak intelligence common to him and his compatriots', is incapable of progressing in civilization.(13) Although it is Friday who obtains fire for Crusoe, he does so merely because his brute strength enables him to rub two sticks together for much longer than Crusoe can. He cannot milk the lamas with which Campe (following Defoe's original error) populates the island. Campe therefore is not tempted to cherish nature above civilization: his confidence merely comes from the fact that he regards civilization as naturally based. Already from this shift of emphasis a social hierarchy and a superior attitude to 'other races' has emerged. Like Defoe, Campe belongs to the age of imperialism in this confidence.

Nevertheless, Campe's novel displays an underlying insecurity when it comes to talk of the relationship of natural man to society, particularly in his fear that the sensual or erotic side of man would assert itself when man was freed from the trappings of civilization, and that morality might not exist in a life rebuilt outside society. It is in this spirit that the narrator reacts to the not unreasonable suggestion of his adolescent daughter that Crusoe must surely wear fewer clothes on his warm island than he did in Europe. The narrator not only claims that Crusoe remains clothed 'out of his own proper sense of modesty'; but Campe invents a particularly irritating variety of 'muskito' which zooms round in swarms, like a vice squad, obliging Crusoe to swathe himself in the thickest clothing(14). How often in colonial fiction hygiene would rush to the help of European civilization and stop those who have left Europe from leaving behind its ethical codes as well. Such episodes showed the insecurity with which Europeans viewed their own adaptation to civilized society.

Another immensely popular eighteenth century work of shipwrecked life, Johann Schnabel's Insel Felsenburg (1776) shows how important a mirror such literature is to the society of Europe. The island in question acts as a magnet to all vessels in distress, and thus as home to a variety of shipwrecks. As the community builds up, it formulates codes of behaviour clearly rooted in a reaction against the world of political intrigue and marital infidelity which prevails in Europe. As an Utopia, the island community is therefore historically specific. No less specifc to its age is the sense of insecurity felt by the community. The worst threat to society lies in the sexual side of human nature. While other island Utopias managed to solve the imbalance of the sexes organisationally by polygamy or polyandry, the author of Insel Felsenburg clearly feels sex to present society with a threat which cannot be solved socially. The problem reaches its climax during the very first settlement, when - as the only survivor recalls - it was horrific.to discover 'that my three remaining compatriots had tamed three female apes for some months past, with which they indulged day and night in the most shameful obscenities'(15). The three men fall to quarrelling over a favourite ape and kill one another.

The scene is interesting for the obvious interplay of sexual fears with the discovery of a new world. The island's jungle is peopled by the fears of the settlers' own nature, fears which, although in one sense archetypal, are historically specific, having been identified and shunned in their influence upon contemporary European society.*

The best known, perhaps even the best nineteenth-century Crusoes were J.D. Wyss' Swiss Family Robinson and Captain Marryat's Masterman Ready, both published in 1841. For today's reader they are hard going. They share a fearful smugness, a readiness to sermonise and to lecture and a reluctance to show any chinks in their heroes' armour which makes the reader wish for catastrophe to strike their island home and feel sorry when they emerge unscathed at the end of the novels. The smugness can be identified with specific features of their age. Whereas Defoe's hero used his hands and wits to survive, Wyss' family merely use their school learning. "I recognized the bush to be the candleberry myrtle (Myrica cerifera)", the father remarks conversationally during a morning stroll, showing that even when you throw a Swiss pedant on to a desert island he remains a pedant. Marryat was very angry with Wyss for the inaccuracies in his book (16) - and with cause, for Wyss' obsession with the introduction of new flora and fauna makes the island more closely resemble Noah's Ark than any natural habitat - but Marryat's group hardly get any nearer to natural survival. They solve their problems in cooking by being shipwrecked with their cook. No making fire, no trying out the local flora for edibles or masticating raw fish - leave that to the servants, seems to be the motto of Marryat's tale.

It is no coincidence therefore that both novels are concerned with group shipwrecks. The Swiss family land in perfect formation, in strict order of age and achievement. The Seagraves add to their family numbers a handyman (Masterman Ready himself) and their cook. Solitude is unthinkable, for the basis of society is the family, with a greater or lesser number of retainers. Their Utopia has left Rousseau far behind; indeed - as the Swiss father assures his sons - 'the life of Robinson Crusoe is only attractive in the pages of the Romanist (...) man is made for the society of his kind: he has need of them and their assistance'.(17)

The contrast is increased by the different presentation of

---

*The archetype is reinforced as the narrative proceeds and the apes take on the roles of slaves and menials which Friday had filled and the 'Natives' were to fill. An act of generosity towards an injured ape creates by a link of servile gratitude reminiscent of that which ties Friday to Crusoe, a new caste of servants, who collect food, build ships and 'show themselves so subservient and clever that they seemed to lack almost nothing but language'. On the ape as an early archetype of black-white race-contact see Winthrop Jordan, White over Black, Chapel Hill, 1968, p.29ff.

the technology needed for survival. Utility remains the god of the island, but whereas Rousseau had seen the opposite pole of utility to be superfluity and had therefore welcomed Crusoe's experience of necessity as a way of stripping life to its essentials, the nineteenth century saw utility in historical and progressive terms. Robinson's superiority over Friday was intellectual and moral: his successors in the nineteenth century added to that a sense of historically inevitable primacy. The Swiss father, needing a kayak, has this to say about the model provided by the uncivilized Greenlanders:

> We thought we could improve upon it; we had already given too many proofs of industrial genius to accept implicitly and without demur from the hands of a savage people an invention which the European intellect might, without any great exertions, notably ameliorate. (18)

Utility has become equated with a complacent belief in Western technology.

Even the threats to society contained in these novels display the same complacency. Masterman Ready sees only two threats to the family. The external threat, a cannibal invasion, is warded off by modern weapons. The internal threat is represented by the implausible naughtiness of little Tommy, whose disobedience provokes a series of crises which culminates in Ready's death. Marryat's contemporaries may have admired his vision of the naughtiness of children, and certainly in comparison to the militarily obedient Swiss Robinsons Tommy is almost a relief. Today, however, we are more struck by the interpretation of all evil as disobedience and by the implicit belief in the wisdom of the dominant father.

The weak spots in the ideological armoury of these families are well hidden. Perhaps Masterman Ready, who has, as a member of the lower classes, achieved personally every worthwhile measure during the family's shipwreck, is killed off lest he request a reward for his services. Certainly the Swiss Robinsons are rescued at great speed as soon as a young lady joins the party, implying that sexual problems greatly disturb its author. Certainly both books deal with group shipwrecks out of their author's fear of the effects of isolation from society on the individual. Marryat's subsequent novel, The Mission, for instance, deals with the dangers to the individual marooned on the shores of Africa, which are not physical so much as moral, a return 'to a state of barbarism' and, more explicitly, a loss of Christian faith(19). The fathers rule their islands with a firm hand and a still firmer morality: in so doing, they reveal both the confidence of their creators and a deeper insecurity at the problematic nature of a world which needs such controls. It is revealing too that the Swiss father, despite his strictures against the life of Crusoe, decides against returning to Europe at the end of the novel(20). At such moments the cultural critique of Europe hidden in the genre is most strongly felt.

IV

To summarise therefore: Mannoni offers an approach to race-relations which is located in an historical understanding of European attitudes. He invites us to read between the lines of the literature describing overseas encounter and to see it as an expression of the starting-point of the colonist rather than as a documentary record of a new world. He shows us the colonial novel holding a mirror up to the old world rather than to the new, showing 'the very age and body of the time his form and pressure'.

We have begun with a major and internationally known author, but soon will need to descend to lower levels of literary achievement. We need to remember, however, that it is not necessarily the literary giants who create those images which remain in a nation's mind or express most forcefully the thoughts of an age. The myth-images of imperialism were the product of repetition rather than of one artistically outstanding statement, just as they were products of widely disseminated opinions rather than of an individual thought(21). The pen which operates as the needle of a seismograph to record tremors not seen on the surface of society does not need to be held in illustrious hands. Indeed it was partly their lack of literary distinction and unthinking acceptance of current attitudes which permitted the colonial novelists to reflect so faithfully the currents of their age.

NOTES

1. B.Parry, Delusions and Discoveries (Allen Lane, 1972). O.Mannoni, Prospero and Caliban, translated Pamela Powesland (New York & Washington, 1964), esp. pp.97/105. For Mannoni's influence see A.P.Thornton, 'Jekyll and Hyde in the Colonies' in For the File on Empire (Macmillan, 1968), pp.328/43. One finds many echoes of Mannoni's ideas, for instance in Fanon – 'for it is the settler who has brought the native into existence and who perpetuates his existence' (quoted by Renate Zahar, Frantz Fanon: Colonialism and Alienation, translated W.F.Feuser, New York & London, 1974, p.18) – and in J.Morris, (Heaven's Command, Penguin Books, 1979, p.8) – 'as though the British had another people inside themselves (...) who yearned to break out of their sad or prosaic realities'.

2. F.W.J.Hemmings, The Age of Realism (Penguin Books, 1974), p.16.

3. Mannoni, p.100.

4. Ibid., p.97.

5. See also Sartre's preface to A.Memmi, Portrait du colonisé (Quebec, 1972), p.23.

6. A.Gide commented on this phenomenon in Voyage au Congo (1927) in Oeuvres Complètes, ed. Martin-Chauffier (Paris, n.d.), vol. 13, p.223.

7. A selection of the various 'national' Robinsons is given by A.Kippenberg, Robinson in Deutschland (Hannover, 1892), pp.39/84.

8. See below, chapter 2. Lebel was explicitly criticized by E.Pujarniscle, Philoxène (Paris,1931), p.171f.

9. Mannoni, p.104.

10. Ibid., p.103 et seq.

11. See I.Watt,'Robinson Crusoe: Individualism and the novel' in The Rise of the Novel (Chatto & Windus, 1957).

12. J.-J. Rousseau, Emile, Bk. 3 (Pléiade edition), p.455.

13. J.H.Campe, Robinson der Jüngere in Sämmtliche Kinder- und Jugendschriften, vol. 11 (Braunschweig, 1831), p.55. Emile is discussed in the preface, vol. 10, pp.iii/xiii.

14. Ibid., vol. 10, p.151.

15. Die Insel Felsenburg, ed. L.Tieck, vol.1 (Breslau, 1828), p.309.

16. J.D.Wyss, The Swiss Family Robinson (Neolson, n.d.), p.167. Marryat criticizes Wyss in letters quoted in the introduction by D.Hannay to Masterman Ready (Macmillan, 1897), p.x. Here too the admiring words on the 'naturalness' of Marryat's description of the appalling Tommy.

17. Wyss, pp. 483,274/75.

18. Ibid., pp.383/84.

19. F.Marryat, The Mission (Rex Collings, 1970), p.9.

20. Wyss, p.562.

21. Cf. L.Fanoudh-Siefer, Le mythe du nègre (Paris, 1968), pp.9/13.

Chapter One

ANTECEDENTS

If <u>Robinson Crusoe</u> offers a model for the reading of colonial fiction, it cannot serve as an introduction to the literary history of colonial writing.   For this we turn to three closely related literary traditions which had an important place in the literary history of the nineteenth century: the exotic novel, the adventure story and the literary exploration of America.

None of these genres were the equivalent of colonial literature, neither being set in the colonial empires nor seeking to portray the everyday tasks of settlement. Nevertheless, all three genres took European fiction overseas and attempted to portray white society and inter-racial relationships outside the constraints of Europe. They exercised a great influence on the reading-public, as well as upon the producers of colonial literature, and in each genre, as I hope to show, the function of the literary work was to filter the encounter with a new world through European perspectives. By the mid-nineteenth century, of course, arrivals in the United States found an existing culture which they could much less mould to their design than, in fiction at least, they could mould the 'primitive' societies which they would encounter elsewhere. The United States less resembled Crusoe's island than did the shores of Africa.   But there are too many similarities between colonial and 'American' literature for us to neglect it entirely, and in any case America stood at the fountain-head of both the exotic novel (Chateaubriand) and the adventure story (Fenimore Cooper). In their treatment of themes which would be crucial to colonial literature - European civilization and its values, race-relations and social organization - the three genres are intimately connected.

I Exotic Literature

Aimer à loisir,
Aimer à mourir
Au pays qui te ressemble! ('L'invitation au voyage')

Exotic literature is back in vogue.   Perhaps it was the age of

14

hippies and gurus which refocussed attention on this vast stream in European literature which ran from de Quincey and Beckford at the end of the eighteenth century well into the hey-day of colonial literature(1). Whether it will prove as durable remains to be seen.

The geographical focus of exotic writing shifted as the tradition developed. The narrow classic view of man bequeathed to the eighteenth century was broken by the great travels of that century, and the characteristic cry of the time - 'Who will deliver us from these Greeks and Romans?' - found its answer in the new world of America.(2) The Noble Savages who peopled the stages of the 1780s were almost invariably American Indians, and Chamfort's Jeune Indienne (1764) and Colman's Inkle and Yarico (1787) were important forerunners of the exotic tradition.(3) Bernardin brought the Indian Ocean into the tradition, while Chateaubriand returned to America. The Germans divided their attention between the East and America. In France the interest in the Middle and then Far East was strong in the late Romantic period, and with the opening of Japan to western visitors in 1853 a new orientalism burgeoned, reaching its highpoint at the end of the century. North Africa came into French fiction in the 1850s, while the Parnassians opened up the South Seas, since Cook and Bougainville's voyages the location of most terrestrial Edens and celebrated later in English letters by Stevenson, Ballantyne and Maugham. The English Romantics' flirtation with the East had been followed by a period of decline in exotic writing, until the pre-Raphaelites' renewed preoccupation with distant places. Indian themes can be found in evocations of the 'mysterious East' from the mid-century onwards, as well as in novels with English settings, but in general the English novel in this period followed a more straightforward practical and European base, partly out of disgust at the sexual licence of the French tradition.(4) In any case, as French and German writers frequently complained, the English were too busy conquering and exploiting the globe to bother writing about it. The French and German traditions were far stronger although, as we shall see, the chief impulse to exotic literature in Germany was a lack of political freedom and national identity at home: a complaint which could hardly be made of France during these years.

Repeatedly the French exotic tradition reflects a dilemma which has particular interest for our approach to colonial fiction. It showed travel to be both an assent to the unfamiliar, involving a loss of identity ('se depayser') and a recognition of the strange as the familiar (Baudelaire's 'pays qui te ressemble'). Such ambiguity went beyond mere scenic impression: it involved assessments of 'primitive' societies and the unity of the human race. At times 'primitive' societies were invested with metropolitan ideas, attitudes and language - so that the 'Noble Savage' was shown to be identical to Frenchmen, possessing one reason and common origin* - and at other times presented as utterly different to metropolitan France. Although this difference began as a vehicle for the cultural criticism of Europe, it quickly became the basis for notions of European superiority. Cultural uncertainty could yield to cultural imperium with disquieting ease.

It was of course Rousseau who did most to encourage the investigation of non-metropolitan cultures, but since as he himself complained 'philosophy does not travel' and since in any case he saw all countries through a kind of 'exotic fog' (the phrase is Chinard's(5)), it was left to the exotic novel to evaluate other ways of life in situ.

Bernardin de St. Pierre's Paul et Virginie (1786) established once and for all the place of the social-critical themes within the exotic novel. A sentimental love-story set in the remotest corners of French territory - the Ile de France - it was convinced of the rottenness of metropolitan France and set out to show that only a child of nature could escape from the curse of mainland society. When Virginie, who had grown up on the island, leaves in search of education and dowry, she discovers that the civilization of Europe is unnatural and her exotic upbringing natural. 'It is not possible,' she concludes, 'for someone brought up in nature to understand the depravities of society.' For her it is France which is 'a country of savages', not Ile de France(6). She is shipwrecked on the shores of her island (victim of a natural modesty which forbids her to strip off her clothes and swim to safety), where Paul, his faithful negro servant Domingo and still more faithful dog Fidèle wait in vain for her return.

The ambiguity of the story emerges in the relationship between the island and France. Bernardin (as befits a future director of the Jardin des Plantes) delights his readers with wonderful descriptions of the exotic flora and fauna of the island, but does so without the slightest suggestion that this profusion of nature was in any way preferable to the intervention of man. Despite the mess made of civilization in Europe, man has a mission to transform this island. By his reason Paul improves the aimlessness of nature and the agricultural methods of Domingo. Bernardin assures his readers that 'in subjecting the plants to his plan Paul did not depart from the plan of nature'.(7) The island comes to reflect Paul's reason, and Bernardin rejects all primitivism

*In the same way the nineteenth century novels dealing with urban and industrial life would pick up the bruised flowers of the proletariat (often remarking, as they did so, on the novelist's role as 'explorer' of the unknown city) and extract from them the drama and excitement of a novelty, only at the denouement of the novel to produce the princess or bourgeoise who has been slumbering under the proletarian grime like a butterfly in a chrysalis, and thus reestablish the cultural norms ostensibly broken by the encounter with the new milieu. This is but one example of the frequent similarities between the treatment of race and social class in the nineteenth century.

as he speaks of the times before Europeans arrived on the island as 'times only of crimes and errors, which fortunately no longer exist'. He includes a long list of the ills of barbarism (those 'colourful atrocities' which future civilization has erased: 'idolatry, magic, oracles, demon worship, human sacrifice, cannibalism, polygamy, incest'). He is pleased to note that these benighted activities have been 'banished to the coasts of inhospitable Africa'(8).

Bernadin, therefore, hovers uneasily between the rationalism with which Crusoe tackled his island and the Romanticism which Rousseau's cult of nature unleashed. He has that lurking desire to penetrate the inhospitable coasts of Africa and that lurking sense of European superiority over the indigene, but remains true to his age in choosing central characters too weak to act on either implication. Paul has nothing of the pioneer and merely dies of grief because Virginie is dead. Bernardin loves the island because it is different, yet loves it also because he can make it like himself.

This kind of ambiguity is present also in Chateaubriand. His work contains numerous accounts of the exotic world of America, and lyrical evocations of the vanishing world of the Indians, among whom René, Atala and Les Natchez are set. He much regrets the passing of this culture, and recreates the language and society of the Indians in each of these works. He presents America as God's gift to man, intended to allow him 'to rediscover that sublime first state from which orginal sin had made him descend'. A gift, therefore, intended to rescue Western man from that ennui which afflicts him 'the more the nations enter into a state of civilization'(9). Rene flees to the American woods after the woes of a tragic love, made worse by that immaturity and rootlessness which is the hallmark of his generation. The New World is both a refuge from the Old and a panacea to its ills; exotic and regeneratingly different. At the same time Chateaubriand's principal contribution to exotic literature was to establish in literature the pathetic fallacy of identification between the European mind and the exotic milieu. Atala was intended to illuminate those 'harmonies between religion, scenes of nature and and the passions of the human heart', to show, therefore, the congruence of the inner world with an external world no longer exotic but made familiar and ultimately subordinate(10).

The exotic's double relationship to Europe, as a corrective to its ills and a mirror to the European self, is taken to extreme lengths in the work of Gautier, Nerval and Flaubert in the mid-nineteenth century. Each of them was inspired by a loathing for European civilization of quite amazing intensity, which drove them into the extremes of exoticism. Gautier, whom Mario Praz calls 'the true and genuine founder of exotic aestheticism', said in earshot of a diarist: 'We are not French, we belong to other races'(11). It was a sentiment all would have echoed. But this belonging involved little or no appreciation for different races from any perspective other than the most egocentric. Nerval's Voyage en Orient (1851) took Gautier's claim literally, both in the narrator's identification with various oriental persona and myths and in his imaginary love-affairs with various women of the Middle East. The identifications involved very little readiness to appreciate other cultures. Nerval remarked that travels 'are a way not of studying exotic countries but of conducting the most secret analyses of the self'(12).

Travel was for the French exotics both an aristocratic and a democratic activity. It highlighted the intense self-concern, such as we saw in Nerval, and suggested that the artist's real self was blocked by the mass-society of Europe. 'I find anyone stupid who has no slaves', Flaubert wrote in a letter:

> Is there anything as stupid as equality? most of all for the people it shackles, and it shackles me desperately. I hate Europe, France, my country, my succulent country which I'd gladly send to all the devils in hell(...)I believe I was transplanted elsewhere, for I've always had something akin to memories and instinctive feelings for balmy shores and blue seas. I was born to be emperor of Cochin-China, to smoke my pipes thirty-six fathoms long, to have six thousand wives and fourteen hundred catamites.(13)

At the same time, however, the interest in other cultures implied a concern for genuine human values and relationships which went beyond this extreme aestheticism and amounted to a serious critique of Western civilization.

This can be seen especially clearly in the work of Pierre Loti, the most widely read of the later exotic novelists. Le mariage de Loti (1874), for instance, contrasts the Tahitians' peaceful and 'child-like' existence with the fact that 'in our wonderful Europe so many poor souls are killing themselves trying to earn their daily bread'(14). In Aziyadé (1879) Loti gives a generous account of the openness of relationships in Turkey which, he believes, amount to an 'equality unknown to our democratic nation and to our Western republics'(15). Such sentiments contrast oddly with the elitist principles on which his travel is based, namely, 'that everything which pleases me is good and that one must always do one's best to spice up life's unappetizing fare'(16). More important still was the relationship between the generosity of his views of other cultures and his obvious acceptance of French imperialism. For Loti at least the criticism of France did not involve scepticism about French expansionism.* Whereas Gauguin, rediscovering primitive colour and experience on Tahiti, felt 'ashamed by my own civilization', Loti managed to remain aggressively proud of it. He was prepared to use other cultures

---

*For Loti's contribution to stereotyped racial thinking about black Africa see below, p. 81.

as an opportunity to comment on his own country, but saw no reason to move from that position to any opposition to French colonial expansion. Instead he focussed his anger at European civilization against the British, blaming them (as Claude Farrère was to) for spreading the evils of civilization across the globe.(17) Exoticism and patriotism could thus co-exist in the shelter of Anglophobia.

The English tradition of exotic writing was, as we said, not strong in the mid-nineteenth century. More practical and down-to-earth writing chronicled British encounters with other cultures, and the imaginative journey, which played such an important part in American fiction of this period, was less prominent in England, save in the more popularized form of the adventure story, which the next section briefly examines. The works of the French exotics were too strong for Victorian taste, and only in the work of Lafcadio Hearn in America did Gautier or Flaubert find a direct successor in the English-speaking world. By the end of the century, however, French influence came to the fore once again, and, partly as a symptom of this, early reviewers of Kipling's work linked him to Loti and spoke of a revival of exotic writing in English. Andrew Young, writing in 1891, welcomed Kipling's work as bringing an entirely new element to Anglo-Indian literature 'because men of imagination and literary skill have been the new conquerors'. He also recognized Kipling's affinities with Romanticism.(18)

Perhaps, however, it was Rider Haggard who came closest to aspects of the exotic novel in France. To say this is not to suggest that he shared the same literary stature as Flaubert or Loti - in any scale of literary importance, Haggard would simply be out of sight - still less any of their more esoteric tastes. But he shared fully in the dilemma we observed in Loti between a Eurocentric superiority and a genuine sympathy for other cultures, notably that of the Zulus. Despite his direct involvement in the British annexation of the Transvaal in 1877, his works preserve an especial contempt for the utilitarian British mentality to which 'a native is just a native, a person from whom land may be filched'(19). He shared the exotics' taste for primitive cultures rather than directionless democracies, and in the same spirit prefaced a Zulu story, in which white deception of the Zulus plays a major part, with the remark that 'all the horrors perpetrated by the Zulu tyrants cannot be published in the polite age of melanite and torpedoes'.(20) Characteristic of the exotic tradition is the ending of <u>Allan Quartermain</u> (1887), in which Sir Henry Curtis decides to keep civilization away from the land of the Zu-Vendi; for, as he explains,

> I am convinced of the sacred duty that rests upon me of preserving to this, on the whole, upright and generous-hearted people the blessings of comparative barbarism(...) I have no fancy for handing over this beautiful country to be torn and fought for by speculators, tourists, politicians, and teachers,(...) nor

> will I endow it with the greed, drunkenness, new
> diseases, gunpowder, and general demoralization which
> chiefly mark the progress of civilization among
> unsophisticated peoples.(21)

The contempt for Africa which lurks behind even this superficially anti-western attitude is soon apparent. Repeatedly the European heroes of Haggard's novels produce demonstrations of the technical sophistication of the West which give the lie to Haggard's repudiation of European standards. In particular the Europeans' rifles, always explained with great technical detail, are used as a kind of shorthand in which the author expresses his fundamental approval for the West. Small wonder that some of the Hausa tribes used to hang guns in the trees and pray to them (22), for they had learnt this mystical attitude towards weapons from a technologically proud West, and the exotic novel's empty gestures of contempt for European civilization did nothing to dent this more fundamental sense of superiority, or to deflect the course of history.

One would expect the exotic novel in Germany to have a rather different relationship to civilization than in France or England. In the first place, the years when French writers were vomiting their hatred for France, German intellectuals had no fatherland to hate. Their early explorations of the world outside were made in the form of cautious sallies, or exuberant and final escapes, from a political and intellectual prison camp erected by Metternich. By the end of the century, however, social changes were taking place in Germany following her unification into the German Empire in 1871 with a rapidity which many found highly disconcerting, and it was more natural in that circumstance for writers to look backwards to pre-industrial days in Germany than to turn aside from Europe in exotic travel.

The two major figures are Charles Sealsfield (1793-1864) and Friedrich Gerstäcker (1816-1872). Both were in different ways rather fascinating people: the former a monk who fled his monastery in 1823 and went to America, where he established himself in bourgeois life and travelled widely, especially in the Southern States and Mexico, publishing under the pseudonym which was only uncovered after his death. His works were well received by the American public, being praised warmly, for example, by Longfellow. Gerstäcker's life seems designed for the dustjacket of novels, for after emigrating from Germany in very straitened circumstances in 1837, he worked as stoker, sailor, lumberjack and took part in the California gold-rush in 1849. His public, much wider than Sealsfield's, was essentially that of the middle-class journals which lionized both him and his works in a way which has done nothing to guarantee his memory.

Sealsfield, in particular, began to write exotic novels at a time when the political radicals were calling for literature to become involved with national life. Instead of writing from the Olympian detachment of Goethe and Schiller, writers were encouraged to portray ' the physiognomy, spirit and tone, the customs and characteristics of entire countries and times'. Because censorship did not permit such enquiries about the mass of the German people, they had to be transferred to overseas countries, just as the major studies of socialism and working-class life in the 1830's were set in England and France. Consequently, writers ascribed to the exotic tradition what they called 'a democratic character'(23). It was out of a similar sense of the democratic values of individuals and nations that the generation of the Young Germans had been drawn to the works of Cooper, and had found there a political message which would not have passed the censors if his novels had not been set in America.

Sealsfield clearly accepted the educative and political role of his fiction. Rather than offering mere entertainment and adventure, his novels set out to portray in the setting of North America 'an entire nation, its social, public and private life, its material, political and religious aspects'(24). It is clear from his juxtaposition of such novels with the 'harmful silly books, called fashion novels, which are written to exacerbate the already unnaturally tense social relations' that the portrayal of other cultures, particularly American culture, had a definite political function. To him the novel had a wider function even than information. The Germans might know all about 'the system of government of China, Japan and Siam', he complained, 'but in the process they entirely overlook their own miserable state'. To understand Japan, therefore, was worthwhile only as the first step towards understanding Germany. Sealsfield was no less anxious to establish for exotic writing a genuine place in literature, and to displace 'the thousands and thousands of immodest, stupid, fantastic and silly books which once covered the dressing-tables of ladies'(25). He moved towards what he called the 'national novel'(26), in which some critics saw a forerunner of the Realist novel of the 1850s, but which no less impressively belongs within and contributes to the exotic tradition. He work set the German novel firmly to the double yoke of the depiction of overseas cultures and the fulfilment of a domestic political task.

Gerstäcker, like Sealsfield, wanted the exotic novel to pursue both scientific and political objectives. His work was hailed by one critic as a contribution to 'comparative ethnology'. It covered a wider geographical sweep than Sealsfield, and included explicit accounts of the problems of German settlement in North and South America, a theme which came up only incidentally in Sealsfield's work. The political dimension is accordingly much greater than in the French tradition, and even his most obviously exotic novels - those set in the Polynesian islands - are strongly marked with European preoccupations.

The Missionaries (1877) is accordingly both an evocation of exotic scenery and a frontal attack on missionary activity. It tells of Bertha, a baron's daughter, who gets so involved in the missionary enthusiasm of her home church that she agrees to go out to Polynesia to marry a missionary stationed there, whom she has never met. Her husband soon reveals himself as a crudely ambitious and egotistical man whose plans for the island spoil the innocence of the society and its members. Bertha has to choose between her theology (which tells her that the Polynesians are in a state of sin) and her more human sense which shows them to be more happy, peaceful and sensually fulfilled than the Europeans. The missionaries break up the organic society and provoke great power rivalry between France and Britain. Bertha, having lost her husband in the fighting, returns to Germany to campaign against the missionary societies and their activity on the island.

The exotic elements in the setting are brought out even more strongly in Tahiti (1868). The hero, René Delavigne (obviously based on Chateaubriand's hero), jumps ship on Tahiti and marries a Polynesian girl, Sadie. Their idyllic relationship is soon destroyed, however, partly by the jealousies and ambitions of the missionaries (Stevenson passed similar judgements during his stay in the South Seas) and in part too by the efforts of the Polynesians to drive the Europeans out of their island. Far from being destroyed in the fighting, as Chateaubriand's hero had been, René abandons his wife and returns to Europe.

Gerstäcker's novel appears, therefore, to establish a contrast between the perfect happiness of Tahitian life and the disrupting and corruptive influence of European civilization and religion. Yet the novel actually contains much greater congruence with European norms than this surface impression suggests. Just as Haggard and Loti only appeared to depart from the norms which imperialism would follow, so Gerstacker acknowledges the idyll only at no cost to his own ideas. He writes conventionally of the warmth and genuineness of Sadie's affections: 'Her skin was brown and her heart beat under a gnatu coat. But it beat warmer there than under the hot black coat of the priests.' He attacks the values of the Europeans as represented by Christianity not merely because they act as a cloak for political ambitions but also because, when compared to the beliefs of the Tahitians, they seem no better than the values of 'primitive peoples'. (One recalls the splendid arguments caused by Colenso, Bishop of Natal, discovering that, as he tried to explain Old Testament stories to his African flock, they struck him as simply absurd.) Conventionally too Gerstäcker contrasts the hustle and bustle of European life with the simplicity of Tahitian life, and predictably comes out in favour of those 'carefree children of the moment, to whom palms and bread-fruit gave each day what the day required'(27). These are the conventional poses of the exotic tradition. Yet the plot of the novel shows a clear current running counter to the exotic sympathy. René is gradually drawn towards Susanne, a Southern States American with violently anti-native opinions. Despite his loyalty and affection for Tahitian society, of which his marriage has made him a part, he finds himself unable to resist the appeal of patriotism and fights for the French against the rebellious chiefs. Although the novel seems to sympathize with this resistance against outside interference, it is a very limited and entirely exotic sympathy, for it portrays the Tahitians who resist as 'fanatics', whereas René fighting for his national interests is obviously a patriot. When Sadie remains in Atiu while René returns to France (the plot is unclear here about exact motives) the explanation of their separation is an almost scientific registration of racial incompatibility. Sadie's beauty, like their love, belonged to a special and exotic environment and cannot be 'transplanted' (a favourite image this) 'like a greenhouse plant torn out of her home soil she was bound to wither and die'(28).

René, therefore, who began the novel feeling 'that he had become a new man and had torn down the bridges which linked him to the world outside', ends the novel with those bridges very much intact. Why was it that nothing came of his escape? It was argued at the time (notably, of course, by the various missionary societies whom the novel had enraged) that Gerstäcker's main purpose in writing the novel had been to further the campaign against the church which Social Democracy was alleged to be waging in Germany(29). But there is little evidence that Gerstäcker was sympathetic to social democracy, and - as we have indicated - the real problem in the novel is not the attack on the missions but the ambiguity in the presentation of the exotic. We need to see his evocation of unspoilt nature, still more than in Sealsfield, as part of a lament for the loss of naturalness in contemporary Germany. The paradise is a construction of the European mind, anxious to escape particular conditions of contemporary Europe, with the organic, tightly knit community of Tahiti corresponding closely to that Gemeinschaft whose disappearance in the face of urbanization and industrialization Ferdinand Tönnies was to describe in 1889. The picture given of natural patriarchal relationships on Bertha's estate, and its contrast to the class-consciousness of the missionaries who become her enemies, show Gerstäcker's sentimental attachment to a past world of value and human relationships which he can only recreate in distant lands.(30) Yet, just as Loti was misled by his Anglophobia into imagining himself an opponent of imperialism, so Gerstacker's work shows only a partial escape from the parochial values of Germany. Indeed, precisely his success with the nationalist middle-class public of Germany implies how grateful public opinion was to have its internal divisions glossed over by being transferred into exotic surroundings. The limitations of his outlook were shared by all his more illustrious predecessors in the genre. Colonial fiction could easily follow the Euro-centric nature of exotic writing. Here, as elsewhere, it did not need actively to destroy humanitarian traditions: if once these had existed, they had eroded from within.

II The Adventure Story

They'd sail to Heaven if they could,
had ships free passage there. BRECHT, 'Ballad of the pirates'.

Nearly all the writers we discuss belonged on the slopes of literary Parnassus. Some sat there as of right, some clung by their finger-nails to the status of 'quality' literature or held themselves aloft by nothing more than the outspokenly middle-class orientation of their taste and by their rejection of the proletarian forms of the adventure story. At the foot of the mountain swirled a vast flood of popular literature, adventure stories, tracts, serialized fiction, pulp literature of every kind, driven on relentlessly by the rotary presses, avidly seized upon by the mass public and frowned upon by critics and by those authors clinging to the higher ground.

In numerous ways this popular literature related to imperialism, both in its plots of travel and adventure and in the themes which it included. Those who have charted this field point to a number of issues which our own discussions have raised: the alteration of insularity and cosmopolitanism, the discovery of national character in exotic milieux, the racial and national stereotypes scattered throughout this literature.(31) To attempt a full account of the relationship between this writing and imperialism would break the introductory function of this chapter, and instead, on the basis of a very few examples (for which no great typicality is claimed), we suggest ways in which the popular adventure story anticipated colonial literature, both in its themes and - more interestingly for our reading of colonial literature - in its internal structure.

Some of these elements form the subject of Martin Green's aptly named study <u>Dreams of Adventure, Deeds of Empire</u>. He has pointed out the way in which popular literature, far more than 'good' literature, propagated enthusiasm for action and national enterprise. The serious Realist novels of the nineteenth century stood back from the militarism of the state and the activity of industrial capitalism either in open criticism or in 'silent resistance'. It was left to the literary second-raters to propagate 'the energizing myth of English imperialism'(32). In the same spirit George Borrow had claimed of <u>Robinson Crusoe</u>, one of the seminal works in the development of the adventure story, that England owed to it 'astonishing discoveries both by sea and land, and no inconsiderable part of her naval glory'(33). Scott continued to write novels with the ambition 'to reinforce the constructive energies of his people', a plan which Green claims, 'makes him, and the other adventure-tellers, so unlike serious writers'(34). Exactly that spirit emerges from the remark of one of those serious writers, the German novelist Wilhelm Raabe in a letter to Gustav Frenssen (whose novel on the Herero war was one of the more violent examples of the 'energizing myth'). Very defensively Raabe claimed: 'Really my works have not done anything to stop people building ships, taking Samoa and conquering China'(35). The argument that they had done nothing to <u>encourage</u> those conquests stands by default.

We accept Green's argument and need not repeat his material. There is, however, a reading of the adventure story, no less important to our own reading of 'colonial fiction, which runs against the picture of the adventure story as a literature merely of noisy assent to European imperialism. The adventure story contained, no less strongly if less conspiciously than 'serious' literature, a silent resistance to European society. It took refuge in the worlds of escape and adventure rather than in that inner world of value to which the 'serious' novelists repaired. The escape of popular literature was from those aspects of European society all too familiar to its readership: the darker sides of the class-system, and we might argue that it was experience of this shadow which made the adventure story plead for a place in the sun.

Something of this resistance had been visible in Crusoe, and in his behaviour towards his slave-boy and later towards Friday there are certainly compensations for his experience at home. The theme of travel was, as we saw, an attempt to guarantee the integrity of the personality in an age ever more inclined to deny it by the division of labour. Defoe's introduction of the bourgeois as adventurer had touched on heroic qualities implicit in the bourgeois ethos but unrealized within the domestic social life of the bourgeoisie. How much more, as literature moved down towards the lower-middle and then proletarian classes, would the genre have to offer those whose chances of self-expression and heroism within Europe were so minimal. Yet here too the liberation into adventure meant to others a new oppression, and involved ultimately an asset to imperialism.

I want to argue, therefore, that the adventure story contains a double structure: a sublimation of the uncomfortable pressures of the European class-system into a positively heroic encounter with the world outside. The nature of that encounter would be conditioned by the intellectual climate of the day, but its function as the expression of a social liberation from Europe would remain constant. As the openness of the late eighteenth century towards other cultures gave way to a more narrowly Euro-centric perspective, the external trappings of the adventure story changed. Just as Biggles flies aeroplanes rather than tramping the veldt and prairie on foot, like the heroes of Cooper or Haggard, so his view of the 'Native' will be different from theirs. Yet these are externals, and the adventure story itself (as the Biggles series demonstrated) can operate successfully even in the age of decolonization, for its inner voice is more important than its adoption of the strident voices of imperialism.

It happens that in many of the early nineteenth century adventure stories the inner and external voices were in harmony in their praise of liberty. Trelawny's Adventures of a Younger Son (1831), for instance, managed to express the author's desire for liberty both in its portrait of Europe and in its relationship to other cultures. The theme of escape from Europe happily coincides with that of respect for the freedom of other peoples. 'Let us change our country and caste', Trelawny's hero is exhorted, 'and find a home amidst the children of Nature'.(36) Both the change and the choice of a new home are rooted in the love of liberty. The hero escapes to the life of a privateer, scorning conventional morality and patriotism, and Trelawny shows the motive for this escape in the vivid pictures he gives of the bondage of school and naval disciplines in England. His hero is thus naturally inclined to the worship of the 'sun of freedom(...) dawning on the pallid slaves of Europe'(37). The freedom of his life-style, the lack of constraint to law, or country or class is the central aspect of the adventure story as such, and it is an historical accident that, writing in the wake of eighteenth century humanism, Trelawny wishes other cultures to express that freedom. To seal that wish his hero marries out of his own culture and finds perfect happiness with an Arab girl. Although, in the style of the adventure story, he is a violent and swashbuckling man (such are the roads to escape from Europe), he teaches a lesson in cultural relativism as strict as any eighteenth century 'philosophe' might have taught:

> 'The light is not less bright because unobscured by, what
> is falsely called, civilization, on these wild children of
> the desert. Though they are not warmed and cooled
> by the same summer and winter, as old Shylock says,
> as Jews and Christians are, yet if you prick them, they
> bleed, - and so forth'.(38)

Ten years later Gustave Aimard remained loyal to this view, and his adventures often involved the demonstration of the common humanity (and indistinguishable appearance) of Europeans and Indians. The eighteenth century's praise for the Noble Savage even took on the modern form of overt praise for the nationalism of the South American Indians, although their struggles with the European conquerors would always be defeated(39). With Aimard's work the liberating structure of the adventure story was beginning to be invaded by the enslaving mentality of imperialism. As the myth of the Noble Savage gave way that of white superiority, such ambiguity became a common-place.

The coexistence of conflicting structures is graphically illustrated in the popular adventure stories of Jules Verne. Just as interest in colonial fiction seems to have revived, as part of the reading of the secret mind of the Victorian period, so Verne, for many years cold-shouldered by literary critics, seems to be coming back into regard. There are plenty of reasons why this should be so. The imaginary journey, the archetypes of the modern age in its mechanical and social-organisational forms, the mythological quests which fuel so many of science fiction's space craft - all these can be found in Verne's work, and their investigation is a particularly interesting key to the nineteenth century mind, grappling with the problems from which the twentieth century has not yet found an escape. Nevertheless, the specific goals of Verne's journeys and the terms in which he describes them, have no less obvious affinities with the time-serving elements of imperial fiction.

Recent study has suggested the close connections between the theme of escape and travel and Verne's personal disillusionment with the political failure of the 1848 revolution. It was as a disappointed revolutionary that Verne took to the road, and with a sensibility attuned to the political unfreedom of Europe that he charted the travel and free adventure of the world. The sea across which his plots move is, as Jean Chesneaux remarks, a sea of liberty, 'a philosophical notion and not simply a piece of tourism'. Verne's preoccupation with imaginary and real travel is 'the negation and antithesis of the policed and constrained society he found on terra firma'(40). Under the black flag of the 'Nautilus' there fly many of the social hopes of the 1848 revolution, together with many of the national ambitions which European intellectuals were anxious to take aboard at the spring-time of the nations. The imaginary journeys of Verne's heroes are real enough when we see them against the background of political disillusion, but they reveal their historical situation no less concretely by assenting to the forms which contemporary oppression adoped outside Europe. While there are still traces in Verne's thought of the earlier stereotype of the Noble Savage, the more negative images of the imperial age predominate.

As Phileas Fogg journeys round the world in eighty days, in pursuit of some freedom of which Mr. Fix, the detective, tries to deprive him, he never bothers to alter his European perspectives or to extend the freedom he seeks to those nations who lack it. He jeers at India with its 'stupid fanatics' and Thugee kings, much as the colonial novel would, and portrays the people of Africa with the same racial stereotypes which can be found in most imperialist fiction. While his liberalism emerges in his sympathetic view of negro emancipation in America, Verne's dismissal of Africans' features as 'squat and preposterous' suggests other sources.(41)

Verne's picture of the exotic world illustrated one other dimension to the literature of adventure which would also play a great role in colonial fiction: namely that travel and exploration are ensnaring the world in the meshes of knowledge and science and that each journey is a step on the road of progress. One novel describes a group of scientists in Africa, measuring the meridian and thus establishing precise scientific standards in a wild continent. For the scientists the journey is one of escape and adventure, escape from the narrow prejudices of Europe (the Crimean War is being fought out in Europe while they work together as free men in Africa) and escape into a larger dimension of manhood and personal meaning.(42) The archetype of adventure is preserved, yet with every triangle which the scientists measure Africa is diminished, the tribal cultures give way and the unknown yields its mysteries. Myth and mystery give way to knowledge, the alchemy of adventure is integrated into the ruthless de-mystification of the world, and the literature which follows adventure condemns its sympathy with the exotic to a decorative function on the sidelines of world-history. If indeed these stories include the energizing myths of imperialism, part of their energy (and most of their usefulness) comes from an implicit acceptance of the separate courses of history and adventure. The Utopian socialism which Jean Chesneaux detects in Verne's work is all the more passionate for being convinced that it is powerless. The passivity of the reception (as well as the creation) of the adventure story seems to imply that the strength of the world will be unshaken.

Just this series of contradictions can be found in Karl May's work, an oeuvre which we must regard as archetypal of the nineteenth century adventure story: passivity and revolt, prejudice towards and identification with the unknown, personal values and historical inevitability. May's own life shows the central role which oppression played in the head of steam driving the adventure story. Perhaps illegitimate, imprisoned for petty frauds, crushed by poverty and the scorn of the established literary figures, May was unable to escape from his own life by writing about it. (Critics have commented on the failure of his attempts at autobiographical social reportage.(43)) Instead he escaped into magical lands of adventure, before all else the Wild West of his Apache hero Winnetou and the mythical East of Kara Ben Nemsi. He had never actually been to these countries (indeed there are amusing accounts of his later visits to the countries he had claimed to know so well: an at times embarrassing encounter between imagination and reality), yet he totally identified with these adventure heroes and claimed first-hand knowledge of their world. 'I really am Old Shatterhand and Kara Ben Nemsi, and I have experienced what I narrate', he wrote in a letter(44). He had said the same thing to the police on one occasion when, to avoid arrest, he had posed as an American citizen (appropriately choosing the name Willkomm would give to his idealized American hero: Burton). Not only did May identify with his hero, but the reader is invited to do the same - with Old Shatterhand, that immensely strong, loyal, gifted and sympathetic German who tells the story of Winnetou - and to use the same gateway of escape as May himself had used. The incredible popularity of the stories implies that the need for escape was widely shared.

In discussing his literary beginnings, May tells how readily available were literary solutions to the frustrations of poverty. His account of the lending libraries of his childhood presents a useful snapshot of the submarine life in the flood of popular literature in the 1840s:

> Rinaldo Rinaldini, King of the Bandits, by Vulpius, Goethe's brother-in-law, Sallo Sallini, the Noble King of the Bandits; Himlo Himlini, the Merciful Bandit; the Bandit's Den on Mount Viso; Bellini, the Admirable Bandit. The Beautiful Bandit Bride, or Innocent yet Unjustly Condemned. The Starvation Tower, or the Cruelty of the Law. Bruno of Lionfield, Priest-Garroter. Hans of Hunsback, or the Mercenary who was Friend to the Poor. Botho of Madrock, Saviour of the Innocent. The Sins of the Archbishop...(45)

It is striking how many of the titles were of the rebel, the outsider, and transposed into crime or adventure the issues of oppression and injustice. May's novels, far from dealing with the steady self-help recommended by the bourgeois novel, handle large-scale and violent adventure themes, where success and happiness rest on criteria utterly different to those of Europe. His heroes are able to redress wrongs for which Europe had found no solution. 'Who will dare to block the way of a free man under God's sky?'(46) - such a claim to independence had enormous appeal to those who knew the dependence of European poverty. Old Shatterhand, who can dash a man to the ground with one blow and shoot straight, is the champion of their rights and turns the frontier into a world luminous with right and wrong, justice and reward. The innumerable happy-ends of May's novels, the cliché from which serious novels backed away in horror, offered a transcendent answer to the unalleviated misery and injustice known by Europe's oppressed.

May, like Trelawny, shows his ancestry to be in the heroic age of the bourgeoisie. At a time when sections of the European novel were retreating from the present into historical plushness and ornament, May plucked the active strain from the popular historical fiction of his youth and went back to the 'ideals which the bourgeoisie had gilded during its rise and struggle with feudalism' - justice and individual rights.(47) So doing, his work is linked to Defoe and the emphatic individualism of Crusoe. Gert Ueding said of May: 'The bourgeois capitalist man of action, blessed with all the virtues that the philosophers of the eighteenth century had ascribed to him, was resurrected in the Wild West.(48)

As he took over this ideal, May also took over the cultural values of the previous century. The Great Spirit worshipped by May's Apaches is the same spirit cultivated in the salons, viewing 'not the different skins of men, but their hearts'(49). The Germans who befriend the Apaches, such as Old Shatterhand and Klekih-petra, have fled to the American wilderness not merely to escape from Europe but to give and teach of the light of civlization. May wishes to spread humanity and justice more widely than to the white poor.

Nevertheless, May belongs firmly to the nineteenth century, and the Great Spirit has Hegelian ancestry too: progress as well as humanity is its progeny. From the opening page of <u>Winnetou</u> we are told that the Apaches' downfall is inevitable, brought low by 'a cruel law, that the weaker must give way to the stronger'(50). Old Shatterhand himself is a man of science, like Verne's explorers, measuring and surveying the traditional homelands of the Apaches for white settlement and for railways. His friendship for the Indians does not hold him back from the plans of the palefaces, nor does his love of their culture make him bend by one inch the railway lines which will oust them from their lands. On Winnetou's grave the epitaph is placed: 'Here lies the red nation: it did not become great because it was not decreed that it should become great'(51). The adventure may include and glorify the Apaches, but it does not contemplate changing their role as losers, or recognize that the rights of the stronger which cause their downfall may be behind the class oppression of Europe.

The adventure story alerts us to processes at work within colonial fiction. The 'energizing myths of Empire' can certainly be found there, far more than in Flaubert or Eliot, so to can a confidence and assurance in travelling beyond the parish pump. The assent to these myths, however, involved a conscious rejection of the existing power-structures of Europe: a rejection which, in its turn, stopped short of radical change. 'We can only lament', comments May's narrator, 'we can change nothing'(52).

In the mid-1930s, when Ernst Bloch evolved his reading of Karl May, he was looking to salvage revolutionary impulses within the bourgeoisie which he might mobilize against the dictators. He argued, as we have, for the truthfulness even of the lies of the adventure story and claimed that the pulp novel's dreams are 'in the last resort always of revolution'.(53) It is my argument that something of this revolutionary heritage passed into colonial literature. The class tensions and that fearing assent to history which speak through the adventure story can also be heard in the still more strident tones of the colonial novel, and without Bloch's example they might not be noticed.

III   Europe in the Mirror of its Vision of America

> America! What name is as weighty as this name? Save in the sphere of imagination there is nothing loftier in the world. The individual speaks of his better self: the globe says 'America'. The word is the final chord and the great cadence in the concert of human perfections. What is impossible in Europe is possble in America: only what America finds impossible has the right to regard itself as truly impossble. I see in America the supreme healthy development of the mature human body: apart from America there is only convulsion and delirium.   FERDINAND KÜRNBERGER

> ...that Republic, but yesterday let loose upon her noble course, but today so maimed and lame, so full of sores and ulcers, foul to the eye and almost hopeless to the sense that her best friends turn from the loathsome creature with disgust.   CHARLES DICKENS

> It was the nightmare of the Old World taking on flesh and blood, turning out to be substance and not dream.

> JAMES RUSSELL LOWELL (54)

For over half a century the United States have been occupied in awakening from the American dream. To the extent that the dream was a domestic American preoccupation it has little relevance to our study, but in its original guise of an European dream transposed to distant lands for its realization the dream demands a brief place. The European literature dealing with America treats of problems of settlement, race-relations and the values of civilization in a way which forces comparison with the colonial literature at the end of the century. I wish to examine that shifting evaluation of America which is shown in the quotations prefacing this section, the belief in the regeneration of western civilization by America which turned sour and then realized that the causes of the failure of the dream lay with the dreamer rather than with America itself. In other words, the European literature dealing with America in the nineteenth century demonstrates not merely the colouring of America with European expectations, but the anticipation of attitudes and problems still only latent in Europe.

America starred from the moment of its known discovery as a vision of paradise, and from 1776 as a vision of political liberty which Franklin's dazzling success with the 'philosophes' did much to consolidate.(55) But the seminal work for the early nineteenth century was St. John Crèvecoeur's <u>Letters from an American Farmer</u> (1786). The book's lyrical evocation of the freedom and dignity of the American farmer endeared it to the English Romantics, and also to Bernardin, who found confirmation of his confidence in those 'northern muses' who by industry and rational labour were transforming the world. Crèvecoeur's letters reveal both the poetry and the ambiguity of Rousseau's cult of nature. He explicitly encouraged the European disillusioned with civilization to believe that in 'the unlimited freedom of the woods' he could shake off the Old Man with 'all his ancient prejudices and manners' and be reborn in the image of nature.(56) The letters reinforced the importance conferred on America by her political achievements as a land of promise and individual and cultural regeneration.

Crèvecoeur has a double interest for the student of colonial literature. He created the idyll of the absolute independence of the colonial settler, and gave currency to a series of potent myths of the frontier which lay behind much later American and colonial fiction. He saw the settler's life as a remedy against the ills of the European class-system: 'For the first time in his life (the settler) counts for something: for hitherto he has been a cipher.' He saw positive and negative sides to this, for the settler 'forgets that mechanism of subordination, the servility of disposition which poverty had taught him; and sometimes he is apt to forget too much, often passing from one extreme to the other'(57). Colonial fiction too would demonstrate the dangers of a frontier individualism which overreached itself. Crevecoeur encouraged this extreme individualism with his claim for the farmer of equality with the emperor of China and his praise for the frontier's lack of moral constraint(58). When he confronted the evil of the frontier mentality shown in slavery, Crèvecoeur's ideology crumbled and with it all belief in the goodness of nature and confidence in the hierarchy of the strong. Instead he merely despaired of all human activity. In a celebrated final letter, fearing the destruction of his farm in the War of 1776, Grèvecoeur decides to take refuge with the Indians. Rejecting civilized norms, he expresses admiration for the Indians' freedom from anxiety and sense of sin, their patience and their philosophy, yet fears the appeal which the life of the savage may have for his children(59). At a moment of such ambivalence, torn between cultural superiority and inferiority Crèvecoeur belongs among the intellectual ancestry of the colonial novel. Perhaps his decision to take up residence in a 'wigwham' suggests a genuine cultural sympathy for the Indians (it need not be interpreted in that way, since, as Lawrence rather contemptuously points out, Crèvecoeur merely travelled to Europe after the final letter 'in high-heeled shoes and embroidered waistcoat, to pose as a literary man'(60)); it at least underlines the ambivalent relationship of civilization and wilderness so close to the heart of American and colonial fiction.

Crèvecoeur's picture of the frontier-life occupies an important place among the myths of American culture. American writers have repeatedly evoked it in order to counteract tendencies in American life of which they disapproved. It is not surprising therefore that Crèvecoeur's Letters made a great contribution to the myth of America emerging in Europe, and that its function there was also the oblique criticism of civilization. We saw aspects of the Letters in Bernardin's juxtaposition of the Ile de France and metropolitan France. In Germany it was particularly Charles Sealsfield who took up Crèvecoeur's farming idyll, and in a series of novels devoted to American provincial life created pictures of domestic life which highlighted all that was wrong in European society.

> Our country life is imbued with a quality which it is hard to define yet which gives it a particular charm. The truly majestic independence, the absence of everything which we call particularism, the unfettered participation in the major issues of the nation and by this means in the events of the world, a participation which gets greater as our republic's influence in the outside world comes to be felt more - all this lends our country life in the absence of all narrowing confines a certain dignity, indeed a sovreignity which is regal. There's tremendous attraction, a magic charm in this country life, differentiated as it is by a cosmopolitan quality and by that self-respect which, bowing only to God and to the Law, is based on the consciousness of inalienable rights. This country-life is the true basis, the foundation of American freedom, and in it alone the citizen of the Union is seen to be great and truly free. In the bustle of the towns his native independence vanishes and we see him as that awkward and inflexible, strangely aristocratic being lacking all naturalness and

> merely imitating the customs and habits of other
> countries.(61)

While this picture obviously derives from Crèvecoeur, it is no less
clear that its approach to American life is conceived within German
terms. Its particular emphasis is political, but it is the politics
of Germany rather than of America which is striking. The escape
from particularism (that proliferation of small states in Germnay
so different from American federalism), the insistence on the
citizen's participation in the currents of world affairs, the
confidence in declaring the birth of an independent and free system
of culture and manners: these elements in this passage reveal its
origins. Whatever truth the picture may have as a report about
America it reveals the truth about Germany, by the nature of its
aspirations and hopes.

It is characteristic also that Sealsfield has little to say about
the Negro problem, or (more significantly, since his setting is the
American West rather than the South) the American Indian. For
an admirer of Fenimore Cooper, Sealsfield is positively silent on
that topic. Admittedly he contrasts the democratic society of the
United States with the corrupt and oppressive 'aristocracy and
hierarchy' of Mexico, and complains that the abolition of slavery
in Mexico is no than a 'legal fiction', but his interests do not
really lie in understanding the oppressed situation of the non-
whites. His narratives focus instead on showing the redemptive
impact of the American soil on the immigrants from Europe and
he concentrates his praise on the 'aristocratic democracy' of the
whites who are building a true republic out of the ruins of the
European class-system.(62) A contemporary German visitor to
America, Leopold Schefer, had already pointed to this dubious
element in German/American conceptions of democracy. His novel
Die Probefahrt nach Amerika (Trial run to America) (1837) had
observed: 'here all the whites are noble, or at least feel themselves
to be such, and all the blacks are canaille'.(63) It is a description
of society such as colonial fiction frequenty gives, more or less
advertently. Pierre van den Berghe coined the phrase 'Herrenvolk
democracy' to describe it, and showed how the term also applies
to colonial social structures in South Africa(64). A biographer was
surely right to define Sealsfield's opinions 'not as democracy in
the sense used by present-day socialists but as a kind of social
aristocracy, which recognizes the rights to power of the
stronger'(65).

This insight into the limited concept of democracy is
interesting not merely as a visitor's opinion on America. It reveals
the extremely narrow conception of democracy which an European
liberal such as Sealsfield held. In the idealized picture which he
gave of America those limitations were much more explicit than
they had become in the Europe of his day. Indeed, it was not
until the reforming liberals confronted the revolutionary proletariat
in Paris and Berlin in 1848 that many of them realized that they
were democrats only in the most limited sense. The portrayal of

America offers in this way an anticipation of developments later in Europe.

Much the same comment can be made on the pictures given of the United States by British visitors in the nineteenth century. Not merely the coexistence of the cult of equal opportunity with a critique of the effects of economic liberalism offers a key to the problems of contemporary Britain. In the all but total ignoring of the Negro problem British visitors gave a clue to the narrow orbit of their social understanding. 'It is incredible,' comments one historian of these visitors, 'to realize the extent to which the visitors(...)managed to ignore the plight of the American Negro'(66). Two generations of Noble Savages had done little to alter social sympathies rooted in economic interest. It is clear also that the frequent comment that America was without pauperization came (like Friedrich Muench's well-publicized promise to German immigrants that there was no proletariat in the United States) from wishful thinking rather than observation.(67) In Martin Chuzzlewit Dickens gives a nice illustration of this point when he shows the ambiguous relationship between British domestic class-relations and British views of American class-relations. Martin Chuzzlewit is very critical of the gap which he observes between the general talk of equality and the thoroughly hierarchical practices of American society. Many visitors made similar criticisms, but Dickens' purpose in this section is not to criticize America but to show Chuzzlewit's appalling snobbishness towards his own working-class companion, Mark Tapley, whom he mistreats even while complaining of America's snobbery. The criticism of America turns round on the critic.

Even de Tocqueville's classic account of Democracy in America (1834) had been written with an eye to events in Europe just as much as to those in America. He regarded as inevitable the onmarch of European societies towards a democracy similar to that already established in America, and his work was intended as a contribution to understanding and preparedness by seeing the future of Europe anticipated across the Atlantic. His subject was the actual historical evolution of nations; ours is the way in which European reporting of America illuminated tendencies latent but as yet unrealized within European society, America therefore as a Crusoe's island on to which Europe projected - wittingly and unwittingly - its fears, prejudices, hopes and therefore its own future. Like colonial fiction, the literary portrayal of America held great scope for the transposition of European problems into exotic settings. Leslie Fiedler has written, for instance, on the role of the Battle of the Sexes (and, for our context more relevantly, on the role of race confrontation) as a transposition into American culture of the class-warfare which the new Americans had left behind in Europe.(68) Both seem more than likely, although, as colonial fiction too will show, the presentation of American sexual relations also owed much to a widespread feeling that European society offered too restricted a role to women. Class-relations were therefore, not the only pressures in play.

This perspective makes one challenge a traditional liberal view of relations between America and (especially) Britain: namely that the example of the United States helped to push Europe down the road towards democracy.(69) We gain an overwhelming impression that visitors to and writers about America projected their own situation into America and what they learned from America was often only self-knowledge. Despite the stereotypes which exist in surveys of European-American relations - the French were 'more enthusiastic' than the British, the Germans 'more encyclopaedic', the British biased by the 'loss in America of a colonial empire'(70) - the process of self projection and self-identification in America holds true for all the European nations across the absolutely enormous volume of literature produced about America in the nineteenth century. While the most notorious visitors were English (Dickens, Captain Marryat, Mrs. Trollope and much later Kipling), the market in Europe for such literature was undifferentiatedly vast. Much of the literature is merely local colour reporting (eating habits, spitting and other trivia playing an important part: 'many men would willingly endure America's vices,' de Tocqueville had commented, 'who cannot supports its manners') and need not concern us. But especially in Germany a stream of literature appeared which focussed on precisely the issues which were to arise in colonial fiction, and which Crèvecoeur's work had discussed.

Such literature was particularly prevalent in Germany because of the enormous flow of emigrants to the Americas out of Germany. Whereas the population of France was in relative decline from the end of the Napoleonic period, Germany's population was increasing rapidly and this, together with the various political set-backs which hit Germany during the first seventy years of the century (as well as the pretty major shocks in the last thirty), drove hundreds of thousands to seek a new home. German writing about America therefore after Sealsfield was coloured by the demands of the emigrants, actual and prospective, who were looking not for adventure or exotic charms but for settlement possibilities. Ever since Gottfried Duden, in a very widely read account of a journey across the United States published in 1829, had harkened rather more to the exotic muse than his readers had wished (for they used the work as a cross between an agricultural handbook and a railway timetable, with disastrous results), writers had been careful to concede nothing by way of accuracy. Even an exotic novelist such as Gerstäcker was closely involved in the practicalities of immigration.(71) Since writers not only assessed America from the immigrant's standpoint, but also evaluated Germans from America's standpoint, as potential citizens, their work was committed to series of complex mediations of domestic problems.

This trend was begun, very naively, by Ernst Willkomm in the novel Die Europa Müden (Tired of Europe) in 1838. Willkomm, a sympathizer with the reform movements of the 1830s who was to write some of the earliest accounts of industrial life in Germany, gave in this novel an image of America as seen by the disenchanted of Europe, who interpret their personal unhappiness as a symptom of general cultural malaise. 'The natural has got lost in man,' the narrator argues, 'Europe has not emerged from the ancien régime; its curse sticks to Europe and holds her down in a sleep of death.'

It is to this world that Burton, an American visitor, comes as liberator and at the end of the novel whisks all the characters off to 'the banks of the Mississippi'. In his own person Burton enshrines all the virtues which are said to be unrealizable in Europe. 'In this man we could find no trace of ennui, no sense of repulsion at the world', the narrator writes in rapt admiration, and goes on to give a portrait of the American made up of everything the Germans wanted to be:

> All his being expressed a healthy clear intelligence, made strong and broadened by the struggle with gigantic nature. No well-bred hypocrisy curled his lips to phrase a courtly lie as we Europeans love to hear. His eye held fast to reality and allowed me, in his practical sense, to see the future of the world in an ideal form.(72)

Comparing this picture with de Tocqueville's remarks of some four years previously ('I found very few men', he complained, 'who displayed that manly candour and masculine independence of opinion which frequently distinguished the American in former times'), we realise how much more Burton owed to Germany than to America. Burton himself is little surprised at the adulation. He's a worthy forerunner of those American boasters lampooned in Martin Chuzzlewit. His explanation of his superiority remains in the Crèvecoeur tradition as he speaks of the social-pastoral life of the 'still undesecrated interior of America', which has made him what he is. He encourages to flee thither all 'whom anguish drives out of Europe and who seek healing for their breaking heart'.(73)

It is no surprise to the reader of Willkomm's novel to learn that he had never been to America. His expectations are such as only ignorance can supply, and the book says little more about America than Goethe's much quoted lines 'America, you have it better/than our old continent(...)'

As the flood of immigrants increased, they formed experiences of America which hardly lived up to Burton's promise, meeting not idealism but corruption and hostility. A prominent member of the disillusioned was the poet Nikolaus Lenau, who made a famously disastrous trip to America in the 1830s, hoping to make money and refresh his soul in the forests. (The commissioner for immigrants in New York greeted him with the cruel comment: 'This young man is looking for inner peace: take him off to a field, give him a hoe and let him ridge potatoes'.(74)) His disillusionment forms the subject of Ferdinand Kürnberger's important counter to Willkomm's novel, Der Amerika-Müde (Tired of America) in 1855: his enthusiasm had furnished the first quotation at the head of this section.

Kurnberger's novel gave a full picture of the abuses which flourished in America. Class prejudice, religious bigotry, fraud and dishonesty are shown to be even more prevalent in America than in the Germany which Dr. Moorfield (the novel's hero) was so pleased to have left behind. Most disturbing to Moorfield is the way in which his own love of culture is irreconcilable with the utilitarian values and 'smartness' of American society:

> The culture of the Americans is a merely mercantile
> one, purely technical. Here practical man evolves in
> his most terrifying earnestness. What we call Fatherland
> is here nothing more than a financial enterprise.(75)

Not surprisingly, Moorfield/Lenau collects around him the few characters who have not lost their lives (all have lost their livelihoods) in the financial, physical and moral hazards of the new world, and takes them on to a ship bound for Europe. The mirage had faded.

America behaved as a 'mirage in the West' for all the European nations, France and Italy no less than for Germany, and it is a truism of American history that the mirage showed its power to disappoint almost as frequently as its power to attract. As the Jeffersonian' democracy in fraternity' gave way to the Jacksonian 'democracy of greed' much that was tangible did actually fade, so that the visitors from Europe happened to report accurately. At the same time, however, there were many factors inside Europe which coloured the visitors' reports no less strongly than did American conditions. It is evident, for instance, from much of the French Romantic historians' preoccupation with America during the 1820s and 1830s - a time when they delighted in regarding America as responsible for the 'collective future of mankind' and as 'in the largest sense the West of the World' - that their view of America was conditioned by their disillusionment with France's development away from precisely those ideals which they had located in the safer, because more distant vision of America. As Durant Echeverria commented, 'the collapse of the American dream went hand in hand with the collapse of the revolutionary dream itself'(76). Conservatives similarly ascribed to America aspects of their own society with which they were unhappy and tried thereby, in attacking American institutions, to express their hostility to developments in France. A notable example of this was given in the many attacks on the power of the mob in America: it is clear that the 'mob' was a Parisian rather than transatlantic phenomenon, and that this approach to America was an attempt to exorcise ghosts at home rather than to give a true picture of American conditions.(77)

Returning to Kürnberger's novel, therefore, we would be mistaken merely to see it as a critique of the new world on the basis of the moral and cultural values of the old. The author had, after all, just been released from prison following his activities during the 1848 Revolution when he started to work on his novel: it would indeed have been odd to champion the 'ancien régime' so soon afterward. His purpose, like that of the exotic novelists, was to criticize his own country via the portrayal of America, and was founded on two particular insights. He saw, first, that the ideal vision of America was the creation of the German liberals who, under the oppression of Metternich and the defeat of the Revolution, 'celebrated the star-spangled republic as the practical realization of ideals outlawed in their own country'.(78) After the initial euphoria of Duden and Willkomm most liberals had come to realize that limitation too. But Kürnberger's second insight was much more far-reaching, for his novel examined in the context of America manifestations and implications of capitalist society such as the majority of the liberals of 1848 had never even suspected. Kürnberger's picture of America was a critique of the liberals themselves. With the defeat of the nationalist aspirations of the liberals of 1848, the idealistic German patriotism of the 1830s (such as Lenau was sorry not to find in the United States) had no role to play in Germany either. The middle-classes, including many of the former liberals, threw themselves into the rapidly expanding industrial and commerical life of Germany as an alternative expression of their patriotism. Economic liberty became a surrogate for political liberty (this was the process which Kürnberger transposed to America) and it was not until much later that the implications of this position struck the middle-classes in Germany. Kürnberger is also notable as the first chronicler of America to focus on those problems of pauperization and urbanization which had just begun to attract attention in the Germany of the 1840s, and whose political dimensions the middle-classes were so anxious to avoid. For him America was a warning and anticipation of the consequences of liberal dreams and liberal compromises in Europe.

This aspect of Kürnberger's novel has often been misunderstood. The novel was published in the period of gradually increasing nationalism in which the turning of the sword of criticism against the fatherland would have been incomprehensible to the majority of critics. In viewing the German settlers' experiences in America, writers tended no longer to stress the remaking of the self by the American wilderness. Instead they portrayed German settlement as the export to America of cultural and racial attributes which were claimed to be essential to American civilization. To preserve linguistic and cultural identity became the priority of German (and French) immigrant organizations. Even a writer as hostile to extreme nationalism as Julius Fröbel spoke of the Germans having a 'civilizing' mission to America, while in a speech greeting the foundation of the German Empire in 1871 Friedrich Kapp launched a bitter attack on 'that sickly cosmopolitanism which has been the result of our previous political disunity and impotence'. He assured his listeners that such attitudes 'will vanish completely from the German national character with the firm founding and certain prosperity of the German nation-state'.(79) If people complained about changes for the worse in America (especially the xenophobia shown by the Know-Nothings in the 1850s) they could hardly claim that their own attitudes were not themselves evolving.

Kurnberger's approach to America was adopted by Reinhold Solger in his satirical novel Anton in Amerika (1862). The author, like Kürnberger, had been a member of the left-wing of the Frankfurt Parliament of 1848. The novel is an Americanized parody of Gustav Freytag's immensely popular middle-class novel Soll und Haben (Credit and Debit). Freytag had put together a mixture of nationalism, antisemitism and the protestant work ethic into what he imagined to be a forward-looking portrait of Germany's economic life. Solger takes to America the son of Freytag's hero and exposes him to the unpleasant results of the gospel of money-making which his father had hawked round in the wrapping of bourgeois values. It is not simply the grand scale of American economic life which is contrasted to Germany, but the blatant abandonment of all ethical values which get in the way of trade. If you want capitalism, Solger argues, here it is. What is important is that the demonstration is not aimed at America particularly, but at the middle-classes in Germany who do not realize the implications of their own chosen path of development. The journey to America hardly crosses the Rhine, let alone the Atlantic.

From the early lyrical evocations of America, therefore, to the later more negative images of it German understanding of America remained domestic in its orientation. Even when Gerstäcker attacked the failures of the German immigrants to America, his focus remained German. When people saw that the German make good settlers, Gerstäcker complained, they really mean that the Germans are naturally 'good vassals'. He was horrified to see those German working-men who made good in America turn into the most conservative of Whigs rather than preserving any of the progressive and democratic ideals which their experience of Revolution and economic disadvantage should have conferred on them(80). This too was therefore a criticism of the shallowness of German liberalism: by observing it transposed to the land of opportunity, Gerstäcker could draw attention to flaws and weaknesses in it as yet unobserved in Europe.

The reporting of slavery provides a final demonstration of the Euro-centric understanding of America, especially with the publication of Uncle Tom's Cabin in 1850. From the time of the Enlightenment, slavery had been a cause for dismay among European observers of America. Yet in each generation the concern for America came back to a concern for domestic problems, most often in the form of an unfavourable comparison with the living conditions of the European proletariat. This can be seen in the 1770s(81), in the 1830s with the notion of 'white slavery', given great currency by the Chartists and, in Germany, by Ernst Willkomm.(82) American anti-abolitionists often picked up these ideas as a way of warding off European criticism of their practices. Mrs. Beecher-Stowe put into the mouth of Augustine St. Clare the comment that there was no difference between the slave and the European proletarian, save that the former is better treated by his master. He shares the view of a fellow-planter that he is 'only doing, in another form, what the English aristocracy and capitalists are doing by the lower classes'. He goes on to make some very observant comments on the relationship between racial discrimination and class prejudice, implying that he sees aspects of the former as being a transference of the latter from European conditions - an insight which many recent studies have come to share(83).

Uncle Tom's Cabin spawned a huge number of translations and pirated editions in Europe. In France, after a generation of sentimental studies of the American black - in which, as the historian of this literature remarks, the impression was given 'that the unhappy love of negroes for white women was the worst of their sufferings' - Beecher Stowe's novel renewed the political interest in America which, as we saw, had waned since the revolutionary days. For many critics the novel appeared to offer a promise of the effectiveness of the vague Christian socialism which had flickered in the July Monarchy;, but had been seemingly laid to rest by Louis Napoleon(84).

Still more revealing than the support for Uncle Tom's Cabin was the opposition to the novel. Some of this had directly economic and (with the outbreak of the American Civil War in 1863) political causes. Great power rivalry began to dictate attitudes on the Negro question, just as the Jamaica Revolt of 1865 coloured British opinion on American issues. But it was in European social structures, rather than in direct response to race-contact situations, that race-thinking began to affect European thinking,(85) the spread of that 'ethnological' concern for the fate of non-whites, furthered in France and Germany by the ideas of Gobineau and in England particularly by woolly notions of Anglo-Saxon racial solidarity, tempered always by the increasing fear lest 'Brother Jonathan' would oust Britain from world supremacy(86). In these ways, 'projecting an America subtly adapted to suit British political and religious beliefs',(87) British opinion-formers, like those in Europe, saw the crusade for abolition in European terms. By this stage anyway the impact of abolition on European colonial practice was too direct to be ignored: Charles Maurras, for instance, blamed Uncle Tom's Cabin for the disastrous policies advocated in Madagascar by the over-philanthropic senator Schoelcher.(88) It was therefore, a fairly striking act for Jules Verne to side so openly with the abolitionists in Nord contre Sud (1887).

In their attitude to the American slave-holders ('the most honest people in America', Maurras called them) and their opposition to abolition, many Europeans revealed a continuing admiration for the myth of the frontier in America. They found in the hardness and ruggedness of the frontier an encouragement to resist the sickly philanthropy which opposed slavery, and to cultivate a new realism in social dealings in their own country. If earlier generations had seen America as the land of democracy, observers in the second half of the nineteenth century were more prone to regard aristocracy as the key-note America struck for Europe (such was the message of Gaillardet's L'Aristocratie en Amérique of 1883). They found in America, in the frontier, in the simple and vigorous virtues which they projected onto it, an antidote to the sickness of their own state, and in the slave-debate they felt that they needed to defend in America that element of ruthlessness which would be their own encouragement to vigorous life in Europe.(89) As, finally, from about 1865 onwards it became fashionable to complain about the growing 'Americanization' of life (setting in motion a circle of arguement which reached its peak at the end of the 1920's) it showed once again how America had to serve as the scape-goat for undesirable elements in European society,(90) and how in transatlantic dreams, both social nightmare and social idyll might lie side by side.

We have seen, therefore, in three types of writing about the overseas world, how strongly pressures felt in Europe expressed themselves in the portrayal of overseas cultures and lands. We have implied that in many respects the journey of the nineteenth century to the exotic and to America were journeys to the interior of Europe, and that, as a result, there was much less chance of actual discovery, of change of heart, of actual contact or real sympathy with other cultures. The tremendously Eurocentric nature of such literature clearly made it unlikely that the colonial writers would start from a more outward-looking position.   Whatever attitudes the 'colonial situation' imposed upon these writers, the literary traditions which preceded them had little power to enlarge their vision for the world outside Europe.

NOTES

1.A.Maler, Der exotische Roman (Stuttgart,1975), p.5f. Maler treats the exotic novel in much the same way Chinard and Jourda approached the topic in French literature. It is a more general approach than that adopted by F. Brie in his important comparativist study Exotismus der Sinne (1920), which drew almost exclusively on the kind of material upon which Mario Praz was to base The Romantic Agony (1933).

2. Berchoux, quoted in P.Jourda, L'Exotisme, vol. 1 (Paris, 1938), p.19.

3. Cf. P.Chinard, L'Amérique et le reve exotique (Paris, 1934), p.399f; E.B.Dykes, The Negro in English Romantic Thought (Washington, 1942), p.43f; H.N.Fairchild, The Noble Savage (New York, 1935), p.80f.

4. Cf. Bhūpāl Singh, A Survey of Anglo-Indian Fiction (OUP,1934), p.268f. The Cambridge History of English Literature speaks, uncritically, of a characteristic English traveller taking with him across the exotic East 'the atmosphere of Eton, Trinity,Lincoln's Inn and the hunting-field' (vol. 14, CUP,1934, p.251).

5. Chinard, p.357.

6. B.de St.Pierre, Paul et Virginie (Paris,1964),pp.187,163 and 163.

7. Ibid.,p.111.

8. Ibid.,p.55.

9. Chateaubriand, Les Natchez (1826) in Oeuvres romanesques et voyages, vol.1 (Paris,1969), p.227; Génie du Christianisme (1802) quoted in Chateaubriand's own preface (1805) to René also in vol. 1 of Oeuvres romanesques et voyages, p.111.

10. Preface to Atala (1801), ibid. p.15.

11. M.Praz, The Romantic Agony (rev. ed. OUP,1970),p.213. Gautier quoted in F.Brie, Exotismus der Sinne (Heidelberg,1920), p.43.

12. Quoted by G.Schaeffer, Le voyage en orient de Nerval (Neuchatel,1967), p.253.

13. Letter of 14 November 1840 to Ernest Chevalier in G. Flaubert, Oeuvres Complètes, vol. 12 (Paris,1974), p.374. In similar vein Leconte de Lisle warns against the 'barbarous clamours of industrial Pandaemonium' in his preface to Poèmes et Poésies (Paris,1855), p.iii.

14. Quoted in M.G.Lerner, Pierre Loti (New York,1974),p.28.

15. P.Loti, Aziyadé (Paris,1879), p.160.

16. Ibid., p.13.

17. P.Gaugin, Noa Noa (Paris,1924), p.88; P.Loti, Lettres à Mme Juliette Adam (Paris,1924) pp.148,150 etc. Cf. C.Farrère, Les civilisés (Paris,1905).

18. A.Young,'Mr.Kipling's stories' (1891) quoted in E.L. Gilbert, Kipling and the critics (Peter Owen,1966),p.2. See also A.Wilson, The strange ride of R. Kipling (Granada,1979), p.194.

19. Quoted in P.B.Ellis, H.Rider Haggard (Routledge & Kegan Paul,1978), p.213.

20. H.Rider Haggard, Nada the Lily (Longmans,1892), p.x.

21. The works of H.Rider Haggard (New York,1928), pp.669/70

22. V.G.Kiernan,The Lords of Human Kind (Weidenfeld & Nicolson, 1969), p.210.

23. W.Menzel on Scott, quoted in G.Friessen, The German panoramic novel (Berne,1972), p.15.

24. Sealsfield, quoted from Friessen, pp.44/45.

25. C.Sealsfield, Morton (Stuttgart,1846), pp.18,6/7, then M.Djordjewitsch, C.Sealsfields Auffassung des Amerikanertums (Weimar,1931), pp.34/35.

26. Friessen, p.45.

27. F.Gerstäcker, Tahiti rev. ed. (Berlin, n.d.), p.104.

28. Ibid., pp.357,451.

29. Ibid., p.96. Cf. G.Jahn, Gerstäcker und die Mission (Halle,1869), p.32f.

30. Maler suggests this general approach (p.70f).

31. See for instance Louis James, Fiction for the Working Man (Penguin Books,1974), pp.120f,151f; and an equivalent study of German reading-habits, R.Schenda, Volk ohne Buch (Frankfurt

a.Main,1970), pp.474/81.
   32. M.Green, Dreams of Adventure, Deeds of Empire
(Routledge & Kegan Paul, 1980), pp.3,57 etc.
   33. Quoted by A.Cruse, The Victorians and their Books
(Allen & Unwin,1935), p.293.
   34. Green, p.109.
   35. Letter of 25.5.1900 in W.Raabe, Briefe (Ergänzungs-
band 2 of Sämtliche Werke, Göttingen,1975, p.413).
   36. E.J.Trelawny, Adventures of a Younger Son, ed. W.St.
Clair (OUP,1974), p.46.
   37. Ibid., p.465.
   38. Ibid., p.172.
   39. Cf. G.Aimard, L'Araucan (Paris,1864), in which an
Indian chief, fighting to liberate his people, successfully
and repeatedly impersonates a Spanish nobleman.
   40. J.Chesneaux, Une lecture politique de Jules Verne
(Paris,1971), pp.78,61f. My whole approach to Verne is coloured by this admirable study, which adds a much needed dimension
to Loutfi's view of Verne as merely a disseminator of imperialism (Littérature et Colonialisme, The Hague & Paris,1971,
p.52f).
   41. J.Verne, Adventures in Southern Africa (Hutchinson,
1879), p.38. See Chesneaux, p.100f. On negro emancipation Nord
contre sud (Paris, 1887).
   42. J.Verne, Aventures de Trois Russes et de Trois Anglais
dans l'Afrique australe (Paris,1872)
   43. H.Wollschläger, Karl May in Selbstzeugnissen und
Bilddokumenten (Reinbek, 1965), p.8f.
   44. Ibid., p.73.
   45. May quoted in A.Klein, Die Krise des bürgerlichen
Unterhaltungsromans (Bonn, 1969), p.72.
   46. K.May, Der Pfahlmann (Vienna & Berlin, n.d.), p.22.
   47. E.Bloch, Erbschaft dieser Zeit (Frankfurt a. Main,
1977), p.172. My indebtedness to Bloch's reading of May is
shared by all the critics in this field. On the more reactionary tradition of plush historicism see James, p.107f.
   48. G.Ueding, Glanzvolles Elend (Frankfurt a. Main, 1973)
p.127.
   49. K.May, Winnetou (Radebeul, 1932), vol.1, p.187.
   50. Ibid., vol. 1, p.2.
   51. Ibid., vol. 3, p.627.
   52. Ibid., vol. 1, p.5.
   53. Bloch, pp. 171,181.
   54. F.Kürnberger, Der Amerika-Müde (Frankfurt a.Main,1855)
p.1; C.Dickens, Martin Chuzzlewit (Signet Books,1965), p.399;
J.R.Lowell quoted by A.J.Torrielli, Italian Opinion on America
(Cambridge Mass., 1941), p.73.
   55. Cf. D.Echeverria, Mirage in the West (Princeton,1968)
   56. H.de St.J. Crèvecoeur, Letters from an American Farmer
(Chatto & Windus,1908), pp.68,54. D.H.Lawrence,'Hector St.John
de Crèvecoeur' in Studies in Classic American Literature

Penguin Books, 1971), pp.28/39.
  57. Crèvecoeur, p.79.
  58. Ibid., pp.28,6O.
  59. Ibid., p. 3o6f. A particularly helpful discussion of
Crèvecoeur's ambiguous attitudes can be found in A.N.Kaul, The
American Vision (New Haven,1963), p.22f.
  6O. Lawrence, p.35.
  61. C.Sealsfield, Morton, vol.1 (Stuttgart,1846), pp.98/99
  62. C.Sealsfield, Das Kajütenbuch (Munich,1963), pp.112/13.
  63. L.Schefer, Die Probefahrt nach Amerika (Bunzlau, 1837)
p.175.
  64. P. van den Berghe, Race and racism (New York,1967),
p.77f.
  65. M.Djordjewitsch, C.Sealsfields Auffassung des Amerikanertums (Weimar, 1931), p.74.
  66. R.L.Rapson, Britons view America (Seattle, 1971), p.
131. See also A.Nevins, America through British eyes (New York,
1948).
  67. F.Muench, Die Zukunft von Nordamerika (Bremen,1860),
p.7. Cf. Rapson, p.59.
  68. L.Fiedler, The Return of the Vanishing American (Palladin, 1972), p.52.
  69. Criticized in Rapson, p.23f. The argument is a benign
version of Arendt's 'boomerang' theory of the behaviour of
settlement colonies. See below, p. 146.
  7O. Cf. F.Monaghan, French travellers in the United States
(New York, 1933), p.viii; Rapson, p.204f; H.M.Jones, O Strange
New World (New York,1965), p.310.
  71. Cf. Gerstäcker titles in footnote 80. Duden's book was
Bericht über eine Reise nach den westlichen Staaten Nordamerikas
(Elberfeld,1829). Many of these themes are helpfully treated in
S.Bauschinger, H.Denkler & W.Malsch (ed.s), Amerika in der
deutschen Literatur (Stuttgart, 1975).
  72. E.Willkomm, Die Europamüden (Leipzig, 1838), vol. 1,
pp.62,16,296; vol. 2, p.81.
  73. Ibid., vol. 2, p.83.
  74. Quoted in G.A.Mulfinger, 'Lenau in Amerika' in Americana Germanica, vol. 2 (New York,1898), p.42.
  75. Lenau quoted in G.A.Mulfinger,'Lenaus Ansichten über
Amerika' in Americana Germanica vol. 3 (New York, 1899), p.8.
  76. Echeverria, p.xi. On French historians' attitudes see
E.C.D. Crossley,'Quelques aspects de l'Américanisme romantique'
in 19th Century French Studies, vol. 6, no. 1 & 2 (1977/78),
pp.82/93. More generally see H.Blumenthal, American and French
Culture (Baton Rouge, 1976), p.56f; and H.M.Jones, America and
French Culture (Chapel Hill, 1927), p.15f.
  77. H.M.Jones, America and French Culture, p.58f. In a
more general context, M.Green has given an interesting account
of the double terms of reference of transatlantic commentators
(A Mirror for Anglo-Saxons, Longmans, 1961, p.128f).
  78. Kürnberger, p.67. Very useful on this theme is Rüdiger

Steinlein's essay 'F.Kürnbergers Der Amerikamüde' in Bauschin-
ger, Denkler & Malsch, pp.154/77.
  79. F.Kapp, Über Auswanderung (Berlin,1871), p.35; J.
Fröbel, Die deutsche Auswanderung und ihre culturhistorische
Bedeutung (Leipzig,1858), p.41f. See also T.S.Baker,'America
as the political Utopia of Young Germany' in Americana Germanica vol. 2 (1898), p.75ff. Also Blumenthal, p.22f and H.
Plischke, Von Cooper bis Karl May (Düsseldorf,1951),p.62f.
  80. F.Gerstäcker, Der deutschen Auswanderer Fahrten und
Schicksale (Leipzig, 1847), p.125; F.Gerstäcker, Achtzehn
Monate in Süd-Amerika und dessen deutschen Colonien (Leipzig,
1863), vol.1, p.106. See also W.F.Kamman, Socialism in German
American Literature (Philadelphia, 1917), p.19.
  81. Cf. J.T.Hatfield and E.Hochbaum,'The influence of the
American Revolution upon German literature' in Americana Germanica vol. 3 (1899), p.377.
  82. E.Willkomm, Weisse Sclaven oder die Leiden des Volkes
(Leipzig,1845).
  83. Uncle Tom's Cabin (Dents,1960), p.232. Cf. P.Mason,
'Class consciousness and imperial aloofness' in Prospero's
Magic (OUP,1962), pp.1/21.
  84. E.Lucas, La littérature anti-esclavagiste au 19ième
siècle (Paris,1930), p.30 etc. See also Torrielli, p.50f.
  85. Cf. M.Biddiss, Gobineau (Jonathan Cape, 1970), p.17f;
and H.Arendt, The origins of totalitarianism (Allen & Unwin,
1967), pp.158/84.
  86. See e.g. T.Carlyle, Occasional Discourse on the Nigger
Question (Thomas Bosworth,1853), p.45. The type of 'ethnological' approach to international and domestic problems can be
widely documented. On American and European lines of thought
see T.K.Penniman, A hundred years of Anthropology (Duckworth,
1965), pp.77f,95f. Within colonial thought see R.Hyam,
Britain's Imperial Century (Batsford,1976), p.80f. For a
random example of race-thinking's place in domestic European
political thinking see J.W.Jackson,'On the racial aspects of
the Franco-Prussian War' in The Journal of the Anthropological
Institute of Great Britain, vol.1 (1871), pp.30/46.
  87. C.Bolt, Victorian attitudes to race (Routledge &
Kegan Paul, 1971), p.31.
  88. C.Maurras,'Feuilles volantes', in Revue encyclopéd-
ique (1896), p.519.
  89. Blumenthal, p.60f. On the place of violence within
late nineteenth century American culture see R.Slotkin, Regeneration through violence (Middletown, 1973), p.5 etc. In
Germany the links between American frontier mentality and
aggressive nationalism can be traced in many of the articles
in Atlantische Studien (Göttingen, 1848f), a magazine notable
for its attacks on idealistic humanism in Africa, America and
at home.
  90. On these attitudes in Renan and the Goncourts see
Blumenthal, p.471. They were, of course, widespread in Germany
too.

Chapter Two

COLONIAL FICTION: A LITERARY HISTORY

In the first thirty years of this century histories of colonial literature enjoyed a vogue. Literary historians, particularly in France and Germany, would collect and classify every page penned in the colonies and mould their material into a 'history of literature' with autonomous movements and trends just like those established in the larger literary scene in Europe. These histories of colonial literature invariably shared much of the ethos of their subject-matter, and often were written with direct political intent: to express nationalism, nostalgia or resentment over the loss of empire. At the same time, however, these works were monuments to an excessive confidence in literary history as such, inheritors of a generation of literary criticism holding to what Rene Wellek has called the 'ingenuous belief in the accumulation of facts'.(1) Certainly these histories are still informative, but they argue for colonial literature as a genre only by the dead-weight of the material they cite. Like a coral reef, colonial literature emerges from the pages of these histories only as an accumulation of corpses.

Although I wish to place colonial fiction in the literary history of its time, I hope it will not disturb too much of the dust which has settled on these older volumes of literary history. I plan no rehabilitation of the genre and unlike Mr. Sanderson, oiling the 'Wheel of Empire' in a recent study, no overall pleading for the 'sophistication and range' of the colonial novel as 'an unduly neglected instrument'.(2) Nevertheless, the literary situation of the colonial writers helped to define and develop their activity, and without trying to write a literary history we need to appreciate that situation. Perhaps too, since even the leading colonial writers of France and Germany are virtually unknown to an English-reading public, a few introductions and signposts may not come amiss.*

---

*At the risk of swamping the reader, short biographies are given of the colonial writers discussed in this book and listed in section 5 of the Bibliography. See below, p. 163f.

I

There is a striking dissimilarity in the place which colonial fiction occupies in the various national literatures. Partly because of the overwhelming pre-eminence of Kipling in English colonial writing there has never been much attempt to delineate the genre as such. Whereas French literature, true to a series of convenient periodicizations, has always been clear about the status and situation of colonial literature, nineteenth-century English literature lacks such convenient chronological divisions and has resisted classification into movements. Bhūpāl Singh's Survey of Anglo-Indian Fiction (1934), for instance, made some contribution towards establishing the continuity and autonomy of this branch of colonial literature. His study listed some nine hundred titles and established distinct periods and schools even within Anglo-India fiction. More representative, however, was the Cambridge History of English Literature which acknowledged colonial fiction in English only by the inclusion of a section on Anglo-Indian literature, and which denied such literature any autonomy as a genre with its definition as 'merely English literature strongly marked by Indian local colour'(3).

Whether English colonial literature existed as a genre or not very largely depended on the viewpoint one started from. French critics found no difficulty in identifying English colonial literature, and the Germans - pastmasters at tracing intellectual influences - instantly saw in the whole of the nineteenth century a continuity which English critics found much harder to discover. Friedrich Brie, in a long essay on nineteenth-century writers from Southey to Kipling, found no difficulty in seeing continuity and autonomous literary evolution behind the individual colonial writers. 'Imperialist tendencies in English literature can be seen to be organically linked,' he concluded, 'and one is justified in speaking of a literary history of English imperialism'.(4)

Detailed objections can be made to Brie's reading of 'mid-Victorian' imperial writing.(5) More telling, however, is to notice how little sense of continuity and intellectual tradition was felt by the English colonial writers at the end of the century. While there are clear affinities between Kipling's work and that of Henry Cunningham, his immediate forerunner in Ango-Indian fiction, neither of them felt any sense of affinity with the Victorian pioneers of Imperial theory. London reviewers compared his early works more readily to Loti, Maupassant and Zola than to other English writers on India, and he himself learnt more from the pre-Raphaelites than from anything in the Anglo-Indian novel.(6) Kipling's influence became dominant among Anglo-Indian writers at the turn of the century, such as Flora Annie Steel (1847-1929), Alice Perrin (1867-1934) and the Frontier novelist Maud Diver (1867-1945) - Bhūpāl Singh rightly speaks of Kipling's 'School'- but the strength of his influence suggests how few other traditions these writers felt themselves to be following. If they participated in a long tradition, they had little awareness of doing so.

This is not to say that Kipling did not form part of the English literary development. Indeed it can be argued that his work exactly corresponded to the situation of English literature in his day. Oscar Wilde, commenting on Kipling's work in 1891, summarized the position of fiction as follows: 'He who would stir us now by fiction must either give us an entirely new background or reveal to us the soul of man in its innermost workings'(7). Wilde felt the need for a new starting-point in fiction since the realist mode seemed to have wrung ordinary life dry as a basis for fiction. Kipling offered that new background and showed one escape from the dilemma confronting metropolitan literature. In a similar manner the renewal of exotic writing with Ste v enson and Rider Haggard appeared to reviewers as an answer to an alleged failure of inspiration within the novel, caused, some felt, by the swamping of literature by science. One reviewer wrote in the 1880s: 'We are to look for no more Sir Walters, no more Thackerays, no more Dickens. The stories have all been told. Plots are exploited. Incident is over'. With a sense of rain after drought, a review of King Solomon's Mines claimed that the novel had rescued literature from potential barrenness in an age when 'it was thoroughly accepted that there were no more stories to be told, that romance was utterly dried up, and that analysis of character was the only thing in fiction attractive to the public'.(8) It would be wrong to overstate the weight of these uncertainties but they serve as a corrective to the view of colonial literature as a mere execrescence on English fiction, or as being 'inhibited by the prestige of the home-grown product'. It is clear that colonial writers recognized the prestige of the metropolitan reading-public (it was the size of that public which had drawn Kipling to London in 1890(9)) but were far less than convinced about the prestige of the main stream of contemporary English literature.

For all its idiosyncracy, Kipling's relationship to his literary contemporaries has a representative importance. His works are poised uneasily between a cheerful philistinism about art and a careful and consistent artistry. He jeers at intellectual theories, and at the arty poets who

> moo and coo with women-folk about
> their blessed souls.

He makes a fetish of presenting his stories in as anti-artistic a manner as possible, what Henry James called 'imitating the amateur'. In the story 'A Conference of the Powers', for instance, a fashionable London writer (always an object of suspicion to the colonials) visits an officers' mess in the Indian Army. The subalterns tell him something of their military exploits. What they have to tell is neatly and wittily related, and at one point the fashionable writer feels that the story is moving into his province, art:

> Cleaver brought his hand down on the table with a
> thump that made the glasses dance. 'That's Art!', he
> said. 'Flat, flagrant mechanism! Don't tell me that
> happened on the spot.'

> The pupils of the Infant's eyes contracted to two
> pinpoints. 'I beg your pardon', he said slowly and stiffly,
> 'but I am telling this thing as it happened'.(10)

While one can see in such mannerisms the distortion of the Realist
zeal for documentation, other stories make clear that Kipling has
inherited from the opponents of Realism a very different view of
the justification of art. In a revealing comment at the end of one
of his stories Kipling writes that

> Truth is a naked lady, and if by accident she is drawn
> up from the bottom of the sea, it behoves a gentleman
> either to give her a print petticoat or to turn his face
> to the wall and vow that he did not see.(11)

The 'print petticoat' is not a product of Victorian prudery. It
testifies to Kipling's genuine belief in an art which goes beyond
realism, and which has the ability to transform and enrich human
experience with beauty and illusion. The famous 'Children of the
Zodiac' elaborates this belief into an overall metaphysic of art
which has nothing in common with Realism. Kipling's philistinism
and his open rejection of 'unwholesome' foreign influences are
deliberate attempts to lay a false scent, but they have their origins
as much in the ambivalence of the literary situation as in Kipling's
personalilty.

German critics such as Friedrich Brie tended to emphasize
the organic unity of English colonial literature and the continuity
of English imperialism because both qualities represented a goal
towards which German literature had laboured in vain throughout
the nineteenth century. Writers and critics alike felt German
culture to be fragmented, out of touch with the currents of history,
and Germany's national life too poor for great literature to be
produced. 'We have no history', Ludwig Börne had written in the
1830s, 'no sense of national identity, no patriotic activity, no trade,
no commerce - how can we expect to have a novel? Nothing
worthwhile ever happens to us small people'.(12) He was accounting
for the absence in the German tradition of novels in the style of
Dickens or Balzac, novels dealing with the social life of the nation
and speaking to the broad mass of Germans. Heine once said that
the Germans lived in the heaven of invention, the imaginative
world of philosophy and music in which the Germans were
preeminent, while the French and English had been storming the
more practical worlds of trade and conquest. The search for a
realism in the novel was therefore, inseparable from a nationalism
which aimed at providing a national life major enough to serve as
the object of fiction.

While German colonial fiction took its place therefore in the line of succession from the exotic novels of the mid-nineteenth century, it also belonged within a movement, nationalist in inspiration, towards the novel of social realism. The military conquests which were needed in Europe and overseas in order to turn Germany into a great power were grist to the mill in the campaign for the realist German novel.

For obvious reasons Germany's colonial fiction was a product of the period 1890-1914. Throughout the nineteenth century Germany had no colonial territory, and no colonial fiction. She lacked even the ambition for overseas territory. Traditionally, the colonizing activity of Prussia, the most powerful of the German states, had been orientated towards Eastern Europe. Public interest in America (and to a lesser extent Britain) was one of the few diversions from a preoccupation with Europe. At various times Bismarck, the entire Reichstag, and most of the opinion formers were of the view that overseas colonies were only a burden to the state. Similar views were current in the mid-century in France and England, as well as in Spain and Portugal, but those countries had at least obtained colonies before deciding that imperialism was not worthwhile. This Germany had not had the foresight to do. It was the efforts of the two prominent colonization propaganda groups, Fabri's Colonial Union and Carl Peters' Society for German Colonization (amalgamated in 1887 as the German Colonial Society) which kept the possibility of colonial activity in the public eye, and only in 1884 with the Congo conference which Bismarck chaired in Berlin, did Germany actually acquire colonies, principally in Africa. The most important of these were South-West Africa (Namibia) and East Africa (now Tanzania).

German colonial fiction therefore came after the scramble for Africa and had no roots in a less hectic period of colonial experience. German missions had been active before the 1880s but had aroused little interest outside professional circles. There was no equivalent to the prolonged French settlement in North Africa, or Britain's centuries of contact with India. In contrast to France and Britain, Germany's colonial literature had in consequence a provisional and make-shift quality. There was a high turnover of civil servants in the German colonies, and fiction was not enriched to the extent of English and French writing by the leisure activities of colonial civil servants. Social life, especially as evinced by the settlement of women, was slow to evolve, and intellectual life slower still. A contemporary observer said that the German colonies had 'nothing much to offer - except fever, hippos and hundreds of German officers, very aristocratic and very drunk'. Hardly an intellectual environment, therefore, and although there are a few examples of writers coming into fiction via colonial newspapers, they and their newspapers fall far behind Kipling or Mille in quality.

Frieda von Bülow (1857-1909) was among the earliest exponents of German colonial fiction. She followed round Africa the Germans' answer to Cecil Rhodes, Carl Peters, and her novels focus on the colonial pioneers rather than on established colonial rule. With the outbreak of major wars in South-West Africa in 1904, however, which focussed public attention on the questions of security and settlement, colonial fiction entered a new phase. Just as the Mutiny in 1857 acted as a watershed in English writing on India, in terms both of its themes and its sheer volume, the events of 1904 caused a veritable flood of literature. The most famous of these products was Gustav Frenssen's Peter Moor's journey to South West (1905). Already an established novelist, Frenssen (1863-1934) brought the war explicitly to the attention of the German public. The same task was performed by Ada von Liliencron, another established writer who, without any experience of colonial settlement, set out to plead the imperial cause. The so-called 'Hottentot elections' of 1907, in which the Centre and Social-Democrat parties' opposition to imperialism lost them nearly half their electoral support, showed the extent of the sympathy colonial literature would find at home. After that time German colonial fiction's political message had a much more defined place in the domestic political scene than the ideas of the colonial societies had ever enjoyed.

The most important German colonial writer was Hans Grimm. Born in 1875 into a Wiesbaden family with close links to Fabri's society, Grimm studied commerce in England before taking up a post in a British trading company in South Africa in 1896, where he remained until 1910. Shortly after his return to Germany he began to publish novels and short stories of colonial life, the best of which stand comparison with anything this literature can offer. In the late 1920s, as an acknowledged expert on the colonies, Grimm revisited South-West Africa and travelled widely through the former colony, to report on its maladministration by the Union of South Africa.(13)

It was Grimm who initiated theoretical debates about colonial literature in Germany, debates which lacked the muscle and public interest of those conducted in France and which culminated in a series of university dissertations rather than widely read histories. Grimm did not need to make writers aware of their distance from exotic tradition, or to inject nationalism into the novel: 1871 and New Imperialism had achieved that. His contribution to German fiction, apart from literary talent, was an almost mystical imitatio Kipling.(14) Since it was traditional and, since the English were blood-brothers of the Germans, racially acceptable for German literature to take English models, Grimm brought Kipling at an early stage into the fold of German colonial writing, and there he tended to stay until 1939, despite his highly embarrassing hatred for the Germans.

II

Literary history did not develop in a vacuum, and the changes in the intellectual and political climate which took place during the years 1830 to 1890 made a greater contribution to the development of the genre than did purely literary trends. A failed revolution, the growth of a class-conscious proletariat, the founding of the German Empire: these events shook European culture to foundations it did not know it had, while the intellectual revolutions of the nineteenth century redrew the intellectual horizons of literature so radically that it was hard to refocus on literary continuity. Figures such as Marx, Darwin, Gobineau and Nietzsche would hardly write in vain for the literature concerned with overseas territory. Two particular trends shaped the situation of the emergent colonial writers: the shift from the universalist humanism of the eighteenth century, and the corresponding political movement from enlightened bourgeois liberalism to a more bigoted nationalism.

These changes in climate left an enormous mark on colonial thinking, and provided the foundation on which virtually all the literature discussed in the next chapters rested. They were gradual, not sudden changes, and there is no magic year from which the attitudes of mind peculiar to New Imperialism can be dated. Agnes Murphy, in her detailed study of the ideology of French imperialism in the decade after the Franco-Prussian War, shows that decade to be the seed-bed of the ideas and attitudes on which New Imperialism was to feed. Friedrich Brie dates the significant abandonment of traditional attitudes in British thinking about overseas countries as late as the time of the Boer War, while Christine Bolt's study identifies a number of diverse focal points of change with a slightly earlier centre of gravity.(15)

At various points a direct link from one or other of these influences will be seen on the colonial fiction. Nietzsche, for instance, had obviously been read by many of the colonial writers and his ideas were mediated by their works. But it is important to be aware of the mediation of these ideas on a less direct level. Not only was much colonial fiction openly contemptuous of abstract ideas; it set out to demonstrate truths from within the orbit of Alexander's soldiers and Caesar's cook. While we cannot ignore the intellectual background to imperialism, we must agree with Alan Cairns 'that the conduct and attitudes of ordinary men cannot be explained as if they were by-products of controversial writings by intellectuals on esoteric subjects'.(16)

Some indication of the mediation of intellectual and historical events into popular consciousness is given, as we saw, by the popular literature of the period, and particularly by the proliferation during the nineteenth century of popular scientific journals dealing with the overseas world. Detailed studies exist of the dissemination of national and imperialist ideas through these journals of popular enlightenment, and in particular the connections between the geographical movement of the nineteenth century and French imperialism have been closely examined, and shown to be an important channel for the mediation of ideas to a very broad middle-class reading public.(17) This is not the place for a similar study in length, but it will indicate something of the change in attitude to take a few illustrations from the German geographical magazines which came into being during the century and which, like their French counterparts, reached a wide public.

A characteristic publication was Das Ausland, which first appeared in 1828 over the sub-title 'newspaper giving information on the intellectual and moral life of nations, particularly bearing in mind related phenomena in Germany'. It proclaimed a belief in progress and in the brotherhood of man which the coming revolution of 1830 would also mark. These attitudes were behind its view of colonial activity. Whereas, it argued, antiquity had known only conquest by the sword,

> it was reserved for our age to see the unfading and eternally victorious power of the Spirit. Civilization forms the inner bonds of nations and conditions their interrelations, independent of the chances of military power, casting a general spiritual bond round all members of the human family...(18)

A belief therefore in the Spirit, in civilizaiton rather than military conquest as the bearer of History, and a warm defence of the notion of one human family - such was the intellectual harbour from which Das Ausland was launched and it was characteristic of its age.

In 1852 another similar periodical appeared for the first time: Die Natur. It aimed at very much the equivalent public to that which Dickens reached with Household Words, which had begun publication two years previously. It still believed 'that the essence of the whole of humanity is one', but began, in keeping with its much more scientific approach, to analyze the material differences between the nations. Whereas Das Ausland had not wanted even to discuss external differences, preferring to concentrate on the ideal unity rather than actual diversity of the world's peoples, Die Natur was fascinated by arguments accounting for such diversity from climate and diet. 'The greatness of a nation is not so exclusively dependent upon its institutions as has been thought', an article remarked in a discussion of the influence of climate on politics in the United States.(19) It was symptomatic of a swing away from the idealist understanding of the world's peoples and their civilization.

Within ten years this anti-idealism had become a weapon in the hands of the ethnologists. When Globus began publication in 1861, it set out to focus on the given and unchangeable nature of the diversity of human societies. Encouraging its readers to plunge into the 'full, fresh life of the nations', it soon made clear that the readers would wear their prejudices and superiority like a diving suit:

The great families of man have very different culture
values; you cannot apply to all of them one and the
same yardstick, you cannot survive on a few general
principles, in the end you are forced to admit that there
are races superior and inferior in their organization,
basic human stocks with very different hereditary
factors and deep-rooted instincts which civilization
cannot displace.

These general statements were soon focussed in an explicit
racial understanding of history. Differences of climate and diet
were not the important thing in explaining the fact that 'between
the various great families of man an inner mutual antipathy reigns'.
Such differences had one origin only: they were 'a question of
race'.(20)

It was on this basis that all the geographical magazines moved
into the scramble for Africa of the 1880s. Even before Germany
possessed colonies the ideology had been established which broke
up the family of man into separate and primevally warring factions
and provided an explanation (and thus a justification) for the
destruction of one race by another. 'Laws of nature' had been
established which took many of the bloodier elements of imperialism
beyond morality. 'The savages of Africa', Das Ausland assured its
readers on the eve of the Berlin Conference, would probably 'vanish
in the face of advancing civilization like snow vanishes before the
sun.' It went on: 'Natural laws rule the history of nations too.
The superior race drives out the inferior'.(21)

Such was the climate of opinion disseminated to the German
middle-classes even before they had, as a nation, acquired colonies
or in all probability ever set eyes upon a 'Native'. The origin of
the ideas lay in Gobineau and others, but their acceptabililty came
less from the political ambitions of Germany in Africa, than from
the situation in Europe and from the type of society which the
European nations were becoming. It is well known that Gobineau's
major impetus in the formulation of his race-theories was his horror
at the revolution of 1848 and his determination to provide
justification for the aristocracy which were not dependent upon
the reactions of the 'mob'.(22) Similar factors, as we suggested,
lay behind European reactions to the causes of emancipation and
republicanism in America. At all events, the ideology of New
Imperialism was widely available to the middle-classes from whom
the colonies would recruit administrators and civil servants, in
Germany without any intervening period of overseas experience.
Not only the reading public at home, but those responsible for
colonial administration were ready to adapt their experience to
these preconceived ideas.

III

We saw in an earlier chapter how continuous and substantial the exotic tradition had been in French literature. There was not, as M. Jourda has pointed out, a single major writer in France who had not significantly contributed to the exotic tradition(23). North Africa was so near that writers could perfectly well explore the country without becoming involved in debates about imperialism. Frescaly's Mariage d'Afrique (1886) and Fromentin's Un été dans le Sahel (1874), for instance, show remarkably little contamination from imperialism and take their reader round North Africa in a mixture of aesthetic and romantic adventure. Writers who lived on other French colonies, La Réunion for instance, could make these countries the subject of their work without needing to reflect upon, still less justify, imperial conquest. Leconte de Lisle was in this restricted sense a colonial writer, although he did not participate in any of the overtly political themes which later writers were forced to consider. French colonies, like the English possessions, included many centres of previous high culture, which exercised an appeal to writers both anterior to and more intense than their appeal to the imperial movement.

There were many historical studies of French colonial literature. The colonies became increasingly important within French domestic politics (partly as a deliberate diversion from the disasters of French policy in Europe), and as a result the literature dealing with them was frequently under debate. Colonial writing was generally accepted as forming a distinct tradition within French literature. Few of these histories have much to offer our study, and their classification of the material according to geographical criteria is useful only to the collector. The debates about colonial literature in France remain interesting, however, for their shifting emphasis on the Realist and exotic traditions. The discussions revealed the diversity of literary response to colonial race-contact.

The colonial novel conventionally turned against the exotic tradition for its lack of realism. Robert Randau spoke for many novelists when he prefaced his novel Les Explorateurs (1907) with a direct assault on the exotic novel:

> Furthermore I wish to say that, quite simply, I have searched in vain through our colonies for those magnificent types the social monsters, those magnificent villians whom many exotic novelists place there. Those products of the imagination may well have a colourful and impressive beauty but no-one has ever seen them in reality. As for those intrigues between Europeans and native women which so many writers base their work on, they come down to a few commercially obtained embraces and they are far from interesting.(24)

In their rejection of the exotic novel many colonial novelists echoed the terms in which, half a century before, the Realists had rejected Romanticism. The Realists too had aimed to present external reality as it was, free from subjective slant and without focussing narrative and description on the sensations which they evoked. Louis Bertrand, with Randau one of the doyens of Algerian literature, drew on this Realist tradition as he complained that exotic literature had failed to discover the reality behind colonial life, portraying exotic backgrounds merely as 'a pretext for emotion or exaltation'.(25)   From this suspicion of subjectivity and unrealism, the colonial novelists tended towards a form of exaggeratedly documentary writing, full of mannered disclaimers about the author's invention of the plot.   Much in Kipling's style, for instance, Pierre Mille ends what is a sentimental and obviously constructed story with the claim that he has told it as it happened,'not wishing to alter by a lie a simple story in which I should blush to introduce art'.(26)

These claims were patently absurd, and it was no less obvious that writers approached the colonies through subjective experience. Despite the efforts of Raymond Lebel, in a series of important studies, to establish the genre as a source of documentary evidence on colonial conditions, it was generally recognised that subjectivity had a proper role to play in colonial fiction.   Eduard Pujarniscle, in his vigorous defence of colonial literature published in 1931, reminded colonial writers of the example of Flaubert, who had shown that it was possible to develop from a subjective starting point towards a literature of psychological realism, without falling prey to lyrical imprecision and the exoticism which inevitably resulted from it.(27)

Despite such attempts to harmonize Realist and colonial fiction, the relationship between the two was bound to be problematic. It had not been the Realists who had first interested colonial writers in their subject-matter;   indeed, as we shall see, some colonial writers felt that Realism had improperly neglected the colonial subjects. Despite their ritual participation in the cult of truth, the colonial novelists included only one writer who breathed the air of pure Realism, Vigné d'Octon.   His work showed how Realism (and the Naturalism which followed it) might influence colonial literature by the introduction of scientific methods of race-analysis into fiction.

It is evident from every page of colonial fiction that the pseudo-scientific tenets of racialism had influenced colonial writers. Skull-shapes, race-classification, monogenesis debates, all featured in colonial fiction whether of naturalist or exotic tendency. Orignally, however, the combination of scientific and literary methods had been exclusively a feature of Realism, following Balzac.   Balzac's novels had explored human social behaviour by analogy with the zoological theories of Saint-Hilaire.   Taine followed this lead, arguing that literature was to explore man 'on a physiological basis', using the methods of the exact sciences to investigate the actual causes of man's actions. In his study of English literature published in 1864 Taine explicitly included the study of race and environment among the tasks of both novelist and literary critic.   Under Zola's leadership the Naturalist movement further identified literary and scientific methods.

These developments created a literature anxious to classify social groups according to scientific principles.   Zola selected various classes and families to be the subject of his novels according to scientific classification of society, attempting to show objectively the various determinants of heredity and environment within each milieu. Vigné d'Octon modelled his work directly on Zola's, focussing his novels on distinct social classes according to their place on what he called an 'ethnological ladder'.(28)   A method evolved on the class-structure of France applied even more happily to the pattern of race-relations in the colonies.   It was Vigné's purpose in Chair Noire (1889), for instance, to establish the division of the race scientifically, as a socio-biological fact, and thus to discredit the picture of harmonious race-mixing given subjectively by the exotic novel. The work was a piece of literary dogmatism as well as a statement of dogmatic racialism, and it is a timely reminder that racialism was accepted and propounded even by writers who, ostensibly, were opposed to French imperial expansion. Liberalism in foreign policy did not need to be matched by liberalism on questions of race.

Pierre Mille argued against the exotic on a more modest basis.   In a series of articles written in the early 1900s, which were to be influential in the subsequent debates, Mille portrayed the exotic style as a danger to colonial fiction. It was not the historical form of exoticism which worried him. Indeed Mille's style owed too much to writers such as Loti and Flaubert for him ever to turn against them. Instead he saw exoticism as an attitude of mind perennially threatening true colonial fiction. He meant by this a metropolitan attitude, based upon the tastes, vocabulary and expectations of a metropolitan reader.   This attitude was producing 'a literature of colonial tourism', in which Mille saw two major drawbacks. First, Mille argued, it would always fail to understand the milieu and mentality of the colonies because it was over-concerned with subjective impressions rather than with objective realities of colonial life. Secondly, this tourist literature would always tend towards an excessive liberalism in its view of the 'Native'. Its roots were in Rousseau, Mille claimed, and the view that 'the savage is always right'.(29)

It was for these reasons that Mille, like Hans Grimm, drew great inspiration from Kipling, who helped him to steer a middle course between dogmatic Naturalism and metropolitan exoticism. He ascribed Kipling's genius for penetrating the 'Native' milieu to the 'fact' that he was himself a half-caste (a rumour which dogged Kipling for much of his life), and he looked forward to a similar mixing of race producing in France a work which would penetrate the worlds of white and black with equal understanding.   It is interesting to note that Kipling too looked for a renewal of colonial literature out of a similar mixing of the races, 'a writer from among the Eurasians who shall write so that men shall be pleased to read of Eurasian life'.(30)

Both Kipling and Mille, therefore, were concerned to develop a colonial literature which was not metropolitan in outlook. Mille shared with Kipling too an aesthetic position which was neatly balanced between the scientific and the anti-rational(31), based on observation and on imagination. Mille did much to propagate this view of Kipling to other French writers, notably Claude Farrère.

In general very few colonial writers applied systematically the Realism which, when attacking exotic writing, they appeared to embrace. Randau, whose criticism of exoticism we quoted earlier, went on to distance himself from Naturalism almost as clearly as from exoticism, and in this was fairly typical of French colonial fiction. Les algérianistes (1911) deals at length with the efforts of a novelist, Cassard, to find a style of fiction appropriate to his country. His comments on the novel can be seen as a statement of Randau's own principles, as he too sought a way to express the distinctive experience of Algeria in art and 'to organize in beauty the artistic tendencies of a nation in the process of formation'. The literature he is looking for will be 'virile and strong, demanding strong feelings and violently spiced dishes', and lacking 'all sickly half-heartedness'. While some of these terms might describe a Zola novel, Cassard explicitly rejects Naturalism for excessive intellectuality and for 'an anarchy of details, chaos'. Cassard looks instead, much as Mille had, for a symbolic literature which would express colonial experience with the appropriate intensity and capture the 'return to barbarism' which Algerian life involved. It is hardly surprising that Cassard concludes his remarks by pointing to Flaubert's Salammbô as his model, with its extraordinary mixture of violence, documentary realism and symbolism(32).

Debates of this kind had considerable importance in the gradual process of defining colonial literature, both by writers and by historians of literature. Both Pujarniscle and Pierre Jourda, in his revaluation of the exotic tradition which began to appear in 1938, were influenced by Randau's emphasis on Flaubert as the model of colonial fiction.

One final reason lay behind the rejection of systematic realism by the majority of colonial writers. Leblond (the name under which Georges Athénas and Aimé Merb published numerous colonial novels) argued that the Realists had been incapable of the cross-cultural sympathies necessary to colonial fiction. 'The Realists', they complained, 'are restricted in their choice of subject to Parisian or provincial life, and they are unwilling to recognise the great social concern and altruism of exotic writing, which comes from its sensitivity to the other, allegedly inferior races of the universe'(33). Perhaps we saw enough of the exotic tradition of France to question the validity of such a claim for its generosity of spirit: in a later chapter we will see how fully Leblond's own work matched up to this altruism.

Another prominent writer to insist on the link of altruism and race-sympathy between colonial and exotic literature was Isabèle Eberhardt, whose beautiful Pages d'Islam date from the early 1900s. She saw the cross-cultural sympathies implicit in exotic writing such as her own as a key to social harmony in the North African colonies she so loved. 'The spirit will not renounce conquest, 'she wrote, defining the strict limits within which her imagination was free to work, 'but it will go further than conquest'.(34)

In rejecting the 'xenophobia' of the Realists, Leblond saw a continuation of the imaginative journey tradition of the eighteenth century into colonial literature. He edited numerous collections of these journeys, and did much to rewrite literary history as an anticipation of colonial fiction. At the same time, however, it was evident that he felt colonial literature to have an important contribution to make to the literary life of metropolitan France, and this view was shared by many colonial novelists.

It was Decadence which most disgusted colonial writers as they looked homewards at the literary life of the mother-country. Oscar Wilde represented the more colourful side of that movement, but there were many other writers lapsing into pessimistic disengagement from life and action. As they viewed such tendencies, colonial writers believed they had a literary mission to Europe. They felt called to divert into literature a stream of fresh experience and to reassert the imagination as an instrument of discovery rather than of dream. While Huysmans' characters imagined foreign places from the comfort of an arm-chair; while Proust made memory rather than action the mainspring of the novel, and while the psychological novel made its triumphal progress through the literary world, colonial writers were convinced of their vocation. Herbert Wild wrote

> It appears to be desirable that writers whose faculty of observation is augmented by a talent for powerful evocation should abandon microscopic analyses and should set out resolutely along the world's road in order to find men to describe.
> We are tired of decadent eroticism(...) and we have had enough of illnesses described by invalids, for France is slowly dying from them.(35)

Roland Lebel, who had quoted these remarks, rounded off his history of colonial literature by underlining its contribution to the regeneration of French culture. He claimed that the whole of colonial literature amounted to 'an affirmation and a moral force' and concluded:

> In the face of sickly over-refinement and the corrupted questioning of an over-subtle civilization, in which the vitality of the race is being drained away, colonial literature points to the remedy which lies in the primitive virtue of effort, in which energy is revived at the fountain-head of ancestral instinct.(36)

The popular novelist Hugues Le Roux defined the task of colonial literature as showing the youth of France a more worthwhile goal in life than seductions and 'a different glory than the destruction of souls'. He saw his own work as an antidote to literary modernism, to which - in a phrase anticipating Gide - he refers as 'that coalition of counterfeiters which for so long has discredited truth'.(37) His novel, Je deviens colon (1895), was full of the naive belief that the description of a simple settler life in Algeria would, at a stroke, redress these faults of culture. A similar view was put forward by Hans Grimm in his widely read essay 'The writer and his age' (1926). Literature in Europe had become obsessed, he argued, with 'the expression of erotic, morbid and frivolous experiences, of a kind which only those would indulge in who do not have a job to keep them busy'.(38) The nationalism of colonial fiction, together with the genre's solid reliance on action rather than reflection, was seen as the natural antidote to these cultural poisons.

There was, of course, a hidden dilemma in claims of this kind. Writers found themselves committed to the defence of the expansion of European civilization, while at the same time offering in their literature an alternative to the malaise which they observed in that civilization itself. In its self-understanding as literary artefact, colonial literature illustrates a dilemma which it would also illuminate thematically: the close connection between cultural imperialism and 'Kulturkritik', which had been anticipated in exotic writing.

Colonial literature therefore drew on both the strengths and weaknesses of the European literary scene in its efforts at self-definition. It reflected the wider insecurities and confidences of the colonial settlers who were to fill its pages.

NOTES

1. R.Wellek, Concepts of criticism (New Haven,1963),p.282. p.282. I have listed some of this histories of colonial literature in section 5 of the biobliography.

2. A.Sandison, The Wheel of Empire (Macmillan, 1967), p.201.

3. The Cambridge History of English Literature, vol.14 (CUP,1934), p.331.

4. F.Brie, Imperialistische Strömungen in der englischen Literatur (Halle, 1916), p.196.

5. For a detailed as well as a general criticism of Brie's study see C.A.Bodelsen, Studies in mid-Victorian

Imperialism (Copenhagen, 1960), pp.24,32.
    6. E.L.Gilbert, Kipling and the Critics (Peter Owen,1966)
pp.1/19. See also A.Wilson, The strange ride of R.Kipling
(Granada,1979), p.332.
    7. Quoted in Gilbert, p.4.
    8. Quoted in A.Cruse, The Victorians and their Books
(Allen & Unwin, 1935), p.308; and P.B.Ellis, H.Rider Haggard,
(Routledge & Kegan Paul, 1978), p.119.
    9. Cf. K. Bhaskara Rao, Kipling's India (Norman, 1967)
pp.31/33.
    10. Many Inventions (Uniform Edition, London 1899), p.39.
The earlier quotation from Kipling's 'In Partibus'. James
quoted from Gilbert, p.12.
    11. 'A Matter of Fact' in Many Inventions, p.141.
    12. Quoted in G.Friessen,'Charles Sealsfield and the
German panoramic novel of the 19th Century' in Modern Language Notes, vol. 84/85 (October 1969), pp.735/36.
    13. Grimm's account of condition in South-West at the
time was given in Die dreizehn Briefe aus Deutsch-Südwest-
Afrika (Munich, 1928).
    14. I have discussed this relationship in the essay 'Hans
Grimm & Rudyard Kipling' in The Modern Language Review, vol.
68 (1973), pp.863/69.
    15. Details of these works can be found in the Bibliogr-
aphy, p.170 f below. D.C.R.A. Goonétilleke makes 1880 the
turning point (Developing countries in British fiction,
Macmillan, 1977, p.3).
    16. H.A.C.Cairns, Prelude to Imperialism (Routledge &
Kegan Paul, 1965), p.91.
    17. See H.Brunschwicg, French Colonialism 1871/1914
(Pall Mall Press,1964), p.24f; and A.Murphy, The Ideology of
French Imperialism (Washington, 1948), p.2f.On the various
Geographical periodicals of France see D.V.McKay,'Colonialism
in the French Geographical movement' in The Geographical
Review, vol. 33 (1943), pp.214/37.
    18. 'Vorwort', Das Ausland, vol. 1 no. 1 (Munich, 1 Jan.
1828), p.2.
    19. Die Natur, vol.2 (Halle, 1853), p.27. Earlier quot-
ation from 'Der Naturmensch - auch ein Mensch', vol. 1 (1852),
p. 207.
    20. 'Ethnologische Beiträge', Globus, vol.4 (Hildburg-
hausen, 1863), p.378. Earlier quotation from 'Vorwort', vol.1
no.1 (1861), p.iv.
    21. 'Die Afrikanische Konferenz in Berlin', Das Ausland,
vol.58 (1885), p.61.
    22. Cf. footnote 34 of previous chapter. Also H.A.C.
Cairns, Prelude to Imperialism, p.92f.
    23. P.Jourda, L'Exotisme, vol.2 (Paris, 1956), p.275.
    24. R.Randau, Les explorateurs (Paris, 1907), pp.6/7.
    25. Quoted in A.R.Lebel, L'Afrique occidentale dans la
littérature française (Paris, 1925), p.226.

26. 'Marie-Faite-En-Fer', Barnavaux et quelques femmes (Paris, 1908), p.23.

27. E.Pujarniscle, Philoxène, ou de la littérature coloniale (Paris, 1931), pp. 15,171/77.

28. P.Vigné d'Octon, Fauves Amours (Paris, 1892), p.iii.

29. P.Mille,'Loti et "L'exotisme"' in Le Roman français (Paris, 1930), p.89.

30. P.Mille,'Littérature coloniale' in Les Nouvelles Littéraires, 2 Jan. 1932, p.1. E.Pujarniscle expressed similar hopes (Philoxène, p.201).

31. Cf. P.Mille, 'R.Kipling et l'invention littéraire' in Le Temps, 15 April 1914, p.3.

32. R.Randau, Les algérianistes (Paris,1911), pp.140/49, 241, 310/11.

33. M.A.Leblond, Les Sortilèges (Paris, 1905), pp.iii/iv.

34. Quoted by V.Barrucand in the preface to I.Eberhardt, Pages d'Islam (Paris, 1920), pp. 10, 12.

35. Quoted by A.R.Lebel, Histoire de la littérature coloniale en France (Paris, 1931), p.172.

36. Ibid., p.212.

37. H.Le Roux, Je deviens colon (Paris, 1895), p.55.

38. H.Grimm, Der Schriftsteller und seine Zeit (Munich, 1926), p.140.

Chapter Three

IMPERIAL LANDSCAPES

Colonial literature, as we have seen, moved between a variety of opposites: objectivity and imaginative empathy, Realism and exoticism, separatist and metropolitan tendencies. These forces can ben seen at work in all colonial literature and in every topic which it took up. We begin by examining colonial literature's presentation of the landscape in the colonies: a morally and politically neutral topic, but one which shows something of the range of relationships possible between the literary imagination and the more concrete aims of imperial conquest.

Landscape had featured prominently in all the genres of fiction which we examined as forerunners of colonial literature, with the exception of the Realist novel. It had symbolized the exotic writers' escape and had been central to the ideology of the early fiction about America. In the adventure story it had played a major supporting role. There was, of course, a vast amount of fiction which continued to treat colonial landscape in this subordinate role, using the splendours of Asia and Africa merely as stage-decoration to bolster a weak score and to revamp those suburban romances which were the authors' only genuine theme. 'Clare made no attempt to withdraw her hands and returned his gaze with eyes that were dark and velvety as the African night sky' - a novel which begins like that will do little to encourage readers to discover how it ends. Even the serious writers, attempting to communicate something of the uniqueness of the colonial setting, all too often fell into the trap of size and merely overshadowed the action of their books by claims about the immensity of the landscape in which it took place. 'Art involves moderation and rejects enormity', Gide remarked as he surveyed the immense expanses of the Congo jungle. 'A description is no more moving if you multiply everything by ten'(1). The cultivation of facile sublimity - 'The spectacle of the great and savage nature delighted him and filled his soul with new emotions' - cut very little ice with the colonial writers. They wanted to show themselves to have been shaped by the experience of the colonial landscape, in that sense at least they were heirs of Chateaubriand and Crèvecoeur, but they wanted to show an acquaintance with the land which was more intimate and utilitarian than that of exotic fiction.

63

Kipling's evocation of the jungle has long been famous, especially the passionate and primitive world of the <u>rukh</u>, in which he brings Mowgli to manhood. Mowgli himself, a child reared by the wolves, is an imaginative tour de force on Kipling's part, a primitive demi-god, 'Adam in the Garden'; and the forest in which he lives shares with him a rich fecundity and a personalized vision of natural forces which spring from the same imaginative vision:

> Then came the Rains with a roar, and the <u>rukh</u> was blotted out in fetch after fetch of warm mist, and the broad leaves drummed the night through under the big drops; and there was a noise of running water, and of juicy green stuff crackling where the wind struck it, and the lightning wove patterns behind the dense matting of the foliage, till the sun broke loose again and the <u>rukh</u> stood with hot flanks smoking to the newly-washed sky. Then the heat and the dry cold subdued everything to tiger-colour again. So Gisborne learned to know his <u>rukh</u> and was very happy.(2)

The passage is distinctive not because of the freedom of Kipling's imagination, but rather because it is harnessed to his understanding of the purposes of colonization. The description is far more than an evocative backdrop to the emergence of Mowgli. It forms part of a wider panegyric to the Department of Woods and Forests, for which Gisborne works. The Department carries out on the Indian landscape precisely the same work which the colonial administrators and soldiers perform in the chaotic human environment of warring and rebellious groups. The vital cycle of the forest is dependent on the colonizing work of the Department, just as the colourful pageant of Indian life depends on the peace-giving presence of the British. The Department has transformed 'denuded hillsides, dry gullies, aching ravines' into a true order, in which primitive nature and man work together. Gisborne, the Forest Officer, smiles on his forest like God in the first garden: he has made it and he knows it to be good. It is no co-incidence that Mowgli should take service with Gisborne and become a game-warden, and it is certainly not a piece of cheap imperialist propaganda transplanted into an imaginative and unpolitical story.(3)The aesthetic vision of the primitive, both Mowgli and the forest, is inseparable from Kipling's pride in the achievements of British rule.

We noted that Pierre Mille drew heavily upon Kipling for his own colonial writing, and that it was the imaginative penetration of the colonies which he claimed most to owe to his English model. He spoke directly of the 'lyricism' which Kipling had contributed to colonial writing(4), and although we shall find him to be as vigorous as Kipling in support of the ideals of European imperialism, the relationship between his imagination and the imperial mentality was much less intimate. Once again a passage of Mille's landscape description will serve to illustrate this.

Landscape is important to Mille's stories, and in the tradition of Flaubert he integrates description and action with consistent skill. His artistry is most apparent in a landscape less full of extremes than Kipling's India, more susceptible to nuance and sensual detail. Whereas Kipling had cursed 'the want of atmosphere in the painter's sense', asserting that in India 'there are no half tints worth noticing'(5), Mille is at his best in the gentle landscapes of Madagascar. His style is typified in the story 'Ruy Blas', in which a French colonial soldier, in an outburst of fever and homesickness, tells the story of the unhappy love which has driven him into the colonial service and landed him in the clammy heat of a Madagascan night:

> The soldier started to swear. The door of the hut stood open and the moon shone outside with an intolerable brilliance. The earth exuded the heat from the sun, which it drank in thirstily during the day, sweating it out now, damp and hot, with a smell of crushed grass, rain, mud and fever. Around a circular clearing, darkened by the shadows of low huts, three sacrificial pillars supported a bizarre and barbarous apparatus: the skulls of oxen, still with their horns attached, as if the oxen had been crucified there(...)The moon poured down its light upon the red and burning earth, lonely and absolute, an all-pervading yet melancholy sight, with its strangely human complexion, its yawning mouth and its treacherous, oriental eyes. Ah! it made you want to weep, the gaze of those celestial eyes...(6)

Reading Mille's landscape descriptions of this kind, we are struck by the entirely European terms of reference. Although it is an imaginative piece of writing and aims to create empathy between the European and the colonial milieu, its focus remains with the individual European and his homesickness. Exotic details, symbolic and impressionistic as they are, have little relationship to the actual landscape, and none whatsoever to the reasons which have brought the Europeans, collectively speaking, to the country. Imperialism plays no part in the canvas that Mille paints. The 'bizarre and barbarous' sacrificial posts remind the sufferer only of his own sufferings: they do not suggest to him anything of the civilization into which he has come, either positively or even in the negative implications of the Europeans' civilizing mission.

In passages of this kind Mille showed how far he was from that 'depaysement' which he wished to encourage, and how close still to the literary tourism he warned others against. He avoided the worst cliches of the exotic tradition and went to Flaubert rather than Chateaubriand for his model, yet this merely changed the style in which a metropolitan perspective was expressed: it did not change the European nature of that perspective. A similar process can be observed in many of the colonial novelists. Even those many writers in the French colonies who, with their particular interest in opium, appeared to have abandoned all pretence at an European perspective soon came round into a style instantly recognizable at as _fin de siècle_ aestheticism. So Jules Boissière, portraying the violence and cruelty of a mythical East through the grey smoke of the opium pipe, remained within the orbit of European literature, and the at times brilliant stories in _Fumeurs d'Opium_ simply belong in the tradition of Poe, Baudelaire and Wilde. However unconventional their 'radiant, sad apotheosis of Death and Beauty'(7), and however far from the superficial orientalism of the Romantics, the stories remain within a European perspective. It was indeed easier to exchange one European style for another than to leave the tradition behind altogether.

The Algerian novels of Bertrand, Randau and Leblond are perhaps the most successful in achieving a shift of perspective from metropolitan France. They argued, as we shall see, for a strongly separatist view of colonial development, and the landscape of Algeria formed an important element in both their novels and their arguments. They show a harsh and rugged landscape which has shaped the mentality of the indigenous peoples for centuries and is no less influential on the personality of the white settlers. Robert Randau's search for a realistic appraisal of colonial experience had stemmed from his observation of the material influence of landscape on personality, and his many portraits of the white Algerian farmer stress a unity of landscape, ideology and imperial mission which, like Kipling's vision of India, is collective rather than merely individual.(8)

For Ernest Psichari, however, the relating of colonial landscape to the overall purposes of imperialism was much more individual, not to say mystical. He begins his account of a military expedition through Chad with the statement that he had decided to abandon himself 'unreflecting to the mysterious charm of the bush'. It seems to announce the relinquishing of the European persona. Yet almost at once Psichari reaches what was to be the central theme of his work: that man creates for himself the beauty of Africa, and that the sole object of the experience of nature is to reach that 'complete harmony with things, in which every nuance seems adapted to the state of our soul'. These ideas mould his descriptions:

> The path follows the right-hand bank. One would have said it was a great road, straight as the Romans built, now abandoned, yet leading to mysterious destinies. The river Logonne is the focal point and logical centre of the country. The river gives architectural shape to the contours of the land and creates their perfect and lasting harmony. That is the hidden reason for its voluptuous charm. Nothing is useless here, nothing distracts your eye. And yet, what sterility there is! Everything matters in this ceaseless monotony, and even the most insignificant object helps you love the river better, with its wonderful nobility and the elegance of its silent banks.

> There was an exquisite freshness in the air. To the
> east, a large sooty red disk slowly rose up the deep
> line of the horizon. Waders and wild duck, quacking
> horribly, rose from the river's surface in sudden flights.
> Everything was clean, well cared for, like a delicate
> water-colour. No obstructions. No violence. Every
> nuance combined to create in us a feeling of well-being
> and contentment.(9)

The writer of these lines cannot be said to be blind to Africa, yet
he touches on only those things which correspond to his own interior
landscape. The river with its mysterious destiny is the river of
his own life. The craving for purity and inner peace projects itself
onto the African landscape: there nothing is useless, excessive,
out of harmony. The sun - one of the principals in all African
dramas - bestows and blesses equally, gives to each object its
proper and satisfying place, to each image a fullness and intensity
which pleases the artist's eye. Later Psichari writes that he
wanted to look on nothing else than 'this lonely, passionate beauty
in which I can shelter any good there may be in myself'(10). The
African landscape is one of self-affirmation, not of discovery.

Psichari has often been compared to T.E. Lawrence, and the
clarity and cleanness of their landscapes had a personal centre
which linked both men. Both held political ideas, and acted on
their behalf, in a way which matched their vision of the landscape.
'I conceive of African landscapes under two aspects,' Psichari
wrote, 'that of action and of dream.' The actions are those forced
marches he describes, the immense and 'noble' efforts which he
undertakes in the cause of imperialism, that national outburst of
health and vitality. Yet that imperialism is itself also a dream,
'an illusion of superiority which drives us out into beautiful actions'.
In what Psichari called the 'metaphysics of Africa' landscape and
self, action and dream, imperialism and the self-revelation of
Africa are one.(11)

I hope to suggest later that the mystical origins of Psichari's
writing did nothing to tone down the political impact which it had
in France, or to change fundamentally his assent to French
imperialism. Nevertheless his work represents a high-point of the
imaginative, inward vision of Africa being in harmony with the
military conquests of imperialism.

So far in this chapter it has been the imagination of colonial
writers which has concerned us, and the extent to which it followed
a course more or less in harmony with imperialism. The German
writer Hans Grimm, however, although no less strongly influenced
by Kipling than Pierre Mille had been, tried to emulate in Kipling
not the literary achievement but the political vision. He argued
that Kipling's vision of imperialism was so all-encompassing that
Kipling was able to relate every situation he wished to describe
to the overall well-being of the British Empire, and that there
was nowhere that Kipling's imagination might alight without
illuminating and furthering British imperial aims. The uniqueness

of Kipling was therefore a political vision rather than an aesthetic or imaginative facility.(12)

Grimm's approach to Kipling may or may not be found persuasive. It clearly echoes the political ambitions which we saw behind the German exotic and travel novels of the mid-nineteenth century. Nevertheless, Grimm's own colonial writing provides an example of the stylistic results of allowing the imagination to be inspired by imperialism as a political idea rather than by the reality of the colonies. A revealing passage comes from Grimm's story about the reviving fortunes of a father and daughter living on a lonely farm in Namaqualand. While the girl has been away at school, her father has lowered his moral standards and taken an African mistress. The girl returns to the farm and sets in motion the recovery of her father's self-respect.

> Autumn and winter had passed across the lonely farm(...), a winter still more dry than the summer; and as the leaves turned colour in far-off Germany and plants and animals made ready their for their long winter sleep through the cold months of shortage and hunger, the spring awoke by the Groot River. Unexpectedly a few drops of rain fell, and the veldt was suddenly green. Within a few days the flowers were open with glowing red and yellow colours, while among the grass and the flowers and cicadas and grasshoppers and other insects took up their song again, until the whole air was filled with their cries and calls and chirpings, like a living organ(...)and everything stretched and moved, as if a new Paradise had sprung up and would continue for ever, a paradise in which everyone had his own significant and rightful place.(13)

It is not merely Kipling's superiority as a stylist which emerges from a comparison with this passage. The relationship between the lyricism and Grimm's imperialism is much more telling than simply Grimm's lesser stylistic abilities. Not only does the plot of the story remain unconnected to this outburst of nature, so that in effect Grimm is merely manipulating nature to comment extraneously on his own story, but the lyricism is itself manipulated in the service of imperialist ideas. It has more connection with Grimm's enthusiasm for settlement than with his love of the scenery of South-West Africa. By means of this evocation of Paradise he wishes to suggest that national problems may be saved by colonial living-space. Germany is deep in winter, a time of 'shortage and hunger' (the date is 1913, the high-point of the 'saturated' economic prosperity of the Kaisers), while the colonies have all the warmth and fullness of spring. Nature parades her riches with the promise that there is room for everyone, and Grimm's imagination reveals itself to be that of the travel-agent.

In one sense it was German misconceptions of imperialism which lay behind the naivety of Grimm's vision. The German colonial movement was notorious for its unrealizable dreams of large-scale colonial settlement and for its determination to attract to German colonies as many as possible of the emigrants who would otherwise flock to the United States. The emphasis on settlement often overlooked factors such as economic viability and even a colony's suitability for European settlement, and there were frequent clashes between colonial administrators and the ideologues about settlement policy. A leader of the German colonial movement summarized the attitudes of his movement as follows:

> We started with(...)a wrong conception of colonial possibilities. We wanted to concentrate on Africa the emigrants we were losing at the beginning of our colonial enterprise. We wanted to build a new Germany on African soil...We tried to assume to ourselves the function of Providence.(14)

Grimm's facile picture of the paradise of colonial nature belonged within unrealistic settlement plans of this kind.

Another important feature of many colonial landscapes emerges from a comparison of Grimm's description of nature as paradise with the frequent, much more negative accounts of colonial scenery. From paradise to hell is a short step. Nature, which we saw acting as the pliant servant of imperialism, shows herself elsewhere to be 'without scruple or sympathy' for the sufferings of the white settlers who are Grimm's heroes. Extraordinarily brutal and cruel scenes flood his novels, and that brutality is claimed to lie no less at the heart of Africa than the facile paradise of the scene we quoted. There are many places in Africa 'where a lonely white man meets his end like a sweating, panic-stricken beast', and Grimm takes his readers to most of them.(15) Why he should do so is less immediately clear. While the Algerian novelists were determined to penetrate into the 'nightmare forests' of Algerian landscape, as a flame to temper the steel of their character(16), they were at least consistent in their cult of the harshness of nature, and their works avoid the sort of mawkish sentimentality which Grimm's style still admitted. Eduard Pujarniscle quotes an interesting account of a writer's efforts to come to terms with this harshness. George Groslier wrote of the experience of Cochin-China:

> Driven back by a wild nature which is so hostile to you, you're forced to cling on to it with all your strength in order to wrest from it some of its mysteries, some of its beauties. It's an unequal struggle - but beautiful and passionate for all that.(17)

Grimm does not struggle for his visions of beauty, and the harshness of nature is not the shell which hides a sweet kernel. It is something Grimm himself imposes on nature, a celebration of his own pain and fears. Like Captain Ahab - 'heal'd of my hurt I laud the inhuman sea' - Grimm was of that peculiar cast of mind determined to banish suffering from the self by locating in it the external world. The psychologist would make much of Grimm's dual picture of Africa in its relation to personal experience: Mannoni gave a neat outline of such responses in the figures of Ariel and Caliban, projected onto the colonial world. Grimm's landscape helps us to see not only the influence of political thinking on the imaginative vision of Africa, but also the inescapable frame of European personal experience which surrounds the pictures given of it.

Our final example of imaginative response to colonial landscape is taken from Paul Vigné d'Octon's La gloire du Sabre(1900). The book is an indictment of the atrocities committed by the French forces in Senegal, and begins with an evocation of the African landscape:

> This is Africa, man-eater, soul-destroyer, wrecker of men's strength, mother of fever and death, mysterious ghost which for centuries has sucked the blood of Europeans, draining them to the very marrow, or making them mad. Over there the smoke of the blue sea, lying in its eternal sleep under the implacable sun. The waves break and beat mercilessly over its narrow coasts and tortured estuaries, a constant terror to the bravest sailor. The innumerable inlets breathing out pestilence, which hide in the sickly shade of the mangroves are the ever-open eyes of Africa, like Sirens ready to engulf those hardy spirits who affront her. At the Equinox, when the moon shines over these swamps, they seem like the white face of dying man(....) Further inland, towards the desert regions, the landscape is still more sad. Huge empty spaces stretch out indefinitely; nothing grows and nothing lives there, except a few meagre shrubs, scanty grass and occasional rubber trees, which beneath the eternal ardours of the sun weep their tears of gold. The sand avidly drinks up the rain which from time to time falls on this sterile land, shunned by birds and animals - even by the jackal, that friend of solitude - because they would die of thirst there.(18)

We have here an archetypal picture of the cruelty and harshness of Africa, repeated ad nauseam in all colonial fiction. Its most obvious feature is the insistence on intensity and violence. There is nothing about it of the passivity of Psichari's internal landscape: Africa is here the active agent, presenting challenges, demanding responses, establishing certain ways of behaving. It does not matter that Vigné himself is horrified by the crimes and atrocities he is about to describe, whereas most writers, introducing their colonial story by such a description, would have taken a much more lenient attitude to these events. In both cases, the landscape and the violence are one. It is an accursed land; the Biblical phrase 'land of Cham' recurs incessantly in colonial fiction. It is to the country itself that are ascribed the crimes and life-style of the invaders. The cliché appeals to Vigne d'Octon in that it helps to preserve the strongly idealistic belief in colonialism which had inspired his attacks on colonial abuses. Men had succumbed to the evil of Africa herself rather than to the inherent brutality of imperialism. For other writers, scene-setting of this kind contributed to the suspension of normal moral judgements which they hoped to achieve in their readers. In the hell of Africa, so such depictions argued, who might be a saint? Where nature is so cruel, can her children be kind?

NOTES

1. A.Gide, Voyage au Congo (1927), loc. cit., p.101. The adjacent quoation is from Jules Verne.

2. 'In the Rukh' in Many Inventions (Macmillans, 1899), pp.304/05.

3. Cf. E.M.Forster's distinction between Kipling's 'Daemon' and his 'job' which Benita Parry developes (Delusions and Discoveries, Allen Lane, 1972, p.255f).

4. P.Mille,'Sur Joseph Conrad' in Les Nouvelles Littéraires, 2 November 1929, p.1.

5. 'Wressley of the Foreign Office' in Plain Tales (Macmillans, 1900), p.310.

6. P.Mille,'Ruy Blas' in Sur la vaste terre (Paris, 1905), pp.150/01.

7. J.Boissière, Fumeurs d'Opium (Paris, 1896), p.149.

8. R.Randau, Les algérianistes (Paris, 1911), pp.275/77.

9. E.Psichari, Terres de Soleil (Paris, 1908), pp.158/59. Earlier quotations pp. 2 and 157.

10. Ibid.,pp.209/10.

11. Ibid.,pp.244,230.

12. H.Grimm,'Vom politischen Dichter: Geistige Begegnung mit Rudyard Kipling' in Das innere Reich, vol. 2 (Munich, 1935), pp.1149/70.

13. H.Grimm, Südafrikanische Novellen (Frankfurt a. Main, 1913), pp.159/60.

14. Prof. Moritz Bonn, quoted in F.J.Maclean, Germany's Colonial Failure (Burrup, Mathieson & Sprague, 1918), p.9.

15. H.Grimm, Südafrikanische Novellen, p.123 etc.

16. Randau, p. 310.

17. E.Pujarniscle, Philoxène, p.31.

18. P.Vigné d'Octon, La gloire du sabre (Paris, 1900), pp. 1/3. For a full analysis of this style of writing about West Africa see L.Fanoudh-Siefer, Le mythe du nègre et de l'Afrique noire...(Paris, 1968), pp.68/106. The reader of this chapter will note how greatly impressed I have been by G.Shepperson's essay on 'The World of Rudyard Kipling', in which he imaginatively explores Kipling's self-projections (in A.Rutherford (ed.) Kipling's mind & Art, esp. p.130f).

Chapter Four

SLAVES AND MISTRESSES

The previous chapter has shown the wide range of imaginative responses which might be evoked by the colonial landscape, the relationship between the imagination, more or less empathetically involved with the strangeness of another world, and the imperial mentality with its unruffled confidence in white attitudes. In responding to the colonized peoples, however, writers faced a more challenging call to reconcile imagination and imperialism. It challenged not merely the artist's eye but also the power of imagination to move beyond the prejudices and narrow experiences of the colonials. At issue was the quality of human response, sincerity of commitment to human values and loyalty to personal experience rather than to received opinions. We shall therefore in this chapter be less concerned to catalogue the brutal stereotypes put forward in colonial fiction than to suggest reasons for their victory over curiosity and imagination. We concentrate on those writers who prided themselves on exploring as well as conquering and who sought intimacy rather than distance in their dealings with the 'Native'.

It is convenient to begin with German colonial fiction since it shows the extent of the imagination's failure to understand, or even to investigate, the otherness of the colonies. Despite a long and honourable missionary tradition, despite the intellectual adventurousness of the German philosophers in the first half of the nineteenth century (Schlegel and Schopenhauer, for instance, had done much to spread the ideas of Buddhism through Europe), and despite the legacy of travellers like Humboldt, German writers achieved next to no sympathetic insight into the lives and minds of the peoples their army had colonized. Although the German colonies were in German hands for as little as thirty years, in which time they learned more about African warfare than about African culture, it was not from ignorance that German writers gave so little account of the African peoples. Indeed, many were anxious to display their inside knowledge of African life and to present themselves as experts on tribal culture. Particularly after 1907, when the discovery of diamonds in South-West Africa brought a flood of whites into the colony, writers were at pains to identify themselves as old hands, 'old Africans' as they said, and inside knowledge of tribal custom, history, law of succession and language was the passport to that status.

This knowledge made little impression upon German fiction, perhaps because of writers' sense of potential inferiority as they compared tribal culture to their own country's history. When the missionary Heinrich Vedder, in his celebrated study of South-West Africa before German rule, traced the lineage of the Herero paramount chief back to 1530, it can have escaped no-one's attention that the Herero people had enjoyed a longer period of nationhood than Germany itself, which was not united as a nation until 1871.(1) Although the tribal wars of the 1840s were often quoted as a justification of the Germans' civilizing mission, the history of Germany was not without bloody and chaotic periods too. The Herero chiefs often showed themselves more experienced and confident in diplomacy and personal authority than their masters the Germans, who, guided by abstract theories of state and historical analogy rather than by experience, often felt at an embarrassing disadvantage. Perhaps it was not surprising that the majority of writers made little use of their knowledge of African history and customs.

Instead, German writers contented themselves with the clichés about the Africans which were to prove so convenient to all the colonizing powers. They fixed their attention almost exclusively on the white community, as if it alone could appeal to the imagination. Their work forms it were a compendium of stereotypes about the 'Native', and the list has a depressing familiarity. The 'Natives' smell, are lazy, are impulsive and childish, they are utterly indifferent to morality, they are said to 'welcome a beating if they have deserved it' - in short, all the shallow, protective clichés of the colonial mind went towards German fiction's account of relations with the Africans. Writers never thought to relax their exclusively European perspective on what they saw, or to rethink the prejudices which this perspective automatically produced. For instance, in Frieda Kraze's Heim Neuland, a very typical settler novel published in 1909, we read of the visit of a German couple to an African celebration. In an often repeated scene the hero and heroine sit wrinkling their noses fastidiously at the gaiety of the dance. Since the early part of the novel had been concerned with the middle-class social round in North Germany in which hero and heroine first met, and which know no celebration more unbridled than an evening of Wagner songs round the piano, we can guess that they are not amused by African ways of enjoyment:

> These people were not human beings. Not even those of them who had become Christians(...) That was proved by the fact that their character had not changed, by their sadistic brutality and their frequent lapses into hereditary primitiveness. Perhaps in a few hundred years time they might become human beings, but for the present they were no better than animals.(2)

The author clearly shares this view, for her novel ignores the

Africans from that moment on. The moment is a characteristic one in all colonial literature, a moment reached after the clichés have been rehearsed: the moment at which writers decided that the colonized people were utterly alien and could be spoken of as if they had no human characteristics at all - the moment, therefore, when the imagination finally capitulated.

Frieda Kraze's novel is characteristic also in that the ultimate repudiation of the Africans was provoked by the alleged sensuality of their culture: a factor which justified their repudiation on both ethical and cultural grounds. British fiction about India, particulary that of the women novelists in vogue at the end of the century (Maud Diver, Mrs. Perrin and Mrs. Steel), often echoed Kraze's repudiation of the sensuality and sexual openness of 'primitive' peoples. Although their works contained far greater detail of Indian life than that which their German contemporaries regarded as worth recording about Africa, these British novelists were no less adamant in withdrawing all sympathy for India because of the apparent licentiousness which they discovered in Hindu art, and more generally in the marriage customs they witnessed in India. Because of what Alice Perrin shyly referred to as 'their present attitude towards the Feminine', she maintained that there could never be 'any true sympathy(...)between two races'.(3) While, in part, such views reflected the greater emancipation of European women, certainly in the matter of the treatment of widows or child-brides, they had a no less important source in the European novelists' highly conservative view of sexuality. Flora Annie Steel, for instance, ascribed the divisiveness of races' 'sense of colour' to differences in sexual temperament. Despite India's rich culture and civilization, she observes in one of her stories that 'the difference between a brown and a white skin was the outward sign of the vast difference between sentiment and sheer passion'(4). Sentiment is the European experience, 'sheer passion' is Indian.

These attitudes had a very long history. From the sixteenth century the encounter with dark-skinned peoples had created in the European mind pictures of semi-humans driven by sensual, bestial passion. Elaborate theories had been worked out to link the 'descendants of Cham' with licentious passion. We saw brief examples of these images among Crusoe's successors. There were, therefore, many antecedents and archetypes for the repudiation of Indian and African culture on the grounds of sex, but we also need to see in such attitudes a reflection of much more recent European developments. The British novelists for instance, were convinced that the movement towards women's emancipation in Europe was inspired by a desire for sexual liberation. Mrs. Steel, who explicitly rejected women's emancipation and the contemporary idea that emotion or passion could be the basis of marriage, showed in her Indian stories the degrading effects which their obsession with sex had brought upon the women of India. In strident reaction against the Victorian New Woman Mrs. Steel proclaimed marriage as 'a duty to the race' and denied that it had anything to do with what she called 'intense personal gratification'. She used her portrait of Indian sensuality as a warning to her British readers of the dangers of the cult of emotion.(5)

There was also, inevitably, a personal aspect. In her autobiography - a splendid account of a vigorous public life in India - Mrs. Steel made it clear that emotional experience had played no part in her own marriage. 'I do not think either of us was in love. I know I was not; I never have been', she wrote(6). Thus, between the ready-made archetype, the social movement in Britain which she wished to oppose, and personal ignorance, her sympathy with India stops short.

Strangely, for their rejection of 'native' sensuality was no less vigorous, many of the German women novelists were far from conservative in their attitude towards sex. Several, most notably Frieda von Bülow, belonged to the movements working for women's emancipation in Germany, a country which had always taken for granted a woman's total dedication to Children, Church and Kitchen. At a time when many writers in Germany were exposing the hypocrisy and unnatural repression inherent in the conventional sexual ethic, many of the women writers saw colonial life as a potential escape into naturalness, into an uninhibited world of genuine feeling and wider responsibilities for women. Yet it is striking that nothing came of this escape. In social terms the women did play a more significant role than they were allowed to in Germany, but emotionally their emancipation was not seen as fulfilling. The heroine of Frieda Kraze's novel, recoiling as we saw from the sensuality of the 'primitive' Africans, soon forgets that she had come out to Africa in search of a liberation which was physical and sexual as well as social. Her early dreams of sexual naturalness are soon forgotten and with relief she takes up the closely-scripted role of motherhood, more matronly and authoritarian even than that from which she had escaped. One cannot but recall Mannoni's observation that the black man 'is the white man's fear of himself', and suggest that some German writers had invested the Africans with the fears and feelings of guilt which accompany emancipation. Their reluctance to talk about Africa was a reluctance to be truthful about themselves.

These subconscious fears were again expressed clearly in the universal condemnation which mixed marriage and inter-racial sexual liaisons received at the hands of German novelists, both the men and the women. While all the writers condemned such liaisons, the reasons given for this condemnation varied somewhat according to the sex of the author. The women writers insisted on the morally degrading aspecats of these relationships and portrayed the African women as depraved, prey to uncontrolled and insatiable sexual appetite. The encounter of German and African women is always presented as a challenge to European moral standards and for that reason German novelists stressed the 'ideal' side of white marriages. Although children are born to white marriages with a regularity which is reassuring for the colony's future, no mention is ever made of the emotional, let alone sexual, side of the marriage. Marriage is not a relationship so much as a business partnership undertaken out of duty to the race. Sex remained the preserve of 'primitive' people, with whom whites should have no contact.

Male views of mixed marriages and of sexual relations with African women departed but slightly from this narrow stereotype. The more honest novelists admitted to the existence of an almost universal custom in German territories of taking African women as wives, with or without benefit of clergy.(7) A few writers even suggested that the settlers regarded an African mistress as proof that one had become emancipated from the irrelevant moral standards of home. There are no accounts whatsoever of sexual relationships between a white woman and an African, at least partly for the reason that civilian settlement remained so restricted in German colonies and European women had settled in such tiny numbers. But these admissions of the problems were immediately counterbalanced by the vitriolic denunciations of all inter-racial liaisons.

A revealing example is the short novel Das Duallamädchen (1908) by Jesco von Puttkamer. Set in the Cameroons, it is a slight and sentimental account of the love between a German trader and a girl from Doula. The novel ends with a striking denunciation of all sexual liaisons with African women, and of mixed marriages in particular. Puttkamer chooses as his mouthpiece for these views a Catholic nun, selecting her no doubt because of the fact that the Missions (higly improperly in the settlers' opinion) preferred mixed marriages to inter-racial promiscuity. The Missions' attitudes had come into public prominence a few years earlier at the time of the so-called Colonial Scandals, in which a district officer of the same name as the novelist (Jesco von Puttkamer) had been disciplined for facilitating sexual relations with local women. It had been the Catholic Mission's insistence on marriage rather than casual promiscuity which led to the scandals becoming public. Puttkamer is noticeably careful that the arguments put forward by the nun against mixed marriages have nothing at all to do with the Christian ethic. The nun explains:

'The alliance of a white man with a black women is a disaster for him and for the colony(....) Look what happens to the man's character in such a long-term relationship. The white man insists that he is master in his own house and gets used to the black women waiting on him. All the time, however, the black's company is altering his whole sensibility. Such a marriage is bound to debase him, however strong-willed he may be.'(8)

There are two distinct elements here, which other writers developed further. One is the danger to the white man and his ethos: the other, the danger to the colony. Many German writers portrayed in graphic detail the degeneration of European customs and ideas in what they usually referred to as as 'a Kaffir marriage'. The mulatto child, 'the swamping of the white man by black customs, by the African family and by dirt', the broken-down farmstead and the poverty of those Germans who fraternise with Africans - all these subjects received full and horrified treatment, and no grain of sympathy alleviated the descriptions.(9)

It is not fanciful to suggest that a major element in German reactions to those who 'go native' was insecurity, a subconscious awareness that they themselves clung to the achievement-oriented ethos of Europe by only the most slender of threads. The lapsed bourgeois featured in much contemporary literature, most famously in the novels of André Gide and Thomas Mann. Although colonial writers were virtually unanimous in their rejection of the ethos of the lapsed bourgeois, they must themselves have known the appeal of 'dropping out'. 'I have become what I am,' Thomas Buddenbrook, near the end of a life devoted to keeping up appearances, explains to his decadent brother, 'because I did not want to become like you.' With these words he expressed tensions similar to those felt by many of the 'respectable' settlers, exhausted by the pressures of always being on show as a member of a master-race, 'living in a glass-house' as one writer expressed it.(10) How many of them must have longed to slip quietly out of the demanding role they had to play and to have deserted ship. The fanaticism with which the novelists depicted the dangers to white men in such drop-out relationships must have been linked to those repressed fears.

No less fanatical was the cult of European habits of hygiene and cooking, which showed themselves often merely as props to an Europeanness which was less than self-assured. A German guide on tropical hygiene illustrates the dilemma clearly. It makes great play on the connections between cleanliness and moral superiority: 'bathing as a moral factor' is a recurring theme. Yet the complacency suggested by these attitudes is soon eroded, for the author is far less certain of himself on the question of sexual hygiene. He flatters his readers by admitting that sexual activity is a sign of manly vigour, but points out that it will not assist their work as 'bearers of culture', and that as soon as the Natives see that 'we have the same passions as they have' white supremacy will be at an end. It hardly shows confidence in white superiority.(11)

Another example which suggests that the fear of mixed marriages was not simply sexual is given by Hans Grimm's story about Mkulu (a white) and Hili (an African). Grimm attacks Mkulu for no other offence than that of living in the same house as a black man. He has 'lost caste' and 'it is a disgrace for everyone who has white skin on his face'. There is no suggestion of sexual impropriety, despite the outraged tone of Grimm's reactions, but the offence implied by the desertion of European standards is felt to be as heinous as any sexual offence.(12)

The other aspect of German opposition to mixed marriages emerges in Puttkamer's phrase 'a disaster to the colony'. Sexual relations between black and white were shown by many writers to threaten the social structure of the German colonies and to 'bring about the collapse of the empire'. Not only would such liaisons end that illusion of god-like ascendancy of the whites on which they felt their authority to be based; they would interfere with the settlement programme, by creating a local population which would ultimately deprive future immigrants of land. Novelists painted grim visions of the future:

> A miserable generation of half-castes, inheriting all the bad qualities of their parents, the criminality and laziness of the black mother in particular, will fill the country and is indeed already threatening its future.(13)

When writers went on to call mixed marriages 'a crime against the blood' (a phrase common in German fiction), they revealed the great usefulness of racial arguments. Without denying that these arguments were part of the intellectual climate of Europe at that time, and that writers would have taken them out to the colonies as part of their intellectual baggage, racism more often fulfilled a secondary function. Racist arguments offered post-hoc validation of socially useful attitudes rather than their starting-point. They modified into a fact of nature the conquest and oppression involved in imperialism. They gave dramatic and unanswerable force to the political threat they felt to exist in mixed marriages. They justified European standards at a level of meaning which was beyond the reach of the counter-arguments against civilization. They gave the special status of treason to otherwise relative questions of shifting cultural standards, and it was for that reason that novelists so readily adoped racial arguments against mixed marriages. It is not surprising that the racist ideologists of the Third Reich should have turned their attention to colonial writers and praised them for their pioneering contribution to racist thought. Frieda von Bülow, for instance, was praised by the National Socialists for making 'a confession of faith' out of her racist ideology.(14) In fact the Nazi theoreticians were wrong, in that these novelists had had no new thoughts and contributed nothing to the development of racist ideas, but, like the Nazis themselves, they had discovered how to mobilize racist ideas in support of social and political aims.

We need to remember that German fiction's account of inter-racial liaisons was profoundly unrealistic. Although German writers' utter failiure to portray African life corresponded exactly to the callous indifference which marked both the policies and the behaviour of the settlers and administrators, their attitude towards more personal relationships had no such equivalent in reality. In this respect, colonial writers were out of touch with settler opinion. This is clearly shown by events in South-West Africa, where the questions of mixed marriages took on great political importance.

Relations with African women were very common in South-West, particularly in the south of the territory, and for years had aroused little or no comment. The pressure for banning mixed marriages originated in Berlin not in South-West Africa itself, and the majority of the settlers accepted the policy only on the basis of the political and social arguments which the Colonial Department put forward. (Much the same balance of pressures affected white sexual behaviour in India, as Professor Ballhatchet's recent study Race, Sex and Class under the Raj has shown.) The ban became law in 1905, and in 1907 was given retrospective force, annulling all marriages which had been concluded with African women before 1905. When therefore writers introduced this retrospective force into their novels and spoke as if race-pride rather than legislation were the inhibitor of mixed marriages, they completely distorted the situation. Not only did they shut their eyes to a series of tragic human problems, as those Germans whose marriage with African women had suddenly been annulled tried to come to terms with the racial discrimination of their fellow-settlers* ; they actually contributed to the worsening relations between races, supplying new settlers especially with a ready-made racist ideology. Racial discrimination itself - in the unpleasant forms of segregation and apartheid which anticipated future South African legislation - did not precede the legislation of 1907 but grew up very quickly afterwards. While it had once been possible to find settlers proud to have attended Herero family and tribal ceremonies, including baptisms and public festivals, after 1905 a new climate of racial discrimination developed in the towns which had no interest in such sympathetic links. This fragmentation of society was further encouraged as writers presented racial separation as a natural expression of ideology or racial self-awareness. Such presentations were self-fulfilling prophecies rather than realistic descriptions of race-relations in South-West Africa. (It was always claimed that a similar deterioration in race-relations followed the spread of racist theories among the colonial administration in India.) In South-West Africa it was noticeable that when the churches and certain social clubs in the townships attempted to follow the line set by extraneous policy and ideology by bringing pressure to bear on the settlers not to indulge in extra-marital relations with African women, the settlers energetically defended their liaisons. They argued that they were not 'ascetics' but normal 'healthy' people with healthy instincts, and that they were not going to let any abstract arguments stand in the way of their natural instinctive satisfaction.(14) Thus while the novelists preferred to hawk round an ideal ethos of race, even to the extent of reviving the ancient idea that sexual intercourse with the Africans should be punished

---

*Helmut Bley includes a most moving letter from one such person, writing to the Governor to plead that the law be not applied in his case. While he obviously accepted the political arguments in favour of the ban on mixed marriages and wanted South-West Africa to remain 'a white man's country', this settler acutely suffered from the dilemma his happy marriage presented him with (South-West Africa under German Rule, p.217f).

as a sexual perversion, the settlers, those unwilling paragons of Aryan virtue, continued their sexual adventures unabated, and novelists learned nothing from them.

It is hard to imagine a greater contrast than with French colonial fiction, in which accounts of inter-racial sexual encounters play a major role. Indeed, it would be amazing had this not been so in a country which had for decades practised in literature a sexual openness almost unheard of in Germany or England. French colonial writers followed the flag to all corners of the globe and gave frank and detailed accounts of the lives of French soldiers and administrators with their consorts: the moresques of Algeria, the moussos of the Sudan, the congaïs of Indo-China. As they moved from colony to colony, their experience of the various races increased and the Grand Tour took on an almost gastronomic quality. French colonial fiction devoted much of its attention to demonstrating the particular qualities of the various races as lovers, with a relish and a delight in voluptuous descriptions which only the most hard-bitten reader (and that certainly included all the German writers, who had nothing but contempt for their French counterparts) could fail to respond to.

French literature contains the clearest accounts of the temptations of that 'dropping out' from European civilisation which German writers so feared. Not only the cult of opium caused a shudder of horror to flicker through the disciplined ranks of the German colonial writers; not only too the sexual profligacy which they saw displayed in French colonial practice, but the explicit readiness to abandon the moral and social props to European civilisation, of which Royer's La maîtresse noire is a particularly clear example. Royer gives the following words to one of his characters:

> 'At the end of the day I think the negroes are right. All our worries and nearly all our unhappiness and disappointment come from the demands we make on life. Ambition, a career - ugh! "You are dust and to the dust you will return." That's truth, eternal truth! Yes, it's the blacks who are right, not us with our stupid, pointless cult of activity(...). They are the ones who have taught us, who have won me over. We all take their moussos, but I have taken over their instinctive laziness, their passive obedience to the law of the minimum effort, which is the source of all wisdom'.(16)

It perhaps was not surprising, in view of what we have seen of German attitudes, that French colonialism had so few friends east of the Rhine.

The influence of the exotic novel on French colonial fiction is at its strongest here. The voluptuous sensuality of the later work is unthinkable without first Chateaubriand, Flaubert and Loti. Many of Loti's novels, like his first, Aziyadé, were simply accounts of the narrator's love affair with a girl of the region which he happened to be visiting. Through these erotic relationships Loti not only contrived to give a picture of the country, he also attempted to show the particular qualities of temperament and outlook which distinguished the race of his temporary election.

Loti's imaginative travelling celebrated the occasional success - a scene which convinces, a character who comes alive - but it would be wrong to think of his achievement as offering an escape from prejudice. His picture of Turkey in Aziyadé is certainly alive with sympathy; although, as most recently Clive Wake has shown, there is a strong sense that Loti's evocation of Turkey is little more than a dramatisation of internal conflicts and dreams, and that in Turkey we are again on Crusoe's island. Loti's picture of Japan in Madame Chrysanthème, however, which uses similar techniques, is full of unpleasant prejudices and dismissive attitudes. The charm falls away fast from Japan: the smile of the narrator's bride becomes 'an old woman's grimace, smiling ugliness, a monkey-face'.(17)

In the same way Le roman d'un spahi (1881), although offering a full account of black-white sexual relations, became a major source of the myths about Africa which continued to prejudice French writing throughout the colonial period. It tells of the love-affair of Jean Peyral, a French colonial soldier, and Fatou-gaye. The beauty of this African girl, her loyalty to her French lover might have been seen as positive qualities traditionally explored by the exotic novelist. Yet the hold she comes to exercise on Peyral is shown to have both disastrous consequences (his gifts to her are carefully juxtaposed with the financial difficulties of Peyral's aged parents in France who need his support) and dubious origins in magic, symbolized by the amulets Fatou-gaye wears. Peyral's 'dignity as a white' succumbs to Fatou-gaye and her 'negro gracefulness, sensual charm and tangible power of seduction: an undefined quality, a mixture of the simian, the virginal and the tigrish'. His disgust at her is, however, ultimately the stronger, and the genre of the exotic novel communicates this sense of disgust no less readily than Aziyadé had communicated the charms of another race.(18)

The striking ambiguity of the exotic tradition towards other races makes one suspicious of the way many colonial writers cherished a sense of continutiy with that tradition, a continuity which went beyond mere stylistic imitation and claimed to follow cultural and moral guide-lines. Leblond gave the fullest account of the possible fruitful relationship which might exist between the exotic and colonial traditions. In the preface to the novel Les Sortilèges (1905) Leblond tried to rehabilitate what, he claimed, had been too often overlooked in exotic writing: namely, 'its social concern and altruism, which came from its sensitivity to the other, allegedly inferior races of the universe'. We saw earlier that Leblond felt Naturalism to be an unsuitable model for colonial literature, and while he was careful to distinguish true exoticism from 'the superficial and demonstrative Orientalism of the

Romantics', Leblond claimed that the exotic tradition gave to
French colonial writing an unique ability to assimilate other
cultures, by means of 'a moral and intellectual conquest, founded
on meticulous analyses'. He predicted for France the emergence
of 'a colonial literature made up of careful depictions, of subtle
psychology and complex intellectual and social understanding'.(19)
We need to ask whether colonial novelists in France managed to
translate the altruism of the exotic novel into their fiction, even
assuming that they managed to identify it in the exotic tradition
itself.

An obvious starting-point for such an enquiry is the story
'Ramary et Kétaka', Pierre Mille's haunting and beautiful account
of the love-affairs between two French soldiers and their Malagasy
mistresses. The story is his most impressive achievement, and
shows very clearly the unique possibilities which the French
tradition gave Mille as a writer and which far surpassed what he
could learn from his other literary model, Kipling.

The story is made up of the pleasures and uncertainties of
two relationships. The pleasures are in the complex and shifting
relationships, in the mixture of childishness, ceremony and
primitiveness which delights the Europeans in their companions,
played out against a brilliant description of the gentle landscape
of Madagascar. The uncertainties, and there are many for it is
a tragic story, came from the different responses to their love
which are dictated by the backgrounds and traditions of the lovers,
the conquered and the conquerors. The Malagasy girls are touched
deeply by the affair; they become utterly dependent on their
lovers, who have uprooted them from family and community.
When Kétaka is abandoned by her lover she cannot re-establish
herself in her old way of life and is broken spiritually by what,
to the soldier, is no more than an episode. At the same time
Mille shows that the Europeans are emotionally disorientated by
their love: one of them remarks that 'we sometimes felt ashamed
to observe that we forgot our old country and that our hearts no
longer beat for the same things as in Europe', and this instability
is contrasted with the security and protective power which they
see in more traditional tribal communities. The Europeans also
lose their bearings and cannot readjust to life, and it is partly
because of Mille's sensitive account of European responses that
his story leads him to a clear and sympathetic vision of the nature
of such relationships and of their effect upon the colonized peoples.
At the end of the story, when death and indifference have broken
both liaisons, a third Malagasy girl takes her leave of the Europeans
and in a moving, if slightly over-dramatic speech, analyses the
plight and future of such relationships:

> 'Ramilina,' she said to me, 'the Malagasy song is true:
> We are to blame and we are dishonoured and we are
> lost, lost! Before, we know nothing of marriage, we
> could not distinguish between a lover and a husband.
> And then you came, you white people, and we loved

you, and you believed in things of which we knew
nothing: fidelity and virtue, which your missionaries
teach to our ignorant little savage girls for long hours
at school, while the handsome officers and the white
planters wait to pick them up at the school-gate. Yet,
by imperceptible stages we come sometimes to believe
that these virtues might exist: and just at that moment
- you leave us!'

For all the pathetic tone of the speech it is, in its age, a clear-
sighted account of the process of abandonment, which Mannoni
was to diagnose as the principal evil left behind by the colonisation
of Madagascar, a type of invisible oppression, discernible only to
the observant.

The transference of dependence from family to lover, and
then the feeling of total abandonment when the dependence is
repudiated is at the heart both of Mille's story and of Mannoni's
analysis. Both see clearly that it is this process which will destroy
Madagascan society, for the lines quoted above conclude with a
vision of the death of that society and of all tribal culture and
government: 'the people will be like dust, the women like mud'(20).

We see the depth of Mille's understanding when we compare
these insights to the explanations offered by colonial administrators
of the external manifestations of Dependence. One contemporary
account of Malagasy life quoted a letter from an Hova girl to the
retiring French governor, which concluded with the words: 'Good-
bye, general, you are my father and my mother. (The form of
address 'Ray aman'd Reny' was widespread at that time.) The
authors of the study, however, authorities on the French colonies,
merely related this humorously to 'the refined coquetry of Hova
ladies', a typically patronising yet unsympathetic view.(21) It was
the exotic imagination rather than the official mind which had
opened the door of understanding.*

Many colonial novels soon moved away, as Mille did, from
merely concentrating upon the excitements of exotic amours. While
Loti had, so to speak, added fuel to the moral disapproval of
primitive peoples in his picture of the animal sensuality of Fatou-
gaye, it became more common to portray and complain of the
sexual passivity of the 'primitive' partners.(22) It occurred to no-
one that this passivity might have its origins in the women's
resentment of a white oppression which reached into their state
of sexual slavery. Sometimes the novelists merely identified this
passivity as a reassertion of the proper status of women, and

---

*It is revealing to compare Mille's imaginative attitude with
Kipling's more limited range. When in the story 'The Head of the
District' Kipling quotes the Indians' similar remark to their white
administrator ('thou art our father and our mother'), he does not
attempt an explanation of this, but merely takes such remarks as
the basis of his paternalist view of colonial administration.

contrasted primitive women very favourably with the more tiresomely demanding emancipated woman in Europe, following prejudices similar to those of Mrs. Steel, albeit reaching a different conclusion. At least primitive partners do not talk literature in bed or expect to order their men-folk around in the day-time - such seems their attraction to many novelists.

Vigné d'Octon portrays sexual passivity as an incompatibility of race. He summarized the message of his novel Chair noire (1889) as follows:

> The black woman has neither the same qualities, nor the feelings nor the same experiences as a woman of the Caucasian race. Between her and the white man there is no possibility that love - in any psychological sense - might exist.(23)

Chair noire studies the sexual relationship between the army doctor, Frantz Varnet, and the Poulh girl, Aïssata-lô. The African girl is shown to be incapable of sexual fulfilment with Frantz, and although both participate in explicitly described and often brutal sexual activity - Frantz assaulting her like a wild beast in the jungle clearings, and Aïssata-lô taking part in one of the 'bestially erotic dances' which feature de rigueur in almost every West African novel - their relationship is one of sexual disharmony. Frantz' frustration is made worse as he watches Aïssato-lô's infatuation with a young man of her own colour. Too late he realizes that the repulsion she feels for him came from 'the withdrawal from contact which was instinctive to her race, following the inflexible law of the preservation of the species', and that it is impossible by means of his own sexuality to awaken a relationship which infringes this law.(24) He may father her child, but he cannot touch Aïssata-lô's innermost nature.

The character of Frantz Varnet implies a critique of the exotic temperament. He is only driven to sexual explorations in Africa because of his perverted and morbid sensuality, a casualty of the corruption that decadence has brought to the metropolitan France of his day. He is one of the over-sensitive, over-introverted weaklings of the fin de siècle, yearning for primitive passion as an antidote to their own weaknesses.

Vigné d'Octon was closely associated with the Naturalist movement and used its methods and belief in inflexible scientific laws governing human behaviour to investigate race relations in the colonies. Clearly Leblond had writers such as Vigné d'Octon in mind when he criticized the Naturalists for a lack of genuine interest in other races and for an intellectual arrogance in dismissing those irrational aspects of behaviour which he regarded as important to an understanding of primitive peoples. It is questionable, however, whether Leblond himself achieves a more worthwhile degree of sympathy.

In his four-part novel Les Sortilèges Leblond portrays four separate inter-racial liaisons, involving not merely Europeans but also Asians and Africans who cross the cultural frontiers. The first novel, Moutousami, reveals the strengths and weaknesses of Leblond's approach. It tells of the love-affair between a Malabrian girl and the son of a European factory-owner, and in particular of the effects of this affair on the girl's father. He is anxious above all to protect his daughter's virginity, so that she may later enter properly upon the traditional marriage and life-style of her people. But she is being alienated from those traditions by her love for the European, while her father is so used to the subservient attitudes which working for the Europeans imposes upon him that he is unable to act decisively on behalf of his daughter. At the moment that she is seduced, he hangs himself.

The novel explores in the manner traditional to exotic fiction both an enchanting landscape and the 'mysterious' soul of the Indians. Implicit in the approach is a certain sympathy to the non-whites, just as Mille could not have diagnosed the plight of the Malagasy girls without a modicum of sympathetic involvement. But just as Mille's achievement was only an occasional insight which in no way ruled out brutal racist opinions, so Leblond's sympathy for the subservient races co-exists with depressingly familiar stereotyped attitudes which he obviously shared with the most unreflective settler. For instance in Moutousami, although Leblond gives a sensitive account of the father's inability to express in words his feelings about his daughter, Leblond goes on to say that the Indians are simply 'degenerate' and 'incapable of action'.(25) He is prepared to admit the interest of his subject, and that marks him off from many of his contemporaries. The exotic tradition makes him an explorer of minds, but the colonial mentality ensures that he will discover merely a cliché.

Leblond's claim that the French colonial novel can best assimilate the rich traditions of the peoples of the French possessions explains his long interest in two particular groups: the creoles (in the strict sense of white people, of European descent, living in the colonies) and the new French nation of Algeria. Erotic and exotic features of his work are important here too, but the novels show most clearly the relationship between nationalism and assimilation and between race-thinking and racism.

His novel Le miracle de la race (1914) tells of the growing to maturity of Alexis Balzamet, a creole in La Réunion. The miracle of which the title speaks is two-fold. It refers to the miraculous awakening within this orphan boy, utterly declasse as he is and surrounded by the influences of native and half-caste cultures, of a pure selfless love for France, her glory, language and civilization. In this sense the book is purely nationalistic: it traces the racial characteristics of this 'young overseas Frenchman (Français d'outre-mer)' and his recognition through love, culture and patriotism of his true nature. The evocation of the colourful life of the island, and the possible affairs with native women (all of whom Alexis repudiates), in other words the exotic framework of the novel, is entirely subservient to its main purpose. The theme involves their rejection. But at the end of the novel that

French identity to which Alexis has successfully strived, that 'almost inaccessible elite' which his mentors have taught him to desire, is shown to contain an element which insists on the assimilation of other cultures. What Alexis has elevated to an ideal of purity is shown in fact to be diverse. Alexis' mentor tells him at the conclusion of the novel:

> 'It is the variety of races which makes the beauty and, one day, the greatness too of our little island, for I am myself certain that it will have a noble place in the history of France as long as we whites learn in the future to remain the superiors of the other races, while yet loving them as our worthy ancestors did. Ah, if only the creole would make the intellectual effort to understand the endemic culture of the peoples which surround him, of the Indians, Chinese, Malagasies and Africans(...)what a rich and brave expression of humanity that would be(...) There can be no doubt about it: the French born on this island will not have achieved the miracle of their race until they have assimilated the genius of all the races which people the colony.'(26)

Algeria provided Leblond with a major illustration of this idea of assimilation. He believed that an entirely new race was being born in Algeria, and the genius of Latin civilization would flower there, enriched by features it had assimilated from Arab culture. He wrote in an essay on 'The Algerian Spirit' (1905):

> The Algerian was born from the mixing of Latin races and from contact with Oriental races. There was no inter-breeding of these races, or at least what there was remained limited and sterile. Instead there took place - by means of the necessarily close contact between masters and subjects which took place in the crowded cities - a slow penetration of the Latin by the Arab.(27)

Clearly Leblond saw assimilation within very strict limits. When he argued for it, he in no sense turned away from the narrow limits of nationalism and racism. Not only does his essay on Algeria use many of the terms favoured by the race-thinkers of the late nineteenth century (as for instance his discussion of the skull types which one may find amongst the Algerians), but his view of miscegenation draws heavily on the popular racist idea that 'hybrids' were sterile. Considerations of this sort make it difficult to see Leblond's ideas as any amelioration of the brutal racism we encounter elsewhere, and his essay on Algeria leaves as the dominant impression little other than ardent separatism. It is only in this spirit of separatism, of the repudiation of the particular racial and cultural standpoint of the metropole that his work breaks new ground. Racism was no less pronounced in the 'brutal, practical and realistic' patriotism of Algeria than in metropolitan France, and in some ways precisely Leblond's interest in the new assimilation of the races in Algeria into a new 'race' made him more susceptible still to racial prejudice.

A similarly enthusiastic account of the benefits of race-mixing in Algeria is contained in Louis Bertrand's novel Le Sang des Races (1899), a novel which in its day received much critical acclaim. It tells of the settlement of Spanish workmen in Algeria, and of their slow emancipation from the political and moral attitudes traditional to their home-country. The central character, Rafael, comes finally to adopt Algeria as his new fatherland and to sever all links with Spain. His grandfather had argued that it was a crime to abandon one's country, using a traditional racist argument: 'whoever deserts his country betrays his blood'. Bertrand's interest is in the new race which is being formed in Algeria, and he shows that the influences of the country and the peoples of Algeria overcome all Rafael's traditional attitudes. 'Intoxicated by the abundance of Africa and carried away by the ardour of the soil', Rafael like the whole colony is 'in the process of transformation', being shaped by Africa into a new Algerian race(28).

One would not wish to deny that these novels - and others like them, notably R. Randau's first novel, Les Colons (1907) - possessed a greater insight into the relationships between races than most English or German fiction. Indeed, French novelists frequently repudiated the intolerant, insular racialism which they observed in the works of their European contemporaries. The exotic tradition had made French novelists imaginative and sensitive travellers, and there was a certain justice in their claims that French imperialism and its literature were concerned with 'the spread of a very noble and admirable sense of humanity'. Yet always the racist attitudes are close to the surface, and the fascination which novelists felt with new racial mixtures certainly did not oust their prejudices about existing races. It is no coincidence that Louis Bertrand's second work on Algeria, an account of a sentimental return to the scene and themes of his earlier novel, should spell out so clearly the racist implications of his theory of assimilation. While he continued to praise in 1930 those 'neo-Africans' (i.e. white Algerians) who would be the agents of social fusion, he makes explicit what the earlier novel had merely implied: that no assimilation and no new Algerian nation could ever cross 'that great divide which separates the African soul from ours', and he claimed that the French in Algeria should take as their motto 'Be on your guard'. He refers to this attitude as a 'corrective which we have always presupposed to exist behind any declaration of fraternity and any programme of collaboration, understanding or union between races'.(29) It was in this spirit that Leblond had argued that humanitarianism was an attitude dangerous in excess, and that it needed to be counterbalanced by a healthy nationalism. These remarks make clear the restrictions which had always been implicit in these assimilative views of race-relations.

Critics in the 1930s tended to be impressed by the assimilative abilities of these writers. Susanne Howe over-enthusiastically praised French fiction for escaping from prejudice through its exotic vein, while Eduard Pujarnsicle argued that the pursuit of eros in the colonies gave 'access to the native milieu', opening 'a series of doors which, without such affairs, would remain inexorably closed'. At the end of his argument, however, he made an admission about such liaisons which underlined the shortcomings of sympathy which we have been at pains to show. None of the liaisons, he admits, amounts to anything approaching equality or in any general way breaks down the barriers of dominance. He accepts as a summary of his view that 'exotic love therefore is love without love'. Philip Mason has rightly pointed to the fact that inter-racial sexual activity far from overcoming racial separation was often a direct product of such discrimination, showing the cheapness of the colonized race.(30)

We noted that even Leblond and Bertrand stopped short of any approval for miscegenation, and it is characteristic of all French colonial fiction that whatever sympathy there may have been for other races, and whatever enthusiasm for inter-racial liaisons, the half-caste is universally disliked. There is no suggestion of political arguments about white supremacy, such as we saw in German colonial fiction; instead the arguments are almost invariably couched in racist terms.

An example of this dislike is the unpleasant story 'The Hare' by Pierre Mille. It is an account of the relationship between a 'blanc-comme-ça-meme' (a Senegalais half-caste) and a white girl. The half-caste is very successful as a suitor, but his success is interrupted by the re-emergence of his 'native soul' at a particularly important point in the seduction. He has just taken the girl to a small hill surrounded by flood-water, when he catches sight of a hare and his hunting instincts are awakened: 'His lips were drawn back, showing his teeth and gums and for the first time I heard the negro's grunt, the deep "Ugh?!" that marks his intense satisfaction when, for instance, the order is given to storm a village'. In a blind blood-lust he races round the islet after the hare, while his European inamorata, horrified at this transformation, suddenly realizes that she had been on the point of making a terrible mistake. Barnavaux, who had witnessed the episode with the distaste of the colonial and therefore tells the story, takes her away from the island and is pleased to see that she has been cured for ever of such suitors. His conclusion: '"I had seen the nigger in him"'.(31)

The story illustrates Mille's growing preoccupation with the possibilities of the 'natives' making off with European women. The great majority of serious fiction tackled the problems of inter-racial liaisons from the position of the white male partner. It was almost exclusively left to sensationalist popular fiction to chart the murky waters of white women's sexual explorations (Pierre Mille recalled that a certain type of publisher tended to reject novels 'because the white woman does not sleep with a

native'(32)) and serious French colonial fiction took a very negative
view of these relationships.

One of Mille's stories tells of an eminent Japanese diplomat,
whom Barnavaux sees in Paris, in the company of a beautiful
French girl who obviously is in love with him. Barnavaux is shocked
at this 'invasion' of France, and shouts an obscene insult at the
girl in Japanese. The narrator, in whom the sight of the couple
had provoked 'a violent feeling of revulsion, a sort of enlarged,
impersonal jealousy which pierced my heart', feels that he ought
to object to Barnavaux' remark. After all, he argues, 'when we
go to Japan we find ourselves little mousmés too'; but he has no
answer to Barnavaux' rejoinder: 'But it isn't the same thing at
all. We are white.'(33)

Two novels in particular explored the theme of a white
woman's marriage with a non-white. Alix de Villemagne in Hors
de sa race (1912) (Outside her race) tells of an upper-middle-class
girl who marries a Vietnamese prince. Their marriage exposes the
utterly different conceptions of the relationship which both hold,
and the novel argues for the impossibility of overcoming the barriers
of race and culture. As their relationship breaks down, her husband
watches her with the feeling of a man peering into a delicate
clock mechanism which he cannot repair. She looks on in horror
as his customs, manners and religion gradually lose the veneer of
Europeanness which they had assumed and he 'becomes entirely
Annamite again'. Her child, unlike the 'entirely white and slightly
pink' baby of her French friends, is yellow and from the earliest
age shows distressing affinities with its paternal grandfather, for
instance by scratching between its toes 'like a monkey'. Despite
the efforts of the parents, both of them sympathetically described
as 'the best of Frenchwomen' and 'the best Annamite husband',
the marriage is a disaster, and although there seems to be a
greater tolerance on behalf of the author than that shown by an
old colonial who reproaches the woman for 'her alliance with that
species of monkey', the ending of the novel makes an appeal for
women never to cross the racial barriers. 'Let my example be of
use to you, my sisters, useful in stopping any of you from marrying
outside your race'(34) - such are the heroine's last reflections, and
it is clear that not only are the races felt to be incompatible,
the Europeans are shown to be superior to the Asians.

The motives for the white woman marrying outside her race
are revealing. Here, as in Chair noire, there is an explicit warning
against the attitudes of the exotic novel. Just as Vigné d'Octon
wanted to deny the pictures of sexual bliss enjoyed by Loti's
'handsome sailor' with Polynesians and Tahitians, Alix de Villemagne
was anxious to show realistically the actual conditions of life in
an Indo-China whose mysteries had charmed many an exotic
novelist. In addition, the novel contains a critique of the class-
attitudes prevalent in France. It is the white girl's mother and
guardian who force her into marriage, out of snobbery, since her
suitor is a prince. Snobbery has replaced race-pride, and the novel
sets out to show that these are false priorities.

The marriage of a white woman and black man in Pierre Mille and André Delmaison's novel La femme et l'homme nu (1924) has similar origins. It too is part of a degeneration in the 'racial pride' of Vania, a nobly born Russian girl, caused by the shocks and disturbances of the Great War. Her marriage to Tiékoro, a Gambian who has come to Europe with the French army, is shown to be extremely superficial. Tiékoro is described as

> a real savage, that is to say the slave of dominant forces, social, religious and magical. Vania perhaps is primitive too but in the opposite direction, in the unleashing of forces. It is this release of energy which she and her race are bringing to the West and which creates her charm - and her danger....(35)

Vania struggles to raise her marriage above the vulgar prejudices which it meets, but once again these prejudices are shown by the end of the novel to be well founded, as Tiékoro succumbs to the lure of the jungle and Vania is left alone to survey the ruins of her life.

Like the German novelists, French writers partly based their response to inter-racial liaisons on a particular view of the role of women. They saw women as the fountainhead of racial strength; they were worried about the declining birth-rate of France, and felt that women had the major part to play in upholding the health of the nation. Leblond often appealed to French women to take up the great national task of increasing the birth-rate, or, in the colonies, what he called 'a heroic and great colonizing work, full of beauty'.(36)   Later we shall see Mille too arguing that the producing of children is an essential contribution to the imperial mission of France.*   It is this 'mother of the race' image which is offended by contact with other races and which thus inspires some of the most virulent racism of French literature.

So far we have examined certain of the more imaginative approaches to race-relations, especially sexual relations. Of course,

---

*Cf. Chapter 5, p. 118. This kind of stock-breeding language (a product partly of the race thinkers and partly of the Naturalists) was very common in colonial writers.   Rider Haggard spoke unashamedly of the need for 'breeding women' in South Africa; Psichari describes his hero's feelings for his fiancee in these terms: 'Claire was simply the women from whom he dreamed of having children later'.   There were, of course, philanthropic societies devoted to the export of marriageable women to the colonies selected according to appropriate ideological and eugenic criteria. A good illustration of these criteria is given by a record of proceedings of a meeting of the French Colonial Union in 1897 (L'Emigration des Femmes aux Colonies, ed. M. Le Comte d'Haussonville and J. Chailly-Bert. Questions du temps present, Paris 1897).

there was in French (as in German and English) literature an immense amount of unthinking prejudiced attitudinizing about 'the Native', and countless cynical accounts of the way to acquire a native mistress without the inconvenience of responding to the relationship, save as 'an instrument of brief pleasure or hygiene'.(37) We are concerned with imaginative insights against a background of general blindness. But it is interesting to see in what circumstances writers turned against the sympathetic insights once offered by their imagination. One might argue, as the colonial cynics did, that it was experience alone which caused opinions to change, and that all newcomers to the colonies lost their 'negrophile' attitudes at the first brush with reality. There is, however, little to suggest that imagination was merely the response of the inexperienced. More likely was that as writers readjusted to life in their home-country, after the experiences of colonial life, they evolved attitudes and relationships towards the home-country which made unnecessary their imaginative penetration of colonial milieu. Thus Bertrand, through the experiences of the Great War, found an identification with France and Europe which made irrelevant his cult of the Algerian. We shall see in Mille and Kipling a similar process taking place. A further factor was that whenever the object of the imagination took on a life of its own and emancipated itself, so to speak, from its purely exotic function, writers saw it in a radically different light, and invariably came to reject what they had first admired.

Some such process lay behind Mille's repudiation of the Japanese diplomat. After France had indulged for fifty years in the cult of the East and French writers (with the exception of Loti) had praised the civilization and art of Japan, Japan suddenly emerged as a threat to the colonial security of the European powers by defeating Russia in the war of 1904/05. Her appeal to exotic writers was at an end, and it became fashionable for writers to portray the East simply in terms of the 'Yellow Peril'. 'Six hundred millions of them on their ant-heaps, at their work', wrote Mille. 'It makes me fear for the future of the white races.' Perhaps it is that fear which makes him so abruptly offensive in his portrayal of the Japanese diplomat,* and leads him to describe the relationship to a French girl as an invasion. It is significant also that Hans Grimm, despite his reluctance to refer to any sexual aspects of race-contact, reserved for the Chinese the ultimate accusation: that they rape German women.(38) Again insecurity

------

*Kipling went through a similar development. Although he admired the Japanese and absolutely detested the Russians whom they obligingly routed, Kipling never lost after 1904 his fear about the world's future when the East 'really wakes up'. While praising Japan's art he had believed that 'Mercifully she has been denied the last touch of firmness in her character that would enable her to play with the whole round world.' 1904 changed that belief.

seems to be the spur to prejudice.

The fear of the reawakened East even crept back into the exotic novel. Claude Farrère, for instance, portrays the Russo-Japanese war with an ambiguity which highlights the problem. He sympathizes openly with Japan, while at the same time showing that the victory over Russia was achieved at the expense of all the exotic aspects of Japanese life. Farrere's sympathy cannot rest with the westernized and victorious Japan, but lies instead with the representatives of the old order, who themselves despise the process of modernization which has led to the victory. The author's mouthpiece is a stock figure of the exotic novel, a French painter trying, in the portrait of an aristocratic lady, to capture the true spirit of Japan. He completes his picture just before the war, in which the lady's husband is killed. His subject withdraws from the world, and only her portrait is left as a memorial to the old order and a symbol of the ending of an artistic relationship to Japan.(39)

English fiction had many years to explore the Empire, and there was both the time and the geographical scope available for writers to differentiate and develop their attitudes. Christine Bolt has given a full account of the different ways in which English writers approached the peoples of Africa, America and India. Cliched though many such opinions were, they contained a wide range of sympathy and outlook. Their diversity underlines the fact that the concept of assimilation plays almost no part in English colonial fiction. Whatever sympathy writers may express for the cultures and personal quality of other peoples, their sympathy remains distant and distinct: 'the Englishman has an instinctive dislike of "assimilation"', wrote a distinguished visitor to West Africa in the 1920s, and his words remain true of the whole of English colonial fiction of the earlier period. Nowhere is this more evident than in the unflattering portraits which English writers gave of the Europeanized, educated 'Native', whom even a sympathetic observer such as Edmund Candler refers to as 'the hybrid Cambridge-type, with the veneer fast wearing off'.(40)

There were various reasons for this. One important factor was undoubtedly that uncertainty about the value of civilization which we examine later, and which led writers to question whether a civilized man was an improvement on primitive man. It belonged to this kind of argument to assume that the English were civilized by racial temperament rather than by the chances of history: it was always a dilemma for writers to show the racial health and strength of the English at the same time as their civilization, and they emphasized the love of sport and hunting in order to bridge the gap. Writers also suspected that education would start a process of rejecting white supremacy and their hatred reflected a determination not to give way.

Another reason for the dislike of assimilation was more purely aesthetic. Writers saw the diversity of race and custom spread out in front of them like an artist's palette and resented any movement which reduced that picturesqueness. Other writers again saw the uprooting effect of Europeanization and, from a most paternalistic standpoint, regarded the assimilated native as an object of pity. Typical was Mrs. Perrin's account of an Indian prince's disorientation when he encounters the moral code of Europe:

> 'Why was I not left alone!(...) Why was I shown a different side to everything, so making me unsatisfied with the ways and customs of my ancestors!(...) How miserable I am, how miserable must I always be -'(41)

No one could argue that sympathy of this kind modified the race-prejudices which underlay Mrs. Perrin's work.

On the subject of mixed marriages British fiction was less forthcoming than the French. Outside the immediate geographical confines of the British Empire (as in Aylmar's Folly, for instance) a writer such as Conrad might at least bring the topic into fiction, but the colonial writers proper had much less to say. Certainly in the much more developed society of British India few writers touched the theme at all. We have already suggested the horror in which such liaisons were regarded by the women novelists. Perhaps the only writer to emerge significantly on this topic in India was Kipling himself.

Kipling's strictures to the whites never to go 'beyond the Pale' and to 'keep to his own caste, race and breed' have been remarked on by all critics. It is also generally accepted that his insights into Indian life reveal a genuine imaginative sympathy with a different race and culture, and that these sympathies occasionally extend to the particular - in other words to individual Indians: not to many, but to some. He obviously dislikes people who lack this sympathy, and in the bitingly ironic story 'Georgie Porgie' it is the English civil servant, who casually deserts an Indian girl in order to marry an English bride, on whom the brunt of Kipling's dislike falls. Indifference is one of the worst vices.

The most revealing story to deal with inter-racial marriages is 'Without Benefit of Clergy'. Despite the tenderness of the story, Kipling cannot be said to approve of the love and marriage of Holden and his Indian bride Ameera. 'By every rule and law she should have been otherwise', and the happiness which they find in crossing the racial frontier is only transient, for fever will rob Holden of both his wife and their child. Yet Kipling tells his story with a gentleness and sympathy, which readers today will find excessive rather than cold. His sympathy is not due to any appreciation of the particular emotional quality of such liaisons, for in fact he profoundly questions the authenticity and emotional realism of the relationship. Nor is his sympathy allied to a psychological interest in the race-factors which threaten the marriage. He mentions Ameera's feelings of guilt at abandoning her own people - albeit showing these feelings as an individual response, and not seeing in them, as Mille had, the symptom of a wider problem - and he refers in passing to the effect of the marriage on Holden's relationship with white society. But the marriage is obviously capable of surviving both pressures. In reality Kipling's sympathy is both humane (for in truth he hates suffering and will not bring his creatures to it with relish that at time he affects) and aesthetic. We suggested in the previous chapter that Kipling's imagination fused his experience of India and his vision of imperialism, harmonizing the artist's eye and the imperial purpose. In his sympathetic picture of a marriage which breaks the rules Kipling, once again, achieves a harmony of imagination and imperialism. His aesthetic imagination which creates this isolated world of happiness outside the norms and the laws of white society is well aware that the picture it paints cannot be more than episodic, and that the laws surrounding the action must remain immutable. It is the acceptance of the racial laws which gives the action its beauty and charm, for as the narrator comments: 'there are not many happinesses so complete as those that are snatched under the shadow of the sword'.(42) Kipling's debt here to Poe and his cult of danger is evident, and it underlines the place of sympathetic moments such as these in his overall outlook. They are in reality simply decorations on a larger imperial understanding: the frame to that picture is given by a strict code from which Kipling does not deviate, and his imagination opens only those doors which he knows greater forces will keep shut.

In English fiction too, the exotic imagination had been content to work within a similarly restricted sphere. In this respect the romances of Rider Haggard, for instance, while appearing to leave behind the accepted norms of colonial fiction, merely flatter to deceive. At first glance the love-affair between the 'dusky' Foulata and Captain Good, surely the ultimate cliché of exotic literature, might appear to be the free exercise of the imagination: love transcending the barriers of race. Certainly the plot of She revealed Haggard's penchant in that direction, with its unbridled fascination with the erotic charm of Africa. It looked at Africa more imaginatively than those to whom, as Haggard himself remarked, 'a native is just a native, a person from whom land may be filched'. In view of this deliberate distancing from conventional attitudes, it is all the more striking that Haggard brings Captain Good safely to harbour in a white marriage (albeit with an African princess) and that Sir Henry Curtis, for whom Haggard reserves a similar white African princess, should emphasize that the first child of his own marriage is 'a regular, curly-haired, blue-eyed young Englishman in looks'. It is an unmistakable emphasis on racial characteristics, and however ready Haggard was to defy contemporary taste and prejudice - his works were often attacked for their sexual outspokenness - he was clearly anxious to assure his readers that in the important matter of race he had remained within the fold.(43)

Stuart Young's novel about an inter-racial marriage, Merely a Negress (1904), revealed that similar attitudes underlay even the more philanthropic and humanitarian accounts of race-relations.

It tells of an English novelist's marriage to a Liberian girl. He is carried away with enthusiasm at the sight of the first black African state, where his support for negro emancipation makes him something of a celebrity. There are emotional scenes when he reads extracts from <u>Uncle Tom's Cabin</u>. When he marries Lily, a local girl, the author at once reassures us that she is 'almost thoroughly Caucasian'(44), or (as a sympathetic reviewer put it) 'a girl of the negro race - but not, of course, black'. Their child, like the offspring of Henry Curtis and those of Loti's heroes, is white also.

Like Vigné d'Octon, Stuart Young sees a link between this marriage and the degeneracy of European cultural life. A thinly disguised Oscar Wilde flits in and out of the novel and its sequel: tastes are depraved, Young implies, and an African bride is a sign of the times. Though his picture of Lily is warm and for the most part sympathetic, he chooses to talk about her character in the language of the race-thinkers and to interpret her behaviour in the light of their prejudices. 'The blood of Hagar ran in her veins'; she is said to be 'tainted with the blood of thousands of years of serfdom'; under stress she reveals herself, physically, to be 'what she was - a negress'.(45) The title of the first of the novels had been defiant, proving that Lily was far more than the popular judgement on her as 'merely a negress'. The second novel, however, vindicates that judgement and traces the influence of her 'dusky origin' on the break-down of her marriage and morals. Once again the novel does not lack sympathy, but its sympathy merely fulfills a cosmetic function and in no way takes back the conventional prejudices around which the plot is built and which are rooted in the novel's language.

The same theme was treated by Maud Diver in the novel <u>Lilamani - a study in possibilities</u> (1911). The possibilities under investigation are those of a mixed marriage between an English painter and an aristocratic Hindu girl. It may well be that many of Maud Diver's regular readers were surprised at the open-mindedness with which she approached this theme, and by the novel's apparent disregard for what its hero calls 'mere accidents of race and creed'. Certainly the novel is sympathetic both to the Indian girl, Lilamani, and to the view forcibly put by one character that there was more to India than met the official eye. The marriage is not the disaster other novelists created, although the couple have to return to India to live, for Lilamani cannot adapt to English life. Nevertheless, it is the language and assumptions behind the plot which give the key to the narrow range of possibilities which Maud Diver envisaged. An Indian girl is argued to belong to a common 'Aryan' race with the English, and this 'racial connection between Indians and Europeans' cannot be mentioned in the same breath as any liaison with 'a Hottentott or an American negro'. When the mixed marriage of the two is not at once productive of children, the reflection is in terms of sexual racial incompatibility: 'Could it be', muses Lilamani, 'that he, her king, shared, even in a small degree his sister's racial recoil from mixed blood? '(46). The unquestioned validity of these assumptions and this vocabulary is in many ways more eloquent than the more open story-line.

The reference to the incompatibility of European and American Negro 'blood' reminds us of the contribution of much American literature to the prejudices and outlook of the colonial novelists. The Negro problem featured centrally in many works which were widely read in Europe at the turn of the century, and one such work to gain the explicit attention of the imperialist thinkers was Gertrude Atherton's Senator North(1900). Like many works it gave strong credence and currency to the idea that notions such as 'the black in the blood' (a reference to the racial determinants of children of mixed marriages) had objective meaning and were accepted even by those working for the social advancement of the Negro. At the same time it offered the European public a commentary on the pointlessness of all efforts to secure rights for the Negro, since the novel showed on the basis of American experience that even equality in law could not bridge the incompatibility and unequal cultural potential of white and black.(47)

We have suggested, therefore, that even the literature ostensibly dealing in inter-racial sympathy rested on foundations of inflexible racial prejudice. As we saw in an earlier chapter, the language of race-thinking was more widespread than simply colonial fiction and it might well be argued that it more truly reflected the basic attitudes of white to black. Perhaps the actual sympathy felt by a novelist for a non-white character is less revealing than the terms of the description, for instance Mrs. Perrin's introduction to an Indian prince:

> A handsome deer-like creature, having the blood of generations and generations of aristocratic ancestors in his veins, linked back and back until it touched at the pure fount of his Aryan progenitors, whose racial stamp was still apparent despite periodical admixtures of lower blood, and the influence of the soil on form and character.(48)

The exploration of 'possibilities' took place on a very tight rein. One might say, as Orwell remarked of the socialist fantasies of the English middle-class some thirty years later, that the explorers drew their strength 'from the secret conviction that nothing will change'.

NOTES
    1. See for instance the character of Governor Leutwein,
as it emerges from H.Bley, South-West Africa under German rule
(Heinemann, 1971). Vedder's book was translated as South-West
Africa in Early Times (OUP,1938).
    2. F.Kraze, Heim Neuland (Stuttgart & Leipzig, 1909),
p.130.
    3. A.Perrin, The Anglo-Indians (Methuen, 1912), pp. 28,
274. The issue is discussed by B.Parry, Delusions and Discoveries (Allen Lane, 1972), pp.52/69, 70/88.
    4. F.A.Steel, The Potters Thumb (1894) quoted by Parry,
p.122.
    5. Cf. Mrs. Steel's contribution to Marie Corelli & others
The Modern Marriage Market (Hutchinson, 1898), pp.95/132, esp.
pp.102, 119. These views can fruitfully be contrasted with
those of H.Le Roux, Nos filles - qu'en ferons-nous? (Paris,
1898), where similar views of 'duty to the race' are used to
counterbalance the debasement of women in the marriage market.
Also notice Mrs. Steel's stories 'Gunesh Chund' and 'At a
Girls' School', which show the humiliation of women in India
(From the five rivers, Heinemann, 1893, pp.1/57, 143/82).
    6. F.A.Steel, The Garden of Fidelity (Macmillan, 1929),
p.29. See also her description of sex as the disharmonizing
curse of Western society (p.263f). On the archetypes of sexuality and negritude see W.Jordan, White over black (Chapel
Hill, 1968), pp.3/41; and, in a more contemporary context,
C.Hernton, Sex and Racism (Andre Deutsch, 1969). Also interesting on the connections between imperialism and the women's
movements: J.Hammerton, Emigrant Gentlewomen (New Jersey, 1979)
pp.75f, 129f, 168f etc; R.J.Evans, The Feminist Movement in
Germany (Sage Publications, 1976), pp.147, 239 etc. (on
counterblasts of conservatism from the imperialist women's
movement), and F.Marrass, Der deutsche Kolonialroman (Vienna,
1935), p.13f.
    7. Cf. J.Dose,Ein alter Afrikaner (Wismar,1913), p.145;
R.Küas, Vom Baum der Erkenntnis (Leipzig, 1911); J.v.Puttkamer
Das Duallamädchen (Leipzig, 1908), etc.
    8. Puttkamer, p.205.
    9. Cf. F.v.Bülow, Im Lande der Verheißung (Leipzig,1899),
pp.122/23; H.Grimm, Lüderitzland (Munich,1934), pp.149/63.
    10. Puttkamer, p.54. Cf. K.Epstein,'Erzberger & the German
Colonial Scandals' English Historical Review, vol.74 (Oct.1959),
pp.637/63.
    11. A.Lion, Tropenhygienische Ratschläge (Munich, 1907),
p.22f.
    12. H.Grimm, Der Gang durch den Sand (Munich,1916),p.361ff.
    13. Dose, pp.358/59.
    14. G.Patzlaff discusses this (admiringly) in Die deuts-
chen Kolonien und der Kolonialgedanke... (Diss. Greifswald,
1938), p.26.
    15. Cf. Bley,p.212. Indian comparisons emerge from K.

Ballhatchet, Race, Sex & Class under the Raj (Weidenfeld,1980).
    16. Quoted in L.Fanoudh-Siefer, Le mythe du nègre (Paris, 1968), p.188.
    17. P.Loti, Madame Chrysanthème (Paris, 1887). Cf. C.Wake, The novels of P.Loti (The Hague,1976), pp.53f, 143f.
    18. P.Loti, Le roman d'un spahi (Paris, 1881), pp. 190/91. See also Fanoudh-Siefer, pp.69/109.
    19. 'Ramary et Kétaka' in Sur la vaste terre (1905), p.91. Cf. O.Mannoni, Prospero & Caliban (New York, 1964), Part III. A.P.Thornton discusses Dependence (Mannoni's 'final heresy' in 'Jekyll & Hyde in the Colonies' in For the File on Empire (Macmillan, 1968), p.343. On Conrad's presentation of the same theme see D.C.R.A.Goonetilleke, Developing countries in British fiction (Macmillans, 1977), p.65f (on Lord Jim).
    20. M.A.Leblond, Les Sortilèges (Paris, 1905), pp.iii/iv; M.A.Leblond, La France devant l'Europe (Paris, 1913), p.321. See also the claim that colonial literature is 'a revelation of humanity' (M.A.Leblond, L'Idéal du XIXe siècle, Paris, 1909, p.303.
    21. G.Bouzeran & C.Lavoipierre, Récits sur Madagascar (Paris, 1905), p.188.
    22. See Pujarniscle, pp.108/62.
    23. P.Vigné d'Octon, Fauves Amours (Paris, 1892),p.ii.
    24. P.Vigné d'Octon, Chair noire (Paris, 1889), pp. 204f, 194,215.
    25. Les Sortilèges, pp. 68, 70, 82.
    26. Le miracle de la race (Paris, 1914), pp.87, 343.
    27. 'L'Esprit algérien' in Revue Bleue, 4th Series, vol. 19 (1905), p.508. It is interesting to note that Leblond makes great play of a comparison between Algeria and America, both in terms of social structure and with regard to the place of race-thinking (p.512).
    28. Le sang des races (Paris, 1899),esp. pp. 23, 135,340.
    29. L.Bertrand, D'Alger la romantique... (Paris, 1930), pp.185,183,188. Cf. M.A.Leblond, La France devant l'Europe,p.12.
    30. Pujarniscle, pp.154,162. See also S.Howe, Novels of Empire (New York, 1949), p.61f; and P.Mason, Patterns of Dominance (OUP,1970?, p.88f.
    31. P.Mille, Louise et Barnavaux (Paris, 1912), pp. 198/213.
    32. P.Mille, 'Avons-nous une vraise littérature coloniale? in Les Nouvelles Littéraires, 9 February 1919, p.1.
    33. P.Mille,'Le Japonais' in Barnavaux et quelques femmes (Paris, 1908), p.163f.
    34. A.de Villemagne, Hors de sa race (Paris, 1912), pp. 152f, 163f, 180, 193.
    35. P.Mille and A. Demaison, La femme et l'homme nu (Paris, 1924), p.118.
    36. M.A.Leblond, 'Le prolétariat francais aux colonies' in H.Béranger et al., Les prolétaires intellectuels en France (Paris, 1901), p.314.

37. G.Pichot, La brousse et ses dieux quoted by L.Fanoudh-Siefer, p.183.

38. P.Mille, Louise et Barnavaux, p.61; and H.Grimm, Volk ohne Raum, vol.1 (Munich, 1926), p.634f. Cf. also V.G. Kiernan, The Lords of Human Kind (Weidenfeld & Nicolson, 1969), pp.170/72.

39. C.Farrère, La bataille (Paris, 1921).

40. E.Candler, The general plan (Blackies ,1911), p.23. Earlier quotation from Parry, p.50. See also A.Wilson, The strange ride of Rudyard Kipling (Granada, 1979), p.425.

41. A.Perrin, The Anglo-Indians (Methuen, 1912), p.275.

42. 'Beyond the Pale' in Plain Tales from the Hills; 'Without Benefit of Clergy' and 'Georgie-Porgie' in Life's Handicap.

43. H.R.Haggard, Allan Quartermain (1887) (New York,1828), p.670. See also P.B.Ellis, H.Rider Haggard (Routledge & Kegan Paul, 1979), p.213 (on 'pro-Native' attitudes) and p.98 (on Haggard's critical reception). For a fascinating discussion of Haggard's adoption and popularization of anthropological discoveries see B.V.Street, The Savage in Literature (Routledge & Kegan Paul, 1975), pp. 57, 149f.

44. J.S.Young, Merely a Negress (J.Long, 1904), p.49.

45. J.S.Young, Passion's Peril (Hermes Press, 1906), pp.14/15, 99.

46. M.Diver, Lilamani (Hutchinson, 1911), p.268. B.Parry has shown how the sequel to this novel makes explicit the doubts my account suggests (Parry, pp.79/82).

47. G.Atherton, Senator North (John Lane, 1900), pp.87, 94, 123, 168 etc. The novel was discussed by E.de Seillière, an eminent theoretician of French imperialism in his Introduction à la philosophie d'Impérialisme (Paris, 1911), pp.34/ 35. Another (more random) example of the infiltration of American racial attitudes into British fiction is given by S.P.Hyatt's novel The little brown brother (1908), which is set in the Philippines under American colonial occupation.

48. A.Perrin, The Anglo-Indians, p.275.

Chapter Five

JUSTIFICATIONS OF EMPIRE

'Cupidity accomplishes what charity would not!'

P. NICOLE

The actual causes of the upsurge of imperialism during the second half of the nineteenth century remain a subject of debate among historians. Controversy seems unlikely to abate between those who believe that the ideologues played a decisive role in unleashing imperial expansion (David Thomson, for instance, argues for a recognition of 'the activity of small groups of people, often intellectuals' in shaping the empires) and those positions which ascribe primacy to certain economic factors as causes of imperialism (Lenin's view of imperialism as 'the highest stage of capitalism'). V.G. Kiernan will continue to make hay with any approach which sees in imperialism an 'idea' formulated by ideologues autonomously(1), and my own approach (although obviously concerned with the manifestations rather than the causes of imperial activity) does not attempt to systematize colonial fiction in isolation from social and economic factors in Europe. The continuing debates about the nature of imperialism naturally lead us to examine colonial literature in the explanation and justifications which it offered for the practices of imperialism.

Certainly colonial fiction spent an inordinate time justifying imperialism. As a genre bridging the twin publics of colony and mother-country and seeing each in the light of the other, colonial fiction was naturally involved in mediating ideas between the two. Its authors were inheritors of the language of idealistic imperialism (the 'civilizing mission') but they saw their works as more down-to-earth contributions to the debates on imperialism conducted in the parliaments and press of the mother-country. They tried to establish on an individual basis the truth of the more sweeping accounts of imperialism made in other types of writing. This involved them in the assent to imperialism within individual lives and within individual parts of the empires.

Marcuse has argued that all culture carries out an 'affirmative' function within society; that by the very fact of portraying a given society's existence literature lends validity to that society and 'thus links itself inevitably to the status quo'. Certainly many writers of the Realist movement were committed to their society and its values at a level which cast doubt upon their ostensible critique of it. Certainly too the 'petty-bourgeois oppositon' to capitalism which lay behind some of the literary movements at the turn of the century was conducted in a way that tended to exacerbate the dehumanising of society against which the literature protested. But very little writing of this period was concerned to justify society in anything like such an explicit manner as colonial fiction. Lukács has rightly said of the literature of the years after 1890 that it acted 'partly as an instrument for disarming political criticism', but we should surely not wish to refer to its authors (Wilde, Gide, Rilke etc.) as 'hired coolies of the pen'. Lenin's phrase can, however, much more justly be applied to the authors of colonial fiction.(2)

This judgement may seem harsh. It sounds as if it implies a contractual relationship between literature and the string-pullers of the City, or a possible tension between what authors were paid to say and what they 'really' believed. Neither needs necessarily to be the case. We shall find, however, that writers were invariably aware that imperialism existed and flourished separately from their accounts of it and their encouragement of it. The moment there was a colonial crisis - it might be the Herero uprising or the Boer War - commercial interests brushed aside other explanations of imperialism. 'We are all burglars now', a British Chancellor grumbled just before the Boer War. 'Financial speculation creates, perhaps without noticing it, the beliefs which it needs for its own purposes', Pierre Mille confessed in 1905, hardly in very flattering assessment of his own life and works. At Leutwein looked back over his time as Governor of South-West Africa, during which his own concern had been with peaceful co-existence and political consolidation, he summarized imperialism much more directly than he had hitherto: 'the final objective of all colonization is to make money'.(3) It was against this background that writers offered their justifications of empire, knowing them to be both justifications after the events and alternatives to more widely accepted interpretations.

It is illuminating to look in this connection at two early accounts of the British rôle in India. The novel Oakfield by 'Punjabee' (W.D. Arnold) published in 1853 and G.O. Trevelyan's semi-fictional Competition Wallah of 1864 both show the growth of idea-centred justifications of British rule in their precarious relation to commercial arguments. Arnold's novel is critical of the open exploitation and coarse commercialism of British India. Oakfield himself, moving from the military to the civilian administration, hopes to turn the Civil Service into a high-minded and idealistic institution which will break with the commercial past. He calls for 'pure, unselfish..., visionary enthusiasm' and continues:

> 'The evil is a money-getting earthly mind, that dares to view a large portion of God's world, and many millions of God's creatures, as a more or less profitable investment, as a good return for money laid out upon them...'(4)

These views, like those Trevelyan was to put forward ten years later, may well have reflected and in turn influenced the self-understanding of the ICS, but in no way did they modify either the initial motive for conquest or the continuing factors of economic life. To talk as if they did was to lacquer over the unacceptable face of imperialism.

In the years after the Mutiny, Trevelyan tried to establish a new wave of idealism in the ICS. We shall see in the next chapter how much he found to attack in the class-system and the appallingly anti-native attitudes of the traders and settlers. No less clearly than Arnold, he recognized the universality of a purely commercial justification of imperial rule. 'No one', he wrote indignantly of Anglo-Indian opinion, 'can estimate very highly the moral and intellectual qualities of people among whom he resides for the single purpose of turning them to pecuniary account.' He, too, pinned his hopes on an idealistic civil service, not because such idealism corresponded to the actual motives behind imperial conquest but precisely because it did not. 'There is not a single non-official person in India', he admitted, 'who would not consider the sentiment that we hold India for the benefit of the inhabitants of India a loathsome un-English piece of cant'.(5)   Maud Diver, also looking back to the period of the Mutiny, attempted to re-interpret events through her idealized heroes and, like Trevelyan, was obliged to concede that the period entirely contradicted the picture her work gave of it.   The majority of colonials were 'dwarfed' by the age and 'its monetary standards, its mean and selfish expedients'.(6)   Little trace of idealism there, yet Maud Diver chose to portray the minority as if it were typical, and in so doing to mask the reality of colonial reality behind idealistic justifications.

It was not only in the colonies that writers were ready to provide unlikely and self-deceiving accounts of contemporary events. Writers have always tended to see historical events from a personal perspective, claiming for them a significance which future historians seldom accept. Writers' attitude to wars, for instance, are not notorious for picking out the actual issues with any clarity, and one needs only to look at the range of explanations offered by writers for the war of 1914 to see how far they would go in self-delusion and wilful blindness to reality. That their attitudes amounted to political nonsense, however, did not make them unpolitical: a fact to bear in mind when considering the justifications offered of imperialism. Historians of this literature have often stressed the extreme complexity of individual authors' understanding of imperialism. A colonial writer such as Buchan, for instance, followed through the high-mindedness of Arnold's thinking and reached a religious interpretation of imperialism so idiosyncratic that it seemed to have forfeited any political relevance. Mr. Sandision has pointed out that Buchan's views had virtually nothing in common with, for example, Kipling's justification of imperialism which started from a completely different standpoint: that of the existentially exposed individual. More recently Angus Wilson has joined those who reject the placing of 'too much emphasis on Kipling's political (in the widest sense) view of man'(7). We need to remember, however, that Kipling and Buchan agreed on the one topic of imperialism, just as Thomas Mann and the Futurists agreed in welcoming the war of 1914, and Ernst Jünger and Hans Grimm in welcoming the Nazis in 1933. The fact that these views probably coincided nowhere else than on the specific political topic in no way invalidated their agreement. Complexity is a writer's trademark, and even highly non-specific theories may express direct political commitment on specific issues.

There was a more particular cause of the complexity of the theories with which colonial fiction attempted to justify imperialism. In that they tried to find individual meaning behind general imperialist statements, writers were led automatically into commenting on the drawbacks and problems of European life to which imperial experience was able to provide an answer. It was in this spirit that Arnold had launched into his moral justification of imperialism. Because British life was materialistic and needed the elevating moral purpose which the Indian Empire could offer, imperialism could be justified as fulfilling a double moral purpose, both within India itself and as a national task for Britain. Arnold's work gives one example of colonial literature's tendency to develop ideological solutions to the problems of nineteenth century Europe, but to do so only obliquely. The indirectness with which these problems were confronted in colonial literature encouraged the flight towards ideological rather than practical solutions. Without the European perspective, however, the justification of colonial life would be incomprehensible.

Not all the justifications we encounter were of great complexity. There are frequent justifications of imperialism offered in the colourless and shallow jargon of the official mind. The paternalism of the 'civilizing mission' rings out hollowly in whatever language, and it would be futile to attempt to read too much into the stereotyped pictures of the colonists as 'representatives of Christ and Caesar', or as 'the legions defending humanity' and 'apostles and heroic pacifists'. While French writers idealized their empire as a rebirth of Latin civilization and compared 'la paix française' to the pax romana, the Germans tended to concentrate on the discipline and moral orderliness of their rule, and the British writers spoke of 'the wonderful order and peace' of the Empire. Official-sounding pronouncements of this sort tended to have one voice, and even when imperial rivalry dictated a criticism of the imperial activity of another European power, writers invariably formulated their criticism in terms of a common purpose to which all imperialist powers had subscribed but which the offending power had failed to live up to.

Nevertheless, statements of this kind were much less important to writers than more personal formulations. Indeed it often happened that the justification of imperialism given by a particular novel clashed violently with the high-sounding generalizations to which writers paid lip-service. Robert Randau's account of the occupation of Senegal demonstrated this possibility.

At one moment Randau parades the official point of view, pointing to all that has been done to civilize the country 'without any brutality towards the natives, relying merely upon the propaganda effect of our goodness'. He portrays the French troops as 'the legions defending humanity'. But no sooner has he made this claim than he turns his attention to the character whom he admires and makes his hero, a colonel who, as rapidly becomes clear, has nothing but contempt for any doctrine save that of the rights of the stronger.(8) It is an extreme example of a tendency inherent in all colonial fiction: that it justifies imperialism locally and individually rather than in official generality, and that its relationship to European values - in this case the sort of humanitarianism which goes down well with parliaments, the civilising mission and so forth - is a critical one. At a less intense level this tendency underlies the most common cliché of colonial fiction: the idea that colonies were a proving-ground for national manhood, a 'providential asylum' for educating younger sons - in Edmund Candler's charming phrase, 'the nurseries of cads'.(9)

A classic illustration is Kipling's story 'Thrown Away'. It tells of a Boy sent out to the Indian Army after a molly-coddling, over-protective education in England. The hardships and suffering which service in India brings do not help the Boy to mature and to gain self-knowledge. Instead he gives up the struggle and shoots himself when he takes offence at some trifling remark. Kipling obviously deplores this, but nowhere does he suggest that the social environment or the heartless attitudes of people in India might be responsible for the Boy's death. Anglo-Indian society and its ways are a fact of life, beyond criticism for its harshness or its insensitivity. The individual must measure up to it or be destroyed.(10)

The educational influence of the colonies took one of two forms. There was a challenge to measure oneself against a harsh and impersonal nature, whether human or non-human. There was also a reshaping of the individual's attitudes to life through the invigorating intensity of colonial life. Both possibilities put into reverse the whole process of justification. Instead of the imperial powers possessing ideas and aspirations which justify the seizure of colonies, the possession of colonies is shown to make possible heroic and manly virtues which are their own justification. The most typical characters in colonial fiction comes to the colonies without ideas, in order to learn there an ethos which gives meaning to their experiences. Psichari explains that the hero of L'Appel des Armes entered colonial service out of a purely private desire 'to perfect himself and to gain a clearer awareness of what he was worth'(11), and this explanation is true of the majority of the heroes of colonial fiction. They are, of course, patriotic about the aims of imperialism, but while their patriotism had been content to stay at home, it was their desire for self-education which took them overseas.

Colonial fiction, therefore, tended to give less emphasis to the idea that imperialism pursued concrete aims in the colonies and emphasized instead imperialism as national self-education. Repeatedly one reads of the colonies as schools, and there are very few differences across the national literatures. Rather than catalogue the values put forward by this open-air, public school colonial ethos(12), we are concerned with the impact of this shift of emphasis on writers' justifications of imperialism.

I

The first casualty of this shift of emphasis was any belief in imperialism as an orthodoxly Christian activity. The stereotyped ethical portrait of the White Man amounted in many important respects to a self-conscious modification of Christian ideals. Colonial fiction in this respect formed part of two more general movements in the nineteenth century. In the first place, it belonged within a widespread secularization of social thinking which ran throughout the nineteenth century. The claims of Christianity were under general challenge and it would have been strange if imperialism and its fiction had not reflected this. The specific religious content of many political movements made the progression from conviction to lip-service, and from there to the scrap-heap. At the same time, however, the growth of an unholy alliance between religion and extreme nationalism proceeded unchecked, and colonial fiction reflected both the nationalist distortion and utilitarian abandonment of religious language. This can be seen most clearly in its portrayal of the representatives of Christianity whom they most frequently encountered: the Missionary societies.

German colonial fiction was outspoken in its attacks on the Missions. It is noticeable that while the French exotic tradition had contained sympathetic portraits of missionaries, starting from Chateaubriand's Aubry, the German exotic novel, as we saw, focussed on the aggressive missionary activity of the South Pacific. German colonial fiction certainly followed up this hostility. In this was reflected the greater radicalism of the movements of secularization in Germany and, more immediately, the explicitly anti-Catholic sentiments provoked by Bismarck's Kulturkampf. There was also a bitter history of bad relations between settlers and missionaries, which meant that the missions were attacked on numerous grounds: because they campaigned for the rights of the Africans; because they criticized the settlers' casual liaisons with native women; because of their hostility to that feudal exercise of personal power for which the settlers yearned. Indeed the Mission emerged as the opponent of every aspect of the settlers' personal ethos and social ideology. When writers turned to consider the political influence which the Missions exercised through the confessional parties in the 'Reichstag', they were unanimous in concluding that the Missions were engaged in 'the systematic undermining of all Germany's colonizing efforts'.(13)

These attacks were surprisingly direct. We need to go back many years in Britain to find similar statements of the Missions' incompatibility with the aims of imperialism, in particular to the attempts to revise the charter of the East India Company so as to forbid missionary activity in India, in the course of which it was explicitly stated that to 'overrun' India with missionaries would bring about 'an end of British supremacy'. More recently, in 1865 the Jamaican revolt had led to widespread public criticism of the role of the Missions, and there were many influential circles in Britain and France who felt, if less explicitly than in Germany, a divergence of aims between imperialism and the Christian missions.(14) Usually writers tried to paper over these divergencies, and even the more radical German critics of the Missions tried to present their opinions as something other than merely anti-Christian. Three main arguments were used: a denial of the efficacy of the Missions, a repudiation of their relevance, and a revision of their moral teaching.

A frequent claim was that the Missions could make no impression on the hopelessly primitive attitude of mind of the 'Natives'. Numerous stories and novels show Christianity as at best a veneer over the unfathomable depths of the 'Native Soul', and at worst simply a cloak for the political intrigues of ambitious chiefs and for the crimes of their people. A typical story is Hans Grimm's 'The Life of John Neukwa' (1913). It tells of an African converted to Christianity for no other reason than that the missionaries flatter him by teaching that black and white are equal in the sight of God. Shortly after his conversion, which has had no effect on his constitutional idleness and his greed for money and spirits, he is cheated at cards by a white man, whom he brutally murders with the help of a witch-doctor. He feels no remorse at his action and returns to the Mission, where he becomes a pillar of the Church, held up by the missionaries as an example of the success of the Christian gospel among the Africans.(15)

This story, and there are many like it, makes explicit colonials' scepticism about their ability in any way to change the racial characteristics of the colonized peoples. The hereditary determinant, usually in the guise of that 'drop of native blood' which emerges at crucial moments in a man's life, was believed to be stronger than the influences of example and changed environment. Religion and civilization would at best therefore only ever be assimilated superficially, and a reversion to savagery would always remain likely. Grimm's story also suggests that the Missions both wittingly (by their doctrine) and unwittingly (by their other-worldy naivety) nurture the seeds of rebellion against white rule.

Writers therefore tried to discredit in every possible way the actual achievements of the Missions, obviously intending to contrast their failure with the solid work of the colonizing forces. But many writers went further and suggested that the Missions' teaching of Christian love and brotherhood could have no relevance to the work of colonization. There is after all very little room for some manoeuvre in this field: as Montesquieu had caustically observed three hundred years before 'either the natives are not human beings or we must admit that we are not Christians'. It was easy to present colonization as the work of God when it was a question of suppressing the slave-trade, or of driving the Mohammedans out of East and West Africa. It was gratifying to include scenes in which a grateful African might thank his white liberators with the words: 'The French are the sabre of God. To help you is to help God.'(16) But there were more moments, of course, when the connections between colonialism and Christianity were far from obvious, and it was these moments which led writers to challenge the Missions' view of the relevance of Christianity.

A much repeated argument was that the Missions should cease attempting to instil complex ethical attitudes into the natives and should instead help them to adapt to European life, especially by learning to work. The phrase 'Education for Labour' was particularly popular in German East Africa, but there were many other colonies in which the missionaries were exhorted to teach the natives the Christian emphasis on work. A typical scene from a novel set in South-West Africa just after the revolt:

> 'True Christianity', said Hardt to the missionary, 'does not express itself merely in singing hymns and in praying, which is all the Herero seem to do. True Christianity isn't a question merely of repeating parrot-fashion phrases like 'Love your enemies'. In any case, you should not teach them to see the Germans as their enemies: they must be taught to see us as their advisers.'
> The missionary laughed contemptuously. 'There may be one or two ignorant heathens,' he said, 'who cannot understand the meaning of Christianity and who instead see personal advantage for themselves in the so-called civilizing work of the Germans.'
> 'If it is only the heathen who think that, they have sounder ideas than the converts. I can see why they do, for the unconverted are happy to work for us, while your converts think themselves too good for that sort of thing. You ought to teach them the meaning of the saying 'Work and Pray'.
> 'Do you think that the Germans here are working? All they do is drink and lead the natives the same way!', shouted the missionary.(17)

This particular conversation goes on for nearly ten pages in this vein, and there are many scenes like it which testify to the bitterness and resentment felt between the settlers and the Missions. The contrast between Christian doctrine and the needs of the colony is quite explicit, as it is also clear that the settler is developing a Christian outlook which fundamentally differs from that of the official church. He makes a distinction between the missionary's religion (which, he says later, is 'concerned with the externals and set forms') and 'a more pure and god-fearing' religion of his own, whose emphasis is entirely practical and which knows no authority other than the individual heart.

The Christianity which novelists found relevant to imperialism had, predictably, little or nothing to do with love. As Gustav Frenssen, a former Lutheran pastor, commented in his famous novel on the Herero war: 'One must either want to love or want to rule'.(18) It was obvious which course writers would choose. It was not surprising therefore that so many colonial writers allowed their concept of love to be modified substantially, in particular by the fashion for attacks on pity which was set in motion by Nietzsche and his followers. For all that they are pioneers of Christian civilization, many of the colonial heroes owe more to Nietzschean ideals. The ruthless pioneers, modelled on Carl Peters or Rhodes, seemed to many writers to express precisely what Nietzsche had meant by his various Antichrist figures. Frieda von Bülow often compared the many characters in her novels whom she modelled on Carl Peters with Nietzschean figures: thus one character is 'an example of Nietzsche's "blond beast"', while Carl Peters himself who appears undisguised in the same novel alongside a whole string of proto-Peters is characterized as Nietzsche's 'Willensmensch (Will-Man)'.(19) Somerset Maugham's early novel, The Explorer (1908), gives a very similar account of the ruthless colonial pioneer with his contempt for the weak and their morality, and his readiness to sacrifice lesser mortals to the accomplishment of his will. It is no coincidence that Maugham speaks in that novel of the increasing influence of Nietzsche upon English letters. Another notable member of this group of Nietzschean imperialists is Robert Randau's Andreotti, who, behind the official justification of himself as 'the sabre of the Lord', behaves with a ruthlessness and an enjoyment of cruelty which is entirely in keeping with his personal ideology. While he talks contemptuously of those people 'idiotic enough to prolong the agony of the weak, the useless and the wretched', Randau's narrator draws the conclusion that all 'official moralities', whether sacred or secular, have the fault that they lead to

> a reversal of values: the weak, the useless and the powerless hold up for centuries the arrival of what is better, by their endless whining about some supposed right to existence and by their hysterical appeals to an alleged common humanity.(20)

The erosion of Christian values by Nietzschean and Social Darwinist ideas is quite unmistakable.

It is hardly surprising that these attacks on the ideas of Christian mission were countered by the missionaries themselves. The fictional missionary who accused the settlers of laziness and excessive drinking was certainly based on a real model. Perhaps more insidious, as part of that gradual harmonizing of national interests with religion which we have discussed, was the way in which the Missions themselves modified their teaching in order to diminish its conflict with settler opinion. This can be seen most clearly in the aftermath of the Herero war of 1904. It was repeatedly claimed that the missionaries had encouraged the Herero to attack the Germans, an impression based on little more than the fact that the Herero paramount chief had placed the missionaries under his personal protection. (Similar accusations were made about the role of the missions in Jamaica before the revolt of 1865). What was particularly striking was that the missions tended to take over the criteria of their opponents and to modify their own work in that light. A leader of the Protestant missionary society in the South-West Africa argued, for instance, that the effect (and very nearly the function) of the mission's work was to provide a work-force for German settlers. Teaching the Herero merely to 'sing and pray' - which had been part of Grimm's accusation - was much less important to the mission than educating them for labour. In addition, the missionary stated categorically that the equality of man did not form part of the mission's teaching, and that instead obedience to the state as demanded by the Apostles formed the basis of their social gospel.(21) While one understands the dilemma of the missions, they showed themselves hardly impervious to the tendencies which created so many new enemies for their work.

The erosion of Christian ideas was not restricted to those areas which overlapped with imperialism. Colonial fiction revealed a perennial fascination for an ethos and a new view of life which transcended Christianity. We saw it, of course, in the cult of men like Maugham's Alec MacKenzie, whose energy and will place him beyond morality. It is a commonplace of colonial fiction to show a man's discovery that the Christian morality which he has brought with him cannot cope with the experiences he undergoes. It is part of the making of a colonial hero that this morality should fall away from him, a process of which Louis Bertrand gives a typical account:

> All the ideas which she had brought from France seemed
> like strangers to her, so insubstantial had they become.
> They had all melted away in the terrible breath of the
> South.(22)

Colonial writers did not merely show Christian morality in dissolution: they showed its replacement. The new ethical sense, that manly, heroic ethos which becomes so tedious in colonial literature, contained highly significant modifications of Christianity. One of these was the idea of sin, which had not

merely come under attack from Nietzsche and the psychologists*
but had also been a bone of contention as the settlers tried to
maintain the ideas of white superiority. The sense of sin had very
little place in a secular active heroism such as colonial fiction
championed, and even a writer explicitly concerned to combine
Christianity and nationalism as Psichari does in his novel L'appel
des armes makes this clear when, in a highly mystical account of
his colonial hero's attendance at Mass, he asserts approvingly thathe
utterly lacks a sense of sin.(23) Similar opinions can be found im
much of this literature.

In revising Christian belief colonial fiction very often attacked
its other-worldliness and asceticism. The colonial ethos was
concerned with the practical problems of here and now, and just
as in colonial life it was the success of one's treatment of the
natives rather than its rights and wrongs which mattered, so colonial
fiction insists that there is no transcendent perspective on life and
men's actions. The conclusion of Kim makes this point, as Kim
embraces the creed of action and rejects the asceticism of the
Lama. Critics have pointed out how considerably Kipling distorts
the teachings of the Lama in order to make his own ideological
stance clear, even to the extent of misleadingly presenting
Buddhism as the characteristic Indian religion.(24) Maud Diver's
frontier novel Desmond's Daughter communicates a similar
message, as its hero, Vincent Leigh, overcomes his admiration for
the teaching of an Indian 'Yogi of outstanding sanctity and wisdom'
and decides to commit himself fully to the tangible and real world
of desire and ambition: a decision which Maud Diver predictably
sums up in the words 'he would up and play the man'.(25)

It may seem odd to discuss modifications of Christianity by
means of critiques of Buddhism, but we must emphasize that there
is no explicit Christian content in these repudiations. Buddhism
and other non-Christian faiths appear in these novels as
representatives of all transcendent religions, and it is umistakable,
for instance, that Kipling regarded Kim's Tibetan teacher as a far
better representative of religion than the Christian priest who
surveys him 'with the triple-ringed uninterest of the creed that
lumps nine-tenths of the world under the title of "heathen"'(26).
Writers take up attitudes to other religions primarily in order to
show the evolution of their own religious thinking.

A particularly clear example is Psichari's comment (in Terres
de Soleil) about Islam. He criticizes Islam's influence on West
Africa, but contrasts it not with Christianity, which is supposed
to be the banner under which French imperialism was operating,
but with primitive Islam which, very obviously, has much in common

---

*In works such as Beyond Good and Evil Nietzsche not only
rejected the notion of moral absolutes, he also attempted in a
'revaluation of values' to show the positive attributes in qualities
which traditional Christianity had condemned as sinful.

with Psichari's own ethical values. He speaks of it as

> a religion of life therefore, much more than Christianity
> is; a religion of life which can come to terms with
> life as it is, without distorting it or making it something
> it isn't, a religion concerned with the earth, very far
> removed from mysticism.(27)

The critique of modern Islam is a fortiori a critique of Christianity.

The colonial ethos was fundamentally secular, and writers were as sceptical of the efficacy of religion as a guide for Europeans as they were of the usefulness of converting 'primitive' peoples. Their work repeatedly emphasized the relativism of all the world's religions, and they loved to tell stories of superstition and the supernatural which showed the powerlessness of organized religion to comprehend the world. It makes for a bizarre mixture as realism and ghost-stories rub shoulders in novels and short-stories. Colonial fiction was very concerned also with the primitive elements in man, with levels of behaviour beneath reason and doctrine. Many writers portrayed the 'regression' into savagery of civilized whites, missionaries even, whose religion proves unable to control the savage instincts which slumber within them. Rider Haggard introduces into one of his novels a peaceful Scottish missionary, MacKenzie, whom first we see caring for his flock and building a second Eden in his lonely district. When Masai tribesmen attack his station, however, he relapses into the broad Scots dialect of his childhood and reveals himself as a terrifying fighter with the bayonet. Pierre Mille too tells of a Catholic mission caught in a local insurrection, when the Father of the Mission, transformed by his anger from a spiritual peace-loving pastor, smashes the skull of one of the rioters and quells the revolt almost single-handed.(28)

Religion therefore is a veneer, both for white and black. Imperialism cannot be justified in terms of the establishment of Christianity, and Christianity itself is not only irrelevant and at times hostile to imperialism: it is out of keeping with that heroic ethos beyond morality, unfitted to that ceaseless struggle for survival within the tangible world which the colonial experience showed to be behind all life.

II

It was not simply the Christian justification of imperialism that writers found impossible to sustain. The idea of bringing civilization to the uncivilized corners of the world seemed hardly less problematic. Both uncertainties, but especially the second, had a long history. Long before Rouseau and Thoreau had turned it into the great truism of the exotic novel, a hostility to civilization had marked those Europeans who had colonized the wild. It is a recurring theme, for instance, in missionary history from the time of the Jesuit settlements in Paraguay. But it was the nineteenth century novel which set the fashion, and which claimed repeatedly to have discovered an earthly paradise which civilization and its discontents must not be allowed to destroy. We saw in the earlier chapter how extreme reactions could be to European civilization in the exotic novel. There were, however, many colonial writers genuinely concerned about the introduction of civilization into the Third World, for reasons that went deeper than a superficial desire for adventure and escape.

In one sense the very pursuit of colonialism implied discontent with Europe. Those who were content with Europe stayed there, and behind each positive claim for colonial experience lay an implicit critique of European civilization. Those who found the colonies adventurous found Europe dull; those who found them simple also complained of the complexities of civilized life; those who found there, like Adela Quested in Passage to India, a fresh concern for personal relationships, did so at least partly because they were tired of European convention and habit. Behind all these complaints and discoveries lay the basic attraction of primitiveness, the sense of dissatisfaction with an excessive and decadent civilization. Much colonial fiction was therefore concerned with regression - both social and personal - and with the re-establishment in the colonies of more authentic and more primitive ways of life. One sees this in the portrayal of so many of the soldiers and administrators in anachronistic terms, as if they were feudal lords, knights-errant, or even re-incarnations of the ancient warriors of the nation. Particularly in descriptions of war, writers were careful to show that their European characters do not lag behind the uncivilized tribes whom they fought in the primitive arts of battle. Wars are more often won in the heady intoxication of a fight to the death than by means of those technical appliances of the civilized Europeans of which, in situations where they wish to impress rather than kill, they are so proud. 'As for the elemental,' observes a victorious commander in a Maud Diver novel, as if he is discussing an ingredient in a cocktail, 'a dash of that is the very tonic we're needing these days.'(29)

The cult of the primitive was a direct critique of industrialized Western society, with its rules, restraints and artificialities. It implied a rejection of the money-thinking, comfort-seeking and security of Europe. All this made writers somewhat uneasy in proclaiming imperialism as the hand-maiden of civilization. Admittedly there were very few writers who took this critique seriously enough to question imperialism itself. Instead they set out to show that the colonies had discovered the primitive centre of life, and had therefore overcome the malaise of civilization. Edmund Candler was one of the few writers to move from a superficial flirtation with the primitive - he said that he had gone to India in order to be 'attacked and overtaken' by Nemesis - towards a questioning of imperialism as much. In a fine passage he sees England through the eyes of the Indians: a s

proud, cruel, insolent, overbearing, mercenary,
Philistine, busy and fussy about little things of the
world, with no sense of the brevity of life and the
enveloping shadow of the Infinite, doing everything for
self-aggrandisement, yet believing themselves to be the
sole inheritors of the three cardinal virtues, which they
dub Christian, and in obedience to which they drill the
weak to the their needs and exploit them to their
material advantage in the name of righteousness.(30)

There are other moments of this sort in English fiction. Kipling's
stories 'A Sahib's War' and 'One View of the Question' use a
similar device, but their purpose is to provide ideological messages
for white society rather than to attack the colonizing power more
centrally. Mrs. Perrin also showed the English through Indian eyes,
but once again without drawing conclusions about the imperial
mission.

The work in which Kipling most played on a juxtaposition of
the civilized and the primitive, The Naulahka (written in 1892 in
collaboration with the American author Wolcott Balestier), showed
by its amusing parody of the West in the figure of a go-getting
American capitalist that Kipling was hardly serious. It was an
intellectual game to play civilization off against 'primitive'
societies. Kipling was only serious in those many stories which
deal with individuals' tendency to revert to primitive beliefs at
times of stress. Complicated theories of life and even Western
rationalism itself were felt by Kipling to be little more than a
charade, which a touch of India could at once put to flight. As
Kipling remarks in the story telling of the 'conversion' of an over-
intellectual civil servant:

...in India, where you really see humanity - raw, brown
naked humanity - with nothing between it and the
blazing sky, and only the used-up, overhandled earth
underfoot(...) most folk came back to simpler
theories.(31)

Claude Farrère's novel Les Civilisés contains perhaps the
most extreme example of the hatred for civilization which underlay
so much colonial experience and which receives such wide attention
in colonial fiction. Its central character is a French naval oficer,
the Comte de Fierce, who epitomizes all the over-refined and
decadent attributes of civilization. His cult of beauty, pleasure
and all the 'artificial paradises' of the mind makes it clear that he
is modelled closely on the aesthete heroes of the late nineteenth

century.*   His realization that, for all his culture, he has achieved or experienced nothing real and worthwhile is one of the clichés of contemporary literature. It opens his eyes to the horror of an imperial mission which aims to spread this artificial civilization more widely in the world. He supports imperialism to the extent that it involves patriotism or enthusiasm for war, and in this novel, as in so many others, it is war that rescues him from the dead-hand of civilization. Farrère is so anxious to make his point clear that he, who is so invariably scrupulous about historical authenticity, invents a French naval campaign against the British. Fierce goes to his death attacking civilizing imperialism in the shape of a British battleship:

> It was Civilization herself that he was attacking on his quivering charger; yes, civilization, the murderess who for twenty-six years had crushed every fibre of his being, ground every nerve in its implacable mill and which soon would end his life with a shell.(32)

It is a melodramatic, but hardly untypical image.

Albert de Pouvourville, an authority on French Indo-China, took up a similar position in describing the collapse of traditional rule in the Far East. Evidently he had little time for an imperialism which merely 'barges out' local customs 'in order to introduce European ways'. His attitude to the smoking of opium showed how far he was from accepting the notion of European cultural superiority. Yet, both as historian and novelist, he assented to the spread of French power. The intensely dramatic presentation of the Tonkin revolt (in L'Annam Sanglante) revealed great sympathy for the old order, and suggested that only by outdoing the old order in heroic and uncivilized ruthlessness could France lay claim to imperial expansion.(33)

There was nothing new at the end of the nineteenth century in writers turning against civilization. In the movements loosely called 'Cultural Pessimism' an increasing discontent found expression at the various negative sides of modern society: cities, mass-production, and political polarization. Imperialist thinkers needed to adapt their attitudes to take account of the unfavourable view of civilization current in their society, and they tended increasingly to portray imperialism as the corrective to the ills of

---

*There is a similar moment in Frieda Kraze's novel Heim Neuland, in which an undesirable German settler is portrayed with precisely the physical attributes Thomas Mann · had used in Buddenbrooks to characterize decadence. The repudiation by colonial literature of the style of the modern literary movement which we examined in an earlier chapter corresponded closely to a recognizable moral and ideological rejection of the civilization which produced them.

civilization rather than as the propagator of its benefits. Their dilemma was highlighted by the widespread discussion in colonial circles of the problem of over-population in Europe.

The basic argument about over-population was essentially Malthusian. The existence of surplus population in Europe was seen as a problem inherent to industrialized societies, a structural problem to which industrial societies knew no answer save mass unemployment and pauperization. By absorbing excess population the colonies could render a valuable service to Europe: - such at least was the thinking behind many emigration movements of the mid-century. Later in the century, however, European great-power rivalry, filtered by the crude theories of the Social Darwinists, brought about the view that over-population was a sign of strength, and that the European powers needed an Empire not to overcome a social evil but to express their national health and vigour. This particularly affected Germany, the late arrival both in nationhood and imperial possessions. Paul Rohrbach, the most celebrated imperialist thinker of the time, summed up the question in these terms:

> Only the German nation has developed in such a way that, like the Anglo-Saxons, she is populous and inwardly strong enough to claim as of right that its national idea should decisively shape the coming age(...) A high birth-rate and the love of children is a direct indication of the inner and external health of a people.(34)

It was this idea which Hans Grimm summarized in the slogan-like title of his famous novel Volk ohne Raum: a nation without living-space.

The cover of Grimm's novel illustrated the theory. It showed a man stretching out his naked body as if it has just been released from chains. He stands in the empty landscape of the colonies, but around his feet are the factory chimneys and the crowded streets of industrial Germany. In the space and freedom of the colonies he has outgrown the shackles of industrial civilization. It showed that Grimm, like so many of his contemporaries, evaluated the colonies in Utopian terms, and that his real motive was pessimism about the state of his own country. The last thing Grimm wished to see was the civilizing or industrialization of the colonies, and the facile argument for imperial expansion on the grounds of a vigorous birth-rate and subsequent over-population had roots in cultural pessimism rather than in the desire to spread the blessings of civilization. Even a reversal of the statistics fell neatly into Grimm's argument. If, as some said, the German birth-rate was declining at the end of the century, then this decline was merely evidence of the effects of over-crowding, and further proof that Germany was 'suffocating through lack of living-space'.(35) This argument also emerged in France, where many writers (among them Leblond, Bertrand, Maurras etc.) were concerned about the declining birth-rate. It was suggested that imperialism was still the answer since the colonies, because of their superior environmental and eugenic conditions, might eventually repopulate a France declining into extinction.(36) The only common thread in these population debates was a discontent with the state of affairs in Europe, and the use of imperialism as a corrective.

III

If colonial fiction had no ambition to explain imperialism in terms either of a Christian or of a civilizing mission, it is reasonable to ask what alternatives were left, save the petty chauvinism which would allow one nation to do anything so long as it got in the way of its rivals. We have seen that colonial fiction was attracted by private justifications of imperialism, and in the next chapter we shall examine the qualities which writers discovered in colonial society and which they felt to be in themselves a justification of imperialism. Even when writers did not make this explicit and merely left open the question of justification, it was obvious that their allegiance to any of the standard excuses for colonialism had worn very thin. Writers were invariably driven to find justifications under the pressure of one of two circumstances: public censure in Europe, or the difficulties of readjusting to European life on their return from the colonies. The importance of the first is obvious, while the second reminds us that the political outlook of the returned settlers was often not simply the extension of their colonial mentality but its unconscious starting-point. We conclude this chapter with two justifications of imperialism made under these pressures.

The works of Pierre Mille contain many examples of unclear thinking about imperialism. Like Kipling's characters, Mille's heroes thrive on colonial life in a way that discourages more profound enquiries into its overall purpose. Like many other writers was was highly ambiguous in his attitude to the values of Western civilization. This is shown, for instance, in some reflections by Barnavaux on a revolt in Madagascar:

> 'I wish I knew why these people are putting up such a resistance. They don't till the soil, they let their cattle roam about in the scrub, most of the time they only eat roots and they shoot from the hip rather than from the shoulder as they ought to. Despite this they get themselves killed and they'll kill you very tidily indeed. People who do nothing with their own country, but don't want anyone else to go there - well, it just doesn't

make sense. In Imérina* it's just the opposite: the
people there know how to read and count, just like
Frenchmen. They've got fields, cattle-food, harvests,
·churches, governors, pastors and curés - all the joys of
civilization. But they take to their heels and run at
the slightest excuse.'(37)

One cannot mistake the ironic tone of these remarks. Barnavaux
is well aware that the bringers of civilization are not welcomed
gratefully by those they pretend to help. At the same time he
admires the spirit of those who remain uncorrupted by civilization:
the savages fight well, while the literate flee for their lives.

This cynical vagueness about the aims of imperialism persists
in Mille's work until the collection of stories Barnavaux et quelques
femmes of 1908. For the first time Mille portrays Barnavaux'
colonial exploits not merely for their own sake, but for something
which lies behind them: 'The things he accomplishes do not make
sense for him on their own,' the narrator observes, 'their only
unity lies in the work of which he is the unknowing tool.'(38) That
work is the imperial mission of France.

The question arises directly in the final story of the collection,
entitled 'The Victory' and dedicated to Kipling, from whose work
'The Greatest Story Ever Told' it obviously derives. Barnavaux is
about to return home after twelve years of continual service
overseas. He demands of the narrator an explanation of the service
he has rendered his nation. He admits that he has lived simply on
a day-to-day basis, without asking for explanations, but now that
he is going into retirement he is anxious lest he should be forced
to conclude that he has wasted his life.

In reply, the narrator tells him the story of the battle of
Actium, as seen from the lower deck of a slave galley fighting in
the battle. In their lowly station the slaves found the great battle
merely confusing and shapeless, and experienced little more than
the tyrannical discipline of the officers directing the ship. At the
end of the battle, however, one of the slaves dares to ask what
has happened and why people are cheering. The overseer replies:
'"Ignorant brute: it is because of the victory which WE have won
at Actium"'. The slaves did not know what was going on, but
they participated in the victory.

The narrator goes on to explain to Barnavaux the relevance
of the story to French imperialism, and in particular to Barnavaux'
part in it. He explains that the battle of Actium was fought in
order to decide

'who would be masters of the world: the Asians and
Africans or the peoples of Europe - that means us,
Barnavaux, us! If they had not won, those people slaving

---

*The Hova region of Madagascar. The 'revolt' in the South
was, in fact, Mille's distorted presentation of the brutal repression
of the Sàkalàvà people by the French forces under Gerard.

117

away in the galley, then you and I would have worked for different masters.'

Barnavaux takes his cue from this, and replies with the crowning argument of Mille's work, in which are combined for the first time civilizing, economic and racist arguments:

'Other masters? The Arabs, the blacks over the Nile, the Syrians with their noses like pick-axes? they would have been the masters? If we had not kept them in their place, they would have been our masters? Yes, it's true enough, we could not have left them alone: it just wouldn't have been possible. If one nation stays still, another always advances. The idea of peace is ridiculous - you are fighting all the time, nation against nation, continent against continent, even in peace-time. You fight by making money, you fight by having more children, you fight with customs officers. And the war you fight with lances, arrows, cannons, guns and battleships is only the necessary climax to all the battles which we call peace. Real war only ever takes place because it is less dangerous, less filled with starvation, hatred and murder than the hypocritical wars of peace. It was a fine battle they fought, the oarsmen of Actium, and if they hadn't won, they wouldn't have been able even to go on earning their livelihood rowing transport-galleys. The others, the enemies, the negroes, Arabs, Syrians, the Yellows from the bottom of Asia would have taken their place. But does that mean that glory - that glory is - bread! ?'
He paused for a moment, almost dazzled by the thought: 'Why does nobody explain this to us in France? Tell me, tell me, have I, Barnavaux, really made, bread, life and glory?'(39).

The narrator assures him that he has done this, and the story ends.
We have quoted this passage at some length for it shows clearly the way in which imperialism is justified by Mille, using arguments which, though they seem little more than rationalizations of colonial experience, have an obvious domestic function. The racial insecurity which was the origin of much brutality is re-expressed as a global rivalry between white and black. If the blacks are not kept in their place they will make themselves masters of the world and infiltrate Europe with their undesirable racial characteristics. The violence and constant action of colonial life no longer needs to rely on a purely personal taste for adventure, nor does it need to fear criticism from liberal quarters: it now appears in the context of a view of history according to which everyone is always at war, engaged in the continuous struggle for existence. No need for Mille to worry about the values of civilization, or about the spread of Christianity: imperialism is

part of a more profound and more ancient struggle. It is also clear that Mille has found a formula which bridges over the many gaps between colony and mother-land which his earlier works had created. A formula has been found by which Barnavaux' return to France may be seen as a continuation of his colonial struggle. It is also an obvious implication of this account of imperialism that the galley-slave (and Barnavaux himself, the proletarian soldier) recognise that their best advantage lies in siding with imperialism.

Mille has therefore jettisoned all idealist ballast. Imperialism is about power. Those who do not display their strength aggressively will lose it. Imperialism serves no immediate economic or military purpose: it is not a policy, which someone might disagree with; it is a way of life. At the same time it defends the status quo. Colonial experience is a dangerous legacy to take to Europe.

The spate of German novels dealing with the suppression of the Herero uprising in South-West Africa demonstrated the pressure exerted on writers to justify to the reading-public at home (and in the colonies too) the acts committed in their name. We have already observed how rapidly all idealistic justifications were dismissed, to be replaced by arguments of economic advantage or crude power. The relation between the various layers of justification emerges most clearly from Gustav Frenssen's novel about the uprising. At the end of the novel a group of soldiers sit around discussing the purpose of the campaign they are engaged upon. Frenssen had described the war in all its sickening horror, and he knew that such events demanded an explanation. One of the soldiers begins the explanation in familiar terms:

> 'These blacks deserved to be killed in the eyes of God and men; not because they murdered two hundred farmers and rose up against us in rebellion, but because they built no houses and dug no wells.'

He goes on to explain why the Europeans' cultural superiority gave them the right of genocide* rather than the obligation to teach and help:

> 'God gave us victory here because we are more honourable and more enterprising than they are. That's not much of a compliment when you compare us with the blacks, but we've got to make sure that we stay superior and better prepared than any nation on earth. The world belongs to the stronger and the more energetic. That is God's justice.'

---

*The word is anything but melodramatic. Numerically speaking, it was the murder of a people, and von Trotha, the German commander, had nothing less in his mind.

The narrator is slow to be convinced by this argument. He looks down at the body of the Herero prisoner whom he has just shot, and he feels uncomfortable at the ruthlessness of his friend's ideas. He misses the idealistic note. His friend continues:

> 'We must be hard, we must kill; but at the same time we must, both as individuals and as a nation, be concerned with lofty thoughts and noble deeds, so that we may make our contribution to the future brotherhood of man.'

At once the narrator's doubts are assuaged, and he feels confident about the purposes of the war:

> ...now I heard a great song, ringing out over the whole of Southern Africa and throughout the world, making sense of everything.(40)

The progression is well marked. The Herero deserve to die because they have not worked and lived in the spirit of European civilization. Yet there is no morality in the world other than a crude Social Darwinist understanding of Strength. Only the strong deserve to rule, and their only justification is strength not culture. Yet these truths, although accepted, need sugaring with idealistic but utterly meaningless phrases. These phrases are obviously empty, but the narrator latches on to them eagerly. It is not simply propaganda for the readers at home: it is reassurance for those whose hands are red with slaughter.

Frenssen's argument did more than paper over the ruthlessness of colonial conquest. It offered the chance to see wars of oppression and exploitation in the more neutral, and morally less questionable, light of race-wars. Many German writers shared this view. They spoke of 'the day which is coming when the Africans will simply wipe us out all across Africa'. Lest anyone should think that this might be in retaliation for what the whites had done to them, the Africans motive was always alleged to be 'Rassenhass', racial hatred. Thus it was 'hatred of our race' which led the Herero to revolt in 1904(41), not a sense of injustice or an understandable response to German land and credit policies. No one was to blame; it was natural and inevitable that the races should be in conflict. However the Germans responded to these actions, they too were acting beyond morality, following the laws of nature.

It is in no way to diminish the callous horror of these actions and their white-washing if we conclude the chapter with the assertion that such events revealed aspects of European life which Europe had yet to recognize in itself. Not simply the indifference to horror and cruelty, the acceptance of transparently insincere justifications for barbarous wars; but the fundamental confusion we find in colonial fiction about the proper basis for society was as true of European life as of European colonial behaviour. It had been Nietzsche, more often picked up at the end of the century for his seeming encouragement of brutality than for his critique of it, who had noted with dismay the unstable tension within his age between post-Christian sentimentality and the acceptance of the brutal truths of Social Darwinism. He had foreseen that his age would wax eloquent about humanity and brotherhood while continuing to organize its society and to conduct its international affairs according to the law of the jungle.(42) No combination of ideas was more lethal than that of brute force disguised by sentiment and greed wrapped up in the tawdry paper of bourgeois ideology. It took the twentieth century to open Europe's eyes to truths about itself from which the oppressed nations of the world had long suffered.

NOTES

1. D.Thomson, Europe since Napoleon (Penguin Books, 1966) 1966), p.496; V.G.Kiernan, 'Farewells to Empire' in Marxism and Imperialism (Edward Arnold, 1974), pp.69/94.
2. H.Marcuse,'The affirmative value of culture' in Negations (Penguin Books, 1972), p.99; G.Lukács, Deutsche Literatur während des Imperialismus (Berlin, 1948), p.7; V.I.Lenin, Imperialism (1916).
3. T.Leutwein, quoted by L.H.Gann & P.Duignan, The Rulers of German Africa (Stanford, 1977), p.44. See also P.Mille, 'La Race Supérieure' in Revue de Paris, vol. 12 (1905),p.834. These admissions are remarkably common in colonial fiction: e.g. J.v.Puttkamer, Das Duallamädchen (Leipzig, 1908), p.37 & H.Rohrmann, Kulturfirnis (Leipzig, 1909), pp.79/80.
4. W.D.Arnold, Oakfield, volume 2 (Longman, 1853),p.223.
5. G.O.Trevelyan, The Competition Wallah (Macmillan, 1864), pp.305, 451. G.D.Bearce discusses these critiques of Anglo-Indian commercialism in British attitudes towards India (OUP,1971), p.272f.
6. M.Diver, The Hero of Herat (Constable, 1912), p.x.
7. A.Sandison, The Wheel of Empire (Macmillan, 1967), passim. A.Wilson, The strange ride of Rudyard Kipling (Granada, 1979), p.172, also p.233.
8. R.Randau, Les explorateurs (Paris, 1907), pp. 62, 153, 168, 341.
9. Quoted by B.Parry, Delusions and Discoveries (Allen Lane, 1972), p.159. Arnold speaks of 'providential asylum' in Oakfield, vol. 2, p.223.
10. 'Thrown Away' in Plain Tales from the Hills.
11. E.Psichari, L'Appel des Armes (Paris, 1912), p.148.
12. Cf. G.D.Killam, Africa in English fiction (Ibadan, 1968), pp.16/34 -on the 'schoolboy master of the world ' - and more from the point of view of an institutional history R.Heussler, Yesterday's Rulers (Syracuse, 1963), pp.19f,62f.

13. O.Holm, Pioniere (Berlin, 1906), p.243. This is a random example, and similar statements can be found throughout German colonial fiction, e.g. A.Funke, Afrikanischer Lorbeer (Berlin, 1907), p.154f; H.Rohrman, Kulturfirnis (Leipzig, 1909), p.33f.

14. Cf. C.Bolt, Victorian attitudes to race (Routledge & Kegan Paul, 1971), p.94f; and S.Neill, Colonialism and Christian Missions (Lutterworth Press, 1966), p.85f. Cf. also Bearce, p.235f.

15. H.Grimm, Südafrikanische Novellen (Frankfurt a. Main, 1913), pp.65/97.

16. R.Randau, Les explorateurs (Paris, 1907), pp.206/o7.

17. O.Holm, pp.244/45. On the 'Education for Labour' strain in colonial fiction see C.Falkenhorst, Jung-Deutschland in Afrika (Dresden, n.d.), p.24; and in reality D.Bald, Deutsch-Ostafrika (Munich, 1970), p.128f.

18. Peter Moors Fahrt nach Südwest (new ed. Berlin, 1936) p.74.

19. F.v.Bülow, Tropenkoller (Berlin, 1896), p.12; Im Lande der Verheißung (Leipzig, 1899), p.37. Peters appears as Dr. Ralf Krome. See also the Carl Peters novel by B.Olden, Ich bin Ich (Berlin, 1927).

20. R.Randau, Les explorateurs (Paris, 1907), pp. 168, 341. See also W.S.Maugham, The explorer (Heinemann, 1908), pp.27,163.

21. J.Olpp, Die Kulturbedeutung der evangelischen Rheinischen Mission für Südwest (Swakopmund, 1914), esp. pp.6,29. For an example of settler attitudes to the mission see e.g. M.v.Eckenbrecher, Was Afrika mir gab und nahm (Berlin, 1907), p.200f.

22. L.Bertrand, Le sang des races (Paris, 1899), p.143.

23. Psichari, p.102.

24. Wilson, p.183.

25. M.Diver, Desmond's Daughter (Blackwood, 1916), p.315.

26. Kim (new edition Macmillan, 1970), p.90.

27. E.Psichari, Terres de Soleil (Paris, 1908), p.115. See also R.Randau, Les algérianistes (Paris, 1911), p.276f. See also Bolt, p.114f.

28. P.Mille, 'Barnavaux Général' in Sur la vaste terre (Paris, 1905), pp.95/148. Missionary MacKenzie can be found in Allan Quartermain.

29. M.Diver, Desmond's Daughter, p.24.

30. Quoted in Parry, p.161.

31. 'The Conversion of Aurelian MacGoggin' in Plain Tales.

32. Les Civilisés (97th Thousand, Paris, 1905), p.307.

33. Compare Mat Gioi (=A.de Pouvourville), Deux Années de lutte (Paris, 1892), pp. 42, 214/17 with A. de Pouvourville, L'Annam Sanglante (Paris, 1912), esp. Part III which describes the French victory. On opium, Mat Gioi, L'Esprit des races jaunes: L'Opium - sa pratique (L'Edition de l'initiation, Paris, 1902) - a handbook full of practical assistance, quite

without any evaluative commentary. See also Pujarniscle, pp. 163/70.

34. P.Rohrbach, Der deutsche Gedanke in der Welt (Düsseldorf & Leipzig, 1912), pp.7/8.

35. The image in Rohrbach's (ibid.,p.178) but occurs repeatedly throughout Grimm's novel.

36. See e.g. M.A.Leblond, La France devant l'Europe (Paris, 1913), pp.106f, 172. Also M.J.Chailley-Bert, L'Emigration des femmes aux colonies (Paris, 1897), p.58f. A.Murphy discusses the lengthy debates on French population statistics in The ideology of French Imperialism (Washington, 1948), p.143f.

37. 'Barnavaux, Général', loc. cit., p.99.

38. 'L'Ile aux Lépreux' in Barnavaux et quelques femmes (Paris, 1908), p.30.

39. 'La Victoire' in ibid., pp.310/12.

40. Frenssen, p.198f.

41. K.Osmann, Buschklatsch quoted in G.Patzlaff, Die Kolonien und der Kolonialgedanke... (Greifswald, 1938), p.153. Also Funke, p.231; F.Kraze, Heim Neuland (Stuttgart, 1909), pp.245,259. Also Bearce, p.235.

42. These were the central arguments of the first of Nietzsche's Thoughts out of season in 1873, devoted to an attack on the popular writer David Friedrich Strauss.

Chapter Six

THE UNEXPECTED ELITE

'I would by contraries execute all things'

(The Tempest)

White colonial society is usually thought of as conservative and traditional. Pictures come to mind of the officers' mess, with its etiquette and regimental silver, or of other corners of the globe made forever England by the habits of dressing for dinner and drinking the Queen's health. But these pictures are somewhat misleading, for as we encounter colonial society through the eyes of its literature the social innovations are more striking than its imitations of Europe. Colonial writers shared with the creators of utopias a certain impatience with the old ways of European society and strove to portray colonial society as new, different and better than what they had known in Europe. Leblond summed up the appeal for many writers of the colonial settler as 'a new man, a brave toiler who(...)leaves behind the ancient soil of Europe, that infertile dust of ruins, made sterile by selfishness and prejudices'; while an earlier French novel set in Algeria comments on the hero's determination that 'the petty demands of society should have no validity in this new country, and that the narrowness of ideas and prejudices from which he had suffered in France should not be able to take root in this young colony'.(1)

These attitudes went further than that general mistrust of civilization outlined in the previous chapter. They involved specific criticism of the mother-country from the standpoint of white colonial society, and a pride in the distinctive social achievements of the settlers. Even on a topic as sensitive as patriotism, writers were highly critical of European attitudes, and the theme of separatism is heard repeatedly, from Algeria to India. Kipling's famous line 'And what should they know of England, who only England know?' neatly summarized the less radical feeling that colonial experience called for a revision of traditional, home-centered patriotism, a feeling which inspired Seeley's famous lectures on 'The Expansion of England'. He explicitly warned his audience that, unless England ceased to regard itself merely as 'an island off the north-western coast of Europe' and learnt to assimilate the political and social thinking of the Empire, the Empire would, like America, break away from the mother-country.(2) He at least had heard the many voices from the Empire which preferred the society and values of the colonies to those traditional to Europe.

Social innovation and reform had always been part of the attraction of overseas territories. This had been the motive of the various sects which established settlements in America, as well as of the majority of the emigrants flooding out of Metternich's Europe, determined to build political and social liberty elsewhere. Settlers invariably dreamt of new men and new societies, and imaginative literature naturally expressed those dreams, both in fulfilment and (as we saw in the European novels about America) in frustration. The final chapter examines the impact of these social dreams on the society and politics of the mother-country; in this chapter we are concerned with the colonials' view of their own white society, and in particular with their understanding of equality, class and the individual's relationship to society.

Very few of the colonial novelists approached the problems of society from a preformed ideological standpoint, or a missionary zeal which predated their colonial experience. Although their ideas had obviously been coloured by Social Darwinism or race-thinking, they had in no way been systematized. Most of them began to write of colonial life for its own sake, because of experiences and situations which had fired their imagination, and the social ideas which they develop came directly from these experiences, filtered always through the subconscious legacy of European life. The characters whom they depict with the greatest interest are those whom the colonies have entirely shaped, either by long experience or because they came out in a state of social innocence, as unwritten sheets which colonial life marked with its distinctive stamp. For this reason so many writers profess ignorance and open-mindedness at every turn: they want to show that their characters are formed by the situation and not by their author. Much loved by writers was any plot which involved the visit to the colonies of a person with preconceived, European ideas about how to behave. These ideas were invariably tested against the realities of colonial life and, in a tragic or comic outcome, found wanting. Aurelian McGoggin, Kipling's implausible follower of Spenser and Comte, goes mad trying to hold fast to his imported theories, and his experience, though extreme, is typical of that of a whole string of similar characters.

Nowhere is colonial fiction more anxious to break away from the 'prejudices' of Europe than in class relations. Virtually all colonial writers portray the experience of colonial life as creating an open and egalitarian white community. Pierre Mille, for instance, in his stories constantly underlines the indifference of the colonials to those distinctions of class and rank which were regarded as important in metropolitan France. Although he describes characters serving within the hierarchical systems of the army and colonial civil service, Mille shows how colonial experience devalues class and hierarchy. One of his early stories, entitled 'Barnavaux, the General', contains an important statement about the experiences of colonial service. Barnavaux, the working-class private soldier, looks back on his service in Madagascar:

> 'Ah, what a time it was for me, living on my pittance as a second-class infantryman, to be the sovereign of my territory. I could look around me at the men, the houses, the estates and rivers and say to myself "I am in command". At that time only two people stood between me and the President of France: the General and the Minister. You know, all my life I shall regret that those years are over. That's what happens when once you have drunk from the cup of power.'(3)

Another of Mille's heroes, the colonial administrator Partonneau, enjoys a similar feeling of prestige and importance. Instead of being a mere cog in the machine of state, preyed upon by his superiors, he feels like a feudal lord. As he remarks, in the colonies 'where the people cannot vote they are your subjects'.(4)

A similar account is given by Jules Boissière of the feelings of an NCO at a lonely guard-post in the hills of Viet-Nam. Here too we see how colonialism has created archaic social conditions, and granted to its more menial servants a status unobtainable in contemporary European society.

> Ferrier's life was one long, happy dream, which he used to dream when he was in the ranks but which he never imagined that he would be able to realize. In every way he savoured his life as a country-gentleman, like a gracious land-owner in Normandy surrounded by his indulgent family. He enjoyed it to the full since he had for so long been bogged down in the dreary rut of life which puts a chain round our neck and burdens us with the shackles of civilization.(5)

These opinions were by no means the private fantasies of individual writers. In an official publication of the French Africa Committee, Maurice Delafosse gave an account of the 'states of mind of a colonial' which obviously drew on Mille's work as an authentic source. Broussard, as Delafosse christens his typical colonial, is filled with an enormous sense of his own importance as he surveys the range of responsibilities which his post in the bush gives him. He is convinced that 'it is better to be number one in a fly-ridden place than to be second-in-command in Rome'.(6) Even for official colonial thinking, such a change in status was welcomed as a liberation.

The important feature of these and many similar portrayals is that they were of people not otherwise in the traditionally governing classes. Writers were anxious to demonstrate the freemasonry among colonials, an equality based upon achievement and responsibility and not upon inherited money or traditional social status. It is this feature of colonial society which has led some historians to modify the negative picture of colonial dominance, claiming that colonial rule was not administered by 'a "ruling class" in the Marxist sense'. In fact what is really meant is that the colonies were not governed by a ruling-class in a non-Marxist sense, not governed, that is, by those who shared through the privileges of birth and wealth in the conspicious social hierarchy of the mother-country. It was only in the colonies that the allegiance of settlers and soldiers to the values of the bourgeoisie became apparent, and Albert Memmi's Portrait du colonisé, shows how the social structure of colonial society imposes on the settler from the lower-middle and working-classes the privileges and ideology of the ruling classes, qualities 'independent of his personal merits and his actual social class'.(7) Memmi's diagnosis forms part of a highly critical account of the proto-Fascist social behaviour latent in colonial society, and focusses on experiences in colonial society which were of particular interest to the colonial writers. In particular, both Memmi and the colonial writers were interested with the phenomenon of the classless society in the colonies. Unlikely though it sounds, colonial fiction portrayed the colonial army and civil service as essentially democratic institutions, in relation to the whites of course and not to the 'Natives'.

The actual word 'democratic' is rare in colonial literature. It smacked of socialism to some and to others, like Kipling, of corrupt and inefficient South American despotisms. In some German fiction the phrase 'aristocratic democracy' was used, the first word guarding against undesirable implications of the second. It expressed very clearly what was the tenor of much of this literature. A democratic association of whites implied that birth and class were less important than race: an aristocratic conspiracy of the whites over the peoples they have colonized gave positive meaning to their experience of equality. French novelists made the same point, adding a comparison between colonial equality and the down-trodden democracy of republican France:

> The whites who arrived in the colonies from the democratic country of France became aristocrats. It is a striking phenomenon: all thought themselves equals at the same time as belonging to a superior race. In Europe they had been separated by class divisions. In the colonies these do not exist, and the simple white clothes in which they all dressed seemed a symbolic representation of this process of levelling-out(...) The nobility of their race was re-established.(8)

In one respect the concept of 'aristocratic democracy' had been anticipated by exotic literature. It had been Sealsfield who first coined the phrase in Germany, and Pierre Loti had used the idea in a similar fashion. In Aziyadé, as we saw, he contrasted his experience of the exotic with the lack of equality in European society and claimed that true equality was 'unknown in our democratic nation and in all our western republics'. But this remark had little or no political seriousness. At most it expressed a yearning for personal relations in an increasingly industrialized society, and it is hardly in confict with Loti's no less characteristic remark 'I have a horror of everything conventionally called civilization and of egalitarian theories'. Part of the appeal of the exotic was to bask in the reflected glory of an uncommon pursuit and thus to fulfil a longing 'to be a seigneur(...)in countries where the laws are not made for everybody'(9).

Colonial fiction was much more consequential in its approach to democracy, and based its ideas upon a sincere critique of the class-system of Europe. It served some of the function which we saw the adventure story assuming. The contrast between colony and mother-land is nowhere stronger than in this regard, and it is German fiction which, perhaps because of the exceptionally rigid hierarchy of German society, most fully illustrates colonial life as an escape into classlessness.

Although German administrators might particularly appreciate their escape from pen-pushing and form-filling, and German soldiers their escape from the rigidly stratified officers' mess, in many other professions people felt that a meaningful life could begin only in the colonies. The various crafts and trades were much more open than in Germany, and individual initiative was far less restricted by tradition. Peasant-farmers not only owned much more land than they had in Germany; they found their social status entirely transformed. From being the underdog in what was often no better than a feudal relationship with the local Junker, they found themselves on a footing of social equality with their farming neighbours and with the officers of the local troops, an equality which they appreciated the more since they in turn could play the role of feudal lord in their dealings with their black subjects.

Women must also be numbered among those glad to have escaped from Germany. Many felt that the active, demanding life of the settler gave to the settler's wife much more responsibility and status than was available to women in Germany. For this reason German colonial fiction remained close to the circles working for women's emancipation. At the same time, however, many women appear to have escaped from Germany for the opposite reason. Because they disapproved of the moves towards emancipation, because the 'modern woman' in Germany horrified them, they set up in the colonies a regressive, peasant style of life, gratefully accepting the simplicity of the demands which this life made on them.

Ironically, even the landed aristocracy were often glad to move to the colonies and saw there much greater room for individual initiative and escape from a society only concerned with nuances of social distinction and court ceremonial. They could become active again, and, paradoxically, gain their freedom by abandoning the privileges of superior birth. Their search for self-expression took on absurd as well as cruel overtones. Aristocratic settlers not only, like almost everyone else, celebrated their new freedom by ill-treating the local people; they went sometimes to extreme lengths to recreate a chivalric freemasonry of landowners, with private armies and many of the habits of the medieval knights. Yet despite these obvious manifestations of the vulgar search for status, German fiction constantly stressed the egalitarian, 'democratic' nature of the social experiment. A character in one of Frieda von Bülow's novels responded angrily to the suggestion that the colonies exacerbated the class differences of Germany:

> 'Recently people have called our African colonies "a paradise for aristocrats" and of all the rubbish which they talk about us over there this is probably the most stupid. In our colonies a German aristocrat differs socially from a German craftsman or peasant so much less than any of them differ from the most nobly-born black that the aristocrat and his German cobbler are for all purposes equals(10).'

The context of these remarks makes it clear that they were more than a reflection of social experience in German East Africa. They served an obvious purpose in defending the German settlers against the unfavourable image which the German press and parliament held of them and which was to culminate some ten years later in the Arenberg commission investigating the colonial scandals. Frieda von Bülow was trying to make the colonies seem attractive to reformers and Social Democrats. When she argues that the 'members of the white elite' would have lacked all status had they remained in Germany and would have been 'members of the herd, a mere number'(11), she was once again offering a justification of imperialism as a corrective to certain social ills in Europe, and by its very nature such a justification implied a major criticism of European society.

English colonial fiction too was convinced that racial kinship created links which obliterated traditional class-distinctions. Maud Diver, for instance, wrote of the Anglo-Indians as 'members of one great family, aliens under one sky', insisting on their equality which was based partly on racial ties and partly on their status as rulers of India. As one writer remarked: 'Everyone in India is, more or less, somebody.' Maud Diver did admit in her picture of India that there were, particularly in certain regiments, vestiges of class-consciousness and a resistance to what, in her novel Desmond's Daughter, one officer contemptuously called '"this new fangled mixing of the classes"'(12), but moments such as these were felt to be exceptions rather than either the rule or the ideal. Class-distinctions were felt to be inherent in the societies Britain had conquered, rather than among the conquerors, and it was in this spirit that novelists attacked the caste-system and the Indian aristocracy. A typical episode is contained in the opening chapters

The unexpected élite

of Flora Annie Steel's novel on the Mutiny, On the Face of the Waters (1893). A high-caste Indian is shown resisting a non-aristocratic member of the British administration, for no other reason than social snobbery. Mrs. Steel is at pains to show the autocratic nature of the leaders of the Mutiny, both in order to underline the superiority of white society and to prevent the Mutiny appearing as a popular uprising. (French writers had attacked Arab society in Algeria on precisely the same ground of its stratification and snobbery.(13)) In portraying the white community the emphasis was on equality and on the proud boast of the Anglo-Indians that their society was open to all, regardless of class and birth.

It is difficult to regard as objective any statement that Anglo-Indian society was classless. From the eighteenth to the twentieth century visitors to India had seen it as 'a land of snobs' and commented on 'the elaborate structure of class distinction', which they often compared unfavourably to the class-system at home. Colonial writers were well aware of these criticisms, and many of their works show up the critics. Alice Perrin's Anglo-Indians contains an episode in which an English gentleman, Sir Rowland Curtice, visits an Anglo-Indian family in the course of their camp expedition round an administrative district(14). Sir Rowland is convinced that the Anglo-Indians live in the lap of luxury, feasting like lords off the fat of the land, with scores of unnecessary servants. A few weeks with the family show him the error of these views, and when the setting of the novel moves to London, Mrs. Perrin is careful to show us just how snobbish, class-ridden and pampered is the society in which Sir Rowland is at home. Her message is clear: if there are gradations in Anglo-Indian society, they have real foundations - race, achievement and integrity - rather than the artificial foundations of money, birth and connections.

Two works in particular deal with the class structure of Anglo-India: Oakfield and The Competition Wallah. Arnold's novel, set in the days before the Mutiny, shows the new type of civil servant not merely reaching a more idealistic view of the imperial mission but asserting himself, as a man from a humble social background, against the class-ridden attitudes prevalent among the army of conquest. Edward Oakfield is determined 'to overlook the merely artificial distinctions of rank and money', and appears to accept that the task is going to involve not only a major critique of English society and attitudes, but also a kind of assent to 'the revolutionary, and let us hope, fertilizing lava stream that flowed from the unrestful Parisian crater'(15) (a reference to the spread of revolutionary ideas after the 1848 revolution). The moral crusade which, as we saw, gave meaning to imperialism cannot help but involve the author in a revision of the class barriers of Europe.

The Mutiny did little to changes these efforts. Indeed, it so widened the gulf between London and Anglo-India in their view of the 'native question' that it actually increased the independence of colonial social thinking. There is a close link, for instance, between Trevelyan's horrified repudiation of the anti-Native lobby in England and his efforts to establish the meritocracy of the ICS. Like Mille and Boissière he sees the colonial administrator as a member of an elite, to which the size of his responsibilities rather than his rank and privilege gives access. The ICS man is 'a member of an official aristocracy, owning no superior, bound to no man; fearing no man'. Trevelyan is a shade suspicious of certain elements in Anglo-Indian society. He hesitates to fill his engagement calendar on the principle recommended by one novelist - that 'if a man has a white skin and a dress-suit, we ask him to dinner'(16), preferring 'to know something of a man besides the colour of his skin before admitting him into the bosom of the family'. Neverthless he has no patience with the norms used in England to make that choice, and stresses that the prizes of real power and responsibility in India are 'open to every subject of the Queen, though his father be as poor as Job subsequently to the crash in that patriarch's affairs, and though he does not number so much as the butler of a member of parliament among his patrons and connexions'.(17)

Colonial writers were prepared to go to enormous lengths in defence of this view of their society. Kipling's 'Ballad of East and West', for instance, ends with a sweepingly egalitarian statement that seems to transcend barriers of race as well as those of class. At that crucial existential moment 'when two strong men stand face to face' differences of rank and colour become irrelevant: 'there is neither East nor West, Border nor Breed, nor Birth'. In this spirit a young man in one of Edmund Candler's stories is sent to India with the advice that 'a gentleman is the same all the world over, whether his skin is black or white or yellow'(18). When Cecil Rhodes called for 'equal rights for every civilized man South of the Zambesi' even he explicitly included the phrase 'whether white or black'. We should see such remarks as a testimony to an intense belief in the democratic nature of colonial experience rather than interpret them as a genuine ambition to extend this democratic ideal to non-white races.

This belief came to be enshrined among the clichés of popular colonial fiction, as well as in its more serious works. One finds increasingly that writers mixed the class-background of their central characters in order subsequently to show that the social differences are levelled out by colonial experience. In this respect colonial fiction merely followed a trend more widely observable in European fiction of the time. Whereas the confrontation of the classes in the first half of the nineteenth century was generally portrayed through love-stories (or crime-stories) in which the differences of class added piquancy and tension to the plot; by the end of the century class differences were introduced in order to be resolved. The technique continued into the adventure stories of this century: in the 'Biggles' stories, for instance, the very pointed class distinctions between two of the central heroes (Ginger, the orphan from the slums, and Bertie, a highly improbable sprig of the nobility) are erased in the common activity of their exciting lives.

G.A. Henty's novel The Dash for Khartoum (1892) contains a particularly absurd example of this trend. The main body of the novel is taken up with the facile military adventures in which Henty specialized, but the adventures are set in a revealing social context. Henty tells of the circumstances in which two boys, one the son of a company commander and the other of a company sergeant and his sluttish wife, are mixed up at birth (like Frederick and Captain Corcoran) so that no one can tell which was the well-born and which the lowly born. Henty seems to find this plot far from ludicrous, so concerned is he to show that the experiences of the two boys in the army in Egypt shape their character so as to obliterate the differences of birth and heredity. Whatever the facts of birth and breeding, Edgar and Rupert become equals.(19)

The sense of equality between white men is an essential part of Kipling's colonial stories. Typical of his early outlook is the story 'His Private Honour'. It tells of the confrontation between an officer and a private in the Indian Army. The officer, newly arrived from England and still very inexperienced, succumbs to the heat and strikes a private soldier. Fortunately for him he strikes Ortheris, one of the three soliders of whom Kipling often wrote, and 'a good man, a proved man, and an Englishman'. At home the pressures of rank and rule-book would have prevented the resolution of their problem, but in that 'true' democracy of white colonials the private is able to satisfy both his honour and the requirements of military discipline by fighting the officer man to man. It is as equals that the private and the officer reach a settlement with their fists. The private, despite his lack of military rank, is 'neither a menial nor an American, but a free man': neither, that is, a windy democrat insisting upon theoretical equality and his 'rights' ('My rights!',says Ortheris contemptuously,''Strewth A'mightly! I'm a man.'), nor yet a cog in an authoritarian system which allows him no individuality.(20) The society is aristocratically democratic, and Kipling feels this to be its important and abiding achievement.

Kipling held on to his vision of the democratic nature of the colonies long after he had returned to Europe. With the outbreak of the Boer War he looked for a regeneration of that classless spirit, both in the South African colonies and at home. He made much play of the fact that all classes were equally involved in the war, as he said in the famous 'Absent Minded Beggar', the poem which raised huge sums for the dependents of ordinary soldiers killed in the war:

> Cook's son - Duke's son - son of a belted Earl - Son of
> a Lambeth publican - it's all the same today!

For Kipling the Boer War was a defence of this democratic ideal against the principle of authoritarianism and Bible-thumping reaction. The colonies were democracies, where ordinary people should be able to make progress and improve their social position, but in Kipling's eyes the Boers had fallen out of line. The story 'Private Copper' (1904) makes this clear. It tells of the encounter of an ordinary British private captured by a member of the Transvaal forces. The South African is openly contemptuous of the private's lowly origins, and feels himself to be the superior of Alf Copper in personal, military and moral respects. He even tries to open Copper's eyes to the degeneracy of '"your own working-classes, the diseased, lying, drinking white stuff that you come out of"'; but just as he is embarking on a further explanation of the evils of the English social system, Copper outwits him and takes him prisoner. Back in his own lines Copper tells his sergeant: '"I caught 'im in the shameful act of tryin' to start a aristocracy on a gun an' a wagon an' a shambuk! Yes, that's what it was: a bloomin' aristocracy."' The war is all about keeping the colonies safe for democracy.(21)*

Kipling's biographers have given an account of the way in which such opinions not merely made Kipling the spokesman of an emotive and populist nationalism but brought him also into opposition to the political establishment in London. As Conservative politicians, and their upper-class representatives in South Africa, showed themselves incapable of learning the political, and above all the social lessons which Kipling felt the Boer War to teach, and as after the death of Rhodes in 1902 South Africa moved further away from the dreams which Kipling had cherished for it, so he found himself less and less able to identify with any of the available political positions, and his search for aristocratic democracy had launched him on a dangerously uncharted ideological journey.(22)

II

Colonial 'democracy' had another important feature. It was not simply dependent on the oppression of other races, the mechanism which allowed white settlers to feel themselves in such a superior position to that they believed they had transcended the European class system. The overcoming of class-distinctions was made easier (indeed, perhaps, made possible at all) by the fact that colonial society was made up of déclassés, by people who had lost their secure membership of any social class. The fraternity of

---

*Conrad wrote in a letter (1899) about the Boer War: 'There is an appalling fatuity in this business. If I am to believe Kipling this is a war undertaken for the cause of democracy. C'est à crever de rire!' But Kipling was by no means alone in his view. Conan Doyle's history of the Boer War, and Henty's novels of the South African campaign agreed with him in portraying the Boers as class-ridden aristocrats and the campaign against them as a crusade for democracy.

white colonial society did not break class allegiance: other factors
had achieved that. Colonial society merely gave identity to those
who belonged nowhere else. The point is made strikingly in Pierre
Mille's story 'Beyond Good and Evil'. It tells of a meeting between
Barnavaux, the narrator and a Russian gentleman who has joined
the French Foreign Legion. The social links between the (middle-
class) narrator and the Russian are very strong, and for a while
Barnavaux' position of equality with the narrator (itself a symbol
of the classless nature of colonial society) is threatened. As the
narrator reflects on the ease which class conventions give to social
intercourse, he shows how little he has escaped from the class-
structure of Europe:

> It is very difficult to explain how we distinguish a man
> who belongs to what we usually call 'good society'. It
> is much more by means of what he does not do as by
> what he actually does: by means of what he does not
> say as by his actual words; by the control which he
> exercises over his gestures, his eyes, his mouth and his
> entire body. Within two minutes I was treating this
> legionary like a gentleman. Poor Barnavaux, usually so
> ingenuously communicative when we are alone together,
> became silent, and took on that sulky detached
> expression which he assumes in the presence of his
> superiors(...) How terribly strong are the forces of
> caste, and the similarities of education and culture!(...)
> The man who had so strangely imposed his company
> upon us inspired in me a mistrust bordering on antipathy,
> yet while it had taken years for me to build up
> confidence between myself and honest, plain Barnavaux,
> this stranger had from the start aroused in me memories
> of books Barnavaux had never read, of men to whom
> he would never have dared to speak, of bejewelled
> ladies, fashionable actresses and exclusive salons.(23)

At the end of the story the atmosphere is broken as the stranger
tells them of the monstrous crime which he committed in his
home-country and which forced him to join the Legion. As soon
as he learns of the stranger's crime, Barnavaux recognises that
both of them are equally excluded from the norms of European
society, albeit for very different reasons, and that although the
stranger belongs to a superior class they are equals. Barnavaux
therefore addresses him with the familiar 'tu'. He is a member
of the community of exiles, a membership which presupposes
already lapsed class-distinctions.

French colonial fiction developed the theme of criminals'
place in colonial society. Whereas Mille's story melodramatically
concentrated on the crime itself, other writers concentrated on
the liberating effect of building a society on the failures and
throw-outs of conventional society. It was a familiar enough
subject in its negative aspects - Gide's Immoraliste would give it

currency far into our own century - but was more striking as, for instance, when Farrère puts into the mouth of a colonial governor a positive evaluation of the colony's function as 'the ultimate sanctuary for the throwouts of every every class and for fugitives from the justice of the world'. The governor continues:

> These who are breaking the virgin-soil of Indo-China never laboured in France; the business-men of the colony were bankrupts at home; the men who give orders to the cultured mandarins did not manage to get a degree in France; while those who judge and sentence in our courts have often themselves been judged and sentenced at home.'(24)

Such openness about the motives and aptitudes of the colonials is not found in English or German fiction. On the occasions that writers admit the existence of 'undesirable' elements in their colonies, they carefully distinguish them from the worthy citizens who people the colony. Yet, almost despite their intentions, English and German novelists also showed all emigrants and settlers to be to a greater or lesser extent the outcasts of European society. A bankruptcy, a failure in love, family disputes about succession to property, an affair of honour, or mere discontent - nearly all the characters in this fiction have some such event in their past which caused them to come out to the colonies. Sometimes it is this starting-point for their adventures which gives them an essentially critical, outsider view of European society. Other novels merely use failure as a catalyst for the start of the plot. Nearly all Henty's settler novels, for instance, begin with the hero's family opening their morning paper to discover that a bank has collapsed and that they are ruined. Membership of the elite club of the colonies, admission to the aristocratic democracy, has therefore two main conditions: personal failure and a white skin.

The obvious exception to the rule of failure was Anglo-India, both civilian and military. Service in India was so much part of a tradition, cultivated by families and institutions, that idealism rather than failure was felt to be the condition of entry. Kipling's Subalterns are schooled for the job, and Mrs. Perrin too goes out of her way to emphasise that the Anglo-Indians are 'normal, self-reliant people, hall-marked with the hereditary faculty for work in exile'(25). Nevertheless, Mrs. Perrin repeatedly points out that their careers are failures by European standards. When they return to Britain they find that, for all the magnificence of their colonial life-style, they must get used to humble mediocrity. From being 'a leader of Calcutta society' the colonial finds himself part of 'the rank and file in the pump room'. Like Broussard, 'who had once been almost a king, commanding vast regions as the unchallenged leader of whole nations', he is obliged to 'live modestly with his wife and children in a humble maisonette'. Administrators who last met on the majestic back of an elephant, catch sight of one another in crowded busses and they die like outcasts in the meanest corners of suburbia.(26) The provisional, tentative nature of colonial society is always clear to them: indeed their loyalty to that society is in part dependent upon their recognition of its frailty, and on their acceptance that its standards are not general.

Still more strong than among the middle-class administrators was the feeling of insecurity among criminals and déclassés in the colonies and among the ordinary soldiers basking in their temporary feudal powers. Pierre Mille constantly shows Barnavaux's fear that the people he governs in such style might one day visit France and realise that a social order exists in which their master is himself a slave. Although he is worried about the implications of this for the continuance of French supremacy, his real fear is that it would have more personal consequences, namely 'the end of prestige'. When he returns eventually to retirement in France, one of his colleagues is horrified at the effect of his return on his social status, and asks: '"How can you live in a country where there are only whites?"'(27)

No one felt this insecurity more keenly than Kipling, for it is the basic experience behind his preoccupation with colonial society. His cult of individuality, of colonial society as a proving-ground for the manhood of Englishmen, implied a rejection of all collective and Europe-based theories of society. He required society to be a continuous challenge to its members, and to provide only the external framework within which they might reach the limits of self-realization. It seems unlikely that a society made up of such full and heroic members should know insecurity and fear, yet Kipling's vision of colonial society was to show that men group together into communities because they have known the 'horror of desolation, abandonment and realized worthlessness'. In their quest for self-realization Kipling's heroes have discovered that even the most heroic individual is as nothing, and that no man can stand secure in the face of an indifferent Nature who 'does her accounts' with the red pencil of massive catastrophe. This realization Kipling sees to be the basis of colonial society and to be the source of the loyalty which that society's members bring to the purposes of Empire. Its obvious metaphysical nature has led critics - most persuasively Mr. Sandison - to argue the complexity of Kipling's imperial opinions. Such a view of society lies behind Kipling's well-known and much discussed cult of the clique and the in-group. Whether he is describing the triumvirate of the 'Soldiers Three', or the 'Great Game' in <u>Kim,</u> or, more simply, the fraternity of the Mess or of the Engine Room, in all these situations Kipling's delight in the paraphernalia of the in-group never obscures his vision of the society as a protective skin against the hardness of life. Behind each law, ethos, convention and private language, behind all the exclusiveness which cliques display, Kipling shows a deep-rooted insecurity and a craving for mutual support and protection.

In a well-known story, 'At the End of the Passage', Kipling describes the weekly meetings of four British administrators in an isolated district of India. At the end of each week, spent in their arduous and lonely official positions, they make long and dangerous journeys for the sake of what appears simply to be a bad-tempered game of whist. They do not particularly like one another and their meetings lack civility and warmth. But Kipling shows that it is their insecurity, their constant encounter with death which makes them so dependent on their ritual meeting and so jealous in its defence. They are 'lonely folk who understand the dread meaning of loneliness'. The heroism of their isolated work, the self-reliance which they need during each week, have paradoxically made them dependent upon society and encouraged them to attach such importance even to its more meaningless rituals. Society, to quote Mr. Sandison's account of this aspect of Kipling's thought, is 'an illusion created by the individual in order to establish, identify and protect the self.'(28)

III

Strangely enough - for it is here that Kipling is at his most personal and furthest from the language of official imperialism - Kipling's vision of society, like that of much of colonial fiction, puts one in mind of certain features of the totalitarian movements of the twentieth century, and it is to these parallels that we now turn. The final chapter examines in greater detail the connections between totalitarianism and the colonial experience* , studying in

---

*I should emphasise that colonial society is seen as an anticipation rather than as a cause of totalitarianism. Recently L.H. Gann and Peter Duignan (The Rulers of German Africa, Stanford 1977, pp. xii, 226-29, 235-38) have taken issue with the idea that significant links existed between totalitarianism and imperialism. They dismiss what they call the Arendt-Bley thesis, put forward originally in Hannah Arendt's pioneering and broadly-based study of The Origins of Totalitarianism and given detailed support in a restricted field by Helmut Bley's South-West Africa under German Rule. They argue from the numerically small German colonial settlements and limited engagement of German capital in imperialism and claim a quantitatively minute link from colonial experience to the mother-country. This approach can be misleading. The so-called 'Hottentot' elections of 1907, for example, showed the enormous influence imperial issues could exercise in domestic politics. Gann and Duignan also fail to take the force of Arendt's arguments. Arendt's study in its relevant sections examines the emergence of a particular ideology and its testing in colonial practice. It was this opportunity, and the links with the bureaucratic machinery of the State which distinguished imperialism from the other intellectual strands from the period of Cultural Pessimism in the nineteenth century in which it is traditional to

particular the many colonial writers who followed their ideas to their equivalents in European politics. Here we are concerned with the parallels in social structure between white colonial and European totalitarian societies.

Colonial society clearly anticipated the political movements of the right in its mixture of insecurity and aggression, exclusiveness and openness, hierarchy and equality. The totalitarian parties exploited fully the desperate longing for identity and security which the broad masses of the middle-classes felt after the horrific and unsettling experiences of war and economic crisis. Like many colonial heroes, the European middle-classes had tasted the 'abandonment and realised worthlessness' of which Kipling spoke, recognising that they were as nothing in face of the catastrophes of war and the impersonal accounting of economic systems. They were glad to find a place in the totalitarian communities, for it gave them an identity and a sense of loyalty, and its fierce rules offered them protection from the alien world outside.

Another proud boast of the totalitarian parties was that they were classless. The 'Volksgemeinschaft' (National Community) which formed a central part of Hitler's propaganda was presented as a community in which all Germans were equal and in which

---

(cont.)
find the 'origins' of totalitarian thought. In their accounts of developments in the German Empire, Gann and Duignan unaccountably fail to take the force of Helmut Bley's presentation of developments in German South-West Africa, with its detailing of just those 'prophylactic' eliminations of populations which they see as a necessary component of totalitarianism. Horst Drechsler(Südwestafrika unter deutscher Kolonialherrschaft, Berlin 1966, p. 273f) - a study to which Gann and Duignan fail to refer - gives further evidence. See also D. Bald, Deutsch-Ostafrika 1900-1914, Munich 1970, pp. 127-40. The parallels to European Fascism are so striking in that they cover not merely a mentality ready to plan atrocities but also the social structure within which such mentality could develop. I find incomprehensible Gann and Duignan's claim that to 'confuse' imperialism and totalitarianism 'subtly excuses the evils of Nazi tyranny'. I confess to less enthusiasm than Gann and Duignan for rescuing the 'progressive' elements in the imperialist heritage, although it is not in order to blacken imperialism that its links with totalitarianism are examined. Just as race-thinking is far from dead, so totalitarianism is by definition neither historically unique nor uniquely horrendous. It was the culmination of a series of movements in the nineteenth and twentieth centuries, movements which expressed themselves and gathered momentum in imperialism. It does not seem unreasonable to explore those affinities.

they might feel a pride and self-respect undreamed of in socialist republics and traditional class-systems alike. The equality of this community encouraged leadership and initiative: it did not 'level men down' to a common denominator, as the Nazi ideologists claimed socialism did, it levelled them upwards, giving them new qualities and making them aware of those they already possessed. It was a model of what colonials meant by democracy.

There are also extremely close parallels between the classlessness of these two societies. We suggested that the insecurity of colonial society depended not only on a recognition of the insignificance of the individual, but also on the fact that the colonials were outcasts from traditional society. Economic failure, crime, or merely discontent had placed a gulf between them and their class which made them ideal material for a social grouping which pretended to have overcome class. But it was precisely from such material that the totalitarian movements created their new communities. They could not abolish class, and indeed the relationships between the Nazi Party and both the German aristocracy and the German working-classes showed that these class-distinctions remained politically influential. The success of the totalitarian parties lay in their ability to give cohesion, identity and purpose to those who had fallen out of the classes to which they had once gladly belonged. The pariahs of the old order became the elite of the new, and they based the experience of 'national rebirth' on a mystification of the process whereby the outcasts found social identity. That men like Goering and Goebbels should have made common cause with Streicher, Himmler or Hitler himself was not a triumph of race over class: it was the triumph of the déclassés over the leaders of the traditional and still active class-structure.

Colonial society obviously anticipated these movements. It emphasized the equality of race in order ostensibly to obliterate the inequalities of society. It also created, by means of a series of ideological arguments which it both developed and took over from others, an inferior race over whom the new elite ruled in such style as to believe in the transformation of society which was claimed. The Jews of Central and Eastern Europe were to learn what countless peoples had learnt in the colonies: that a sub-human status was worse than no status at all. However, as we shall see, the transition from imperialism to totalitarianism was not merely a question of casting different races and minorities in that role of victim tried out within colonial society.

Many critics have remarked on the way in which colonial stereotypes of the 'Native' resembled the pictures of the working-classes current in Europe at that time. The same childish, impulsive emotional character was invariably ascribed to both groups, and the same prejudices about their morals, their appetites, and their smell. Leblond illustrates this by giving an account of how a white creole, visiting Paris for the first time, establishes his reaction to the European working-classes (whom he has not encountered before) solely according to his experience of the

139

negroes of La Réunion.(29) This suggests that, in examining the transition from colonial attitudes to totalitarianism, it will be the survival of class-distinctions as well as the transference of race-thinking which must be considered. It was not simply the attitude towards racial inferiors which was common to both situations, but the interchangeability of racial and class discrimination. When Hilter wrote in Mein Kampf that 'it must be held in greater honour to be a citizen of the German Reich, even if only a road-sweeper, than to be a king in a foreign state', his remark not only used race to give meaning to every member of the German nation, it also presupposed that road-sweepers would show their gratitude for the honour of being German by remaining content with the humble position of road-sweeper. The classless, racial society rescued the casualties of the class-system only to push them back still deeper into subservience, and the status quo was ingeniously restored. In precisely the same way, the colonial writers, arguing that the racial status of their characters as 'Englishmen', Aryans or Latins raised them high above the coloured peoples of the world, implicitly assumed that by so doing the domestic class-structure would remain unchanged. To give the Englishman a pride in his race as 'the highest rank that a man can reach upon this earth' - Rider Haggard's characteristic summary in Allan Quartermain of that status - was an excellent brake upon ambitions to improve rank and status by other means.

When right-wing thinkers claimed class and race as alternative poles for social grouping they did not merit serious consideration. But it was a sign of the pressures of the society within and for which they wrote that their views were received with such interest. It was not because they discovered race, or introduced an absolute belief in race into a society not otherwise that way inclined, that they contributed to the growth of ideologies which were to terrorize our century. It was much rather that they demonstrated the kind of longings created by the class system, and the kind of stereotypes which those longings would in turn create. It is as people conditioned by the European class-system, rather than as escapees from it, that the white colonials and their court-poets are of interest to us, and it follows that we shall want to look at European totalitarianism in a similar light.

An important indicator of the relative strengths of social and racial criteria in colonial thinking is provided by the problem of violence. Violence, so fundamental a part of colonial life, formed an obvious link with the totalitarian systems of the twentieth century, and it is clear that in both situations violence was possible and acceptable on such a large scale primarily because of racial ideologies which placed groups of people into a sub-human category. But as one looks at the violence reported in colonial literature very little of it has its origin in explicit racial ideologies, even if it drew on such ideologies for its justification. Much violence was a direct result of the particular nature of white society and its interrelations.

We need to distinguish between functional violence and what

- to coin a rather clumsy phrase - we might call a self-justifying violence. By functional violence we mean those actions which were concerned with internal security, and described by clichés such as 'teaching them a lesson' or 'keeping them in their place'. While it is usually present in colonial fiction as a sort of ground-bass, justifying the day-to-day brutality and insensitivity of white rule, functional violence occasionally features much more prominently. In one story, for instance, Karl Dove (an agricultural expert working in the German colonial service) describes the killing of a group of bushmen, including women and children. In a horrific scene they are caught in a cave, fires are lit at the opening and the bushmen are choked to death. 'The shrieking and crying, which at the beginning came out of the depths of the cave, soon died away.' When they go in to examine the bodies, they notice very ancient cave-paintings; evidence of culture, one might have thought, but not to the white killers who casually comment that the pictures were 'not bad'. Indeed, 'if anyone had happened to regret that a few women and children had choked to death along with the men', there is a ready explanation in terms of the function of the violence in clearing the district of hindrances to farming and settlement:

> 'Do not forget that between the white man and the coloured there can never be peace until one is the master and the other his servant. It is a question of "them or us"'...(30)

The justifications of imperialism which we discussed in the previous chapter extended therefore to the explicit defence of white violence. The need for security built on dismissive attitudes to the lesser races who were the objects of violence.

Neverthless, there were other links between imperialism and violence. On many occasions physical violence is described and relished in situations which involve no threat to whites. Barnavaux, casually beating up an Annamite soldier at the Colonial Exhibition in Paris, does so not because he felt threatened, but in order to prove something about himself. His violence was an assertion of membership in the colonial elite, re-established despite his return to France.(31) Violence here was not the result of white insecurity in the face of the blacks, but stemmed from the whites' insecurity and disorientation in their own community. Violence was shown here, as it was so often under the Nazis, to be a kind of initiation into an in-group, the racial elite. Imperialism showed what the age of the dictators was to underline: that the oppressor is best served, not by the murderer and the sadist - although they will thrive - but by 'the man from the streets without hope'(32).

Interracial violence was not only a prop to personal security and a passport to the in-group: it was also a prominent virtue in the ethical systems developed by colonial fiction. Karl Dove's narrative ends with the claim that such actions need to be defended against elements 'back home' which have differing ethical and

141

ideological values, 'all those spineless hearts and pious little groups who don't know how people like us feel...'.(33) Violence was part of the colonial ethos, in competition with other values, and colonial writers even felt a certain pride in violence and certainly no compunction at the thought that they were using other peoples as objects in a process of ideological education. Just like the landscape and the climate, the Native fitted in at moments with an educational process, and writers gave it no thought if, at such times, white education demanded a schooling in violence.

'War is a primitive art', says Mrs. Steel's soldier hero, while putting down the Indian Mutiny, 'and needs a primitive people'. To 'kill somebody' is not simply a military necessity, it is a spiritual drive and a proof of manhood.(34) Henry Daguerches, in his novel about the construction of the Siam-Cambodian railway (which took a great toll of the lives of the coolies in the construction gangs) also believed that indifference to suffering was a sign of national health, an essential condition of manhood, proving 'the strength of my blood and the strength of my race'(35). 'We must be hard, we must kill', Frenssen had written of the Herero war: 'must' as a point of honour, as a seal on the nation's virility, and much less as part of a military or security necessity.(36)

Nowhere is this clearer than in German fiction's account of the extermination of the Herero nation at the end of the war of 1904-06. After their defeat at the battle of the Waterberg, the Herero were pushed out into the arid wastes of the Kalahari desert, where tens of thousands who had escaped the German gunfire were to perish miserably. German fiction contains some of the most harrowing descriptions of the realities of colonial conquest that one finds anywhere. Yet it is almost inconceivable that they should have wanted to give such detailed descriptions of the carnage. Public opinion in Germany was swinging strongly against the military policies applied in South-West Africa, and writers merely added fresh fuel to the damaging criticisms already being made. Most of the novelists did not even notice that the German settlers had called upon General von Trotha, long before the battle of the Waterberg, to stop slaughtering the Herero, because they were frightened of losing the entire work-force of the colony. If it was neither in the interests of the settlers, nor to the liking of the German public to fight the battles which German colonial writers described with such realism; if, in short, they represented the interests of neither group of their readers, the only explanation of their attitude was they they saw an ideological message behind these depictions, and that even the most pointless violence suggested to them a view of life which they wanted to communicate.

We have seen enough of the infiltration of the popularized and cheapened Nietzschean heritage into colonial thinking not to need to look further for the ideological message which writers found in violence. The idea that it was ennobling to face the bestial and the hellish in life without flinching or weakening is very close indeed both to the ingenuous 'public school' ethos of the colonials and to a cultivated inhumanity. 'To have done these things', said Himmler approvingly of his SS guards, 'and not to have become hard' - that was the spirit towards which colonial literature was moving. Daguerches spoke for many writers when he claimed that the most exhilarating of the colonial experiences was 'to have been set free from compassion'.(37)

Violence, therefore, came from the whites' view of themselves just as much as from their view of the blacks. Just as people wanted to show that they were masters - though in their hearts they knew how close they were to being victims - so they wanted to prove that their society was virile and not decadent, although (as we saw in the last chapter) they knew that it was. Not until the outbreak of the First World War did Europe realize how violence and decadence might yet go together; not until the totalitarian states of the 1920s and 1930s did the violent masters see the price they had paid for their power.

NOTES

1. M.A.Leblond,'Le prolétariat français aux colonies' in H.Béranger (ed.), Les Prolétaires Intellectuels en France (Paris, 1901), p.334; and M.Frescaly, Mariage d'Afrique (Paris, 1886), p.34. See also C.Farrère, Les hommes nouveaux (Paris, 1922), p.46 (defining the 'new man' as 'a man who previously was next to nothing and has just grown'). For a view of European society as conservative see A.Martinkus-Zemp,'Europécentrisme et exotisme' in Cahiers d'Etudes Africaines, vol. 13 (1973), p.60f.

2. J.R.Seeley, The expansion of England (Macmillans, 1895), p.184f.

3. P.Mille, 'Barnavaux Général' in Sur la vaste terre (Paris, 1905), pp.101/02.

4. P.Mille, L'Illustre Partonneau (Paris, 1924), p.149.

5. J.Boissière, Fumeurs d'Opium (Paris, 1896), p.189f.

6. M. Delafosse, Les états d'ame d'un colonial (Paris, 1909), pp.39,13.

7. A.Memmi, Portrait du colonisé (Quebec, 1972), p.35; L.H.Gann & P.Duignan, Rulers of British Africa (Croom Helm, 1978), p.201.

8. P.Mille, Mémoires, quoted by W.J.Everts, The Life and Works of Pierre Mille (New York, 1938), p.41.

9. Quoted by R.Maunier, The sociology of the colonies vol. 1 (Routledge & Kegan Paul, 1949), p.41.

10. F.v.Bülow, Tropenkoller (Berlin, 1896), p.137.

11. Ibid., p.136.

12. B.Parry, Delusions and Discoveries (Allen Lane, 1972) pp.38,24,34; M.Diver, Desmond's Daughter (Blackwood, 1916) p.45.

13. M.Frescaly, p.162f; F.A.Steel, On the face of the waters (Nelson, 1907), p.59f.

14. Parry, pp.31,32; A.Perrin, The Anglo-Indians

(Methuen, 1912), p.60f.

15. W.D.Arnold, Oakfield, vol.2 (Longman, 1853), pp. 141, 43.

16. C.J.Cutcliffe Hyne, Atoms of Empire (Methuen, 1923), p.1. German colonies also experienced a cooling of social relations, cf. F.v. Bülow, Im Lande der Verheißung (Leipzig, 1899), p.398.

17. G.O.Trevelyan, The Competition Wallah (Macmillan, 1864), pp. 143/44,25,147.

18. E.Candler, The general plan (Blackies, 1911), p.18.

19.G.A.Henty, The Dash for Khartoum (Blackie, 1892).

20. 'His Private Honour' in Many Inventions.

21. 'The Comprehension of Private Copper' in Traffics and Discoveries. Conrad quoted in J.Myers, Fiction and the colonial experience (Boydell Press, 1973), p.56.

22. See C.Carrington, Kipling (Penguin Books, 1970), p.359f. Gann & Duignan call Kipling 'as bitter a critic of the establishment as Karl Marx' (Rulers of British Africa, Croom Helm, 1978, p.205).

23. P.Mille, 'Au delà du Bien et du Mal' in Barnavaux et quelques femmes (Paris, 1908), pp.220/21.

24. C.Farrère, Les Civilisés (Paris, 1905), p.91.

25. A.Perrin, The Anglo-Indians, pp.15/16.

26. Ibid., pp.18/19; Trevelyan, p.154; Delafosse, p.80.

27. P.Mille, Barnavaux et quelques femmes, p.77; Sur la vaste terre (Paris, 1905), p.185.

28. A.Sandison,'The Artist and the Empire' in A.Rutherford (ed.), Kipling's Mind and Art (Oliver & Boyd, 1964), p.164. See also Kipling's essay 'Independence' of 1923. 'At the End of the Passage' is in Life's Handicap.

29. Cf. R.Maunier, The sociology of colonies, vol. 1 (Routledge & Kegan Paul, 1949), p.83; M.A.Leblond, En France (Paris, 1910), pp. 9, 123 etc.

30. K.Dove, Die Kobra (Berlin, 1911), pp.114/15.

31. 'Barnavaux, Homme d'Etat' in Sur la vaste terre (Paris, 1905), pp.175/85. Cf. his remark 'All these dirty savages should never leave their home country, they should not even know that we have a country like theirs, a country with earth, stones and trees just like in their own country, and white slaves you can buy for twenty sous behind the Invalides' (p.178).

32. The remark of a contemporary observer of the Congo scandals, quoted by G.D. Killam, Africa in English fiction (Ibadan, 1968), p.96.

33. Dove, p.115. Cf. Cutcliffe Hyne on 'those canting, whining fools' in Europe who put at risk colonial activity (Hyne, p.7).

34. F.A.Steel, On the face of the waters (Nelson, 1907), pp.476.473.

35. H.Daguerches, Le Kilomètre 83 (Paris, 1913), p.554.

36. G.Frenssen, <u>Peter Moors Fahrt nach Südwest</u> (Berlin, 1936), p. 199.

37. Daguerches, p.139.

Chapter Seven

COLONIAL THEORY AND DOMESTIC PRACTICE

There was a certain irony in the fact that many of the colonial writers returned to Europe in time for the Great War. They had spent much time on the little-known battlefields of the empire, convinced that life's real frontiers could only be encountered in Africa and India, not in the comforts of European civilization. 'Chivalry could not attain full stature in a milieu of pavements and chimney-pots', Edmund Candler had remarked scornfully.(1) Yet suddenly the world which they had affected to despise for its security was engulfed in war and, worse still, in social change and revolution.

All travellers have something of Rip van Winkle about them. They step back into a world which they have known only from out-of-date newspapers and letters, and are amazed to find that it has changed. The colonials returning to Europe felt this very strongly. They had been proud to be representatives of their country, glowing examples of their national way of life, albeit on their own terms, and it hurt their self-esteem to find that great changes had taken place in what they had been seen to represent. It smacked of ingratitude, and further encouraged the colonial writers to translate into radicalism the ethos and social attitudes which the colonies had given them.

As we examine these reactions, we shall inevitably stray some distance from literary considerations. The material we consider includes letters and autobiographies, speeches and pamphlets. It takes us again into the sensitive area in discussions of imperialism, its relationship to totalitarianism. Hannah Arendt has put forward the aptly named 'boomerang' theory to account for this relationship: that the colonial praxis of a nation, harsher and more extreme than its home policies, trickles back to the home country and infects the conduct of its domestic affairs. We have tried to show how the colonial praxis reflected in colonial literature was an acting-out of domestic pressures and unconscious attitudes. Colonial literature was in that respect a boomerang which had never left the hand. Writers had experienced a kind of accelerated awareness in the colonies, discovering truths about their own attitudes more starkly than those who had stayed at home. When they returned to confront the society they had left, colonial experience meant that they were forearmed by a type of response which their contemporaries would be slower to adopt.

146

A typical example of the process of adaptation was the German writer Hans Grimm, who returned to Germany in 1910. He had left a sleepy provincial town for Africa in the previous century, and when he returned to live in the industrial cities of Munich and Hamburg it must have seemed as if a hundred years had passed since his departure. His impressions of Germany provide a fascinating insight into colonial reactions:

> Returning home he found his own country confusing. Out in the colonies energy, action and success had been the factors which determined a man's reputation, and his place in a bureaucratic system or his social rank paled into insignificance in the face of such essential criteria. At home, however, rank and office were pre-eminent; and a man's worth in the life of the community appeared to depend on the extent of his recognition by the local prince or court(...) Apart from a few long-established aristocratic and peasant families, well over half the nation (and in particular the traditional middle-class) had succumbed to this strange, restrictive subservience. But what had most confused and frightened him was that scarcely anyone in Germany seemed to know or care about his neighbour; the various professions and classes lived quite independent of each other, as if they were separated by invisible and unscalable fences...(2)

Grimm was, in fact, still more horrified by the urban working-classes who dreamed of challenging this 'subservience' than by that condition itself, but it is clear that his initial discontent was with his own class. He contrasts the hierarchical and restrictive society of Germany with the open meritocracy of the colonies, and observes that those who preached democracy in Germany were as unable to emancipate themselves from 'subservience' as was the rest of society. Whatever development took place in Grimm's ideas after his return home, it would be in response to his feeling that German society should live up to the ideals of white colonial democracy.

Pierre Mille responded in almost identical terms to the conditions of life in France after 1910, the date at which, in fiction, Barnavaux returned to his native country. Barnavaux has overcome his fear of living in France by marrying Louise, 'a white woman of his own blood'. They live simply, and have adapted to life in France the insights which Barnavaux gained overseas. The narrator comments:

> From their behaviour I might have imagined that I was among people in a far higher class of society. This seems to me to prove that we French, who are a very ancient people, are on the way to becoming a nation of aristocrats; forty millions of us, each having a pride and reserve of our own, a need for a certain kind of

leisure, and with the ability to control our impulses and
inclinations(...)

Another thing which appeared to me to have an
aristocratic quality was the quite irrational but sincere
and unmovable conviction shared by both Louise and
Barnavaux: namely that they were of the same rank
as anyone in France and superior to any foreigner.(3)

Mille goes on to explain that, while such a belief was natural
to Barnavaux who has been 'a white man in the colonies', it was
remarkable that Louise should share his opinion, since she has
never left France.

The application of colonial experience to life in France had
brought Mille immediately to the view that a racial 'democracy'
would guarantee the stability of the social hierarchy. Barnavaux
accepts his inferior position in society because he believes that
his racial status is more important than social improvement. Just
as the galley-slaves in 'The Victory' had accepted slavery as
preferable to the defeat of their nation, so Barnavaux persuades
himself to remain a slave at home by means of arguments which
concern his relationship with other races. It is noticeable too that
the middle-class narrator, previously so proud of his equality with
the working-class soldier, feels no longer compelled to assert that
equality. He theorizes about racial equality but upholds traditional
class-distinctions. Mille gives these ideas an explicitly reactionary
slant, for he tells us that Louise, as a student at the 'Université
populaire', had been indoctrinated with dangerous left-wing ideas
about the emancipation of women and the evils of militarism and
imperialism, and her conversion to the cause of racist conservatism
is highly significant. What Barnavaux has to teach her from his
colonial experience cures her of these ideas, and thus advances
the spiritual 'health' of the nation. Earlier in his colonial writing
Mille had not merely preached a form of egalitarianism: he had
even admitted that 'in face of the crises which are tearing our
unhappy nation apart, I have adopted the opinion of the anarchists,
and that means that I don't have to agree with anyone'.(4) On
his return to France, however, colonial experience had ranged him
with the extreme right-wing of committed political thinkers.

Mille's ideas had a great similarity with those of Maurice
Barrès, the intellectual leader of the 'Action Française'. The two
men knew and respected each other's work. Barrès' concept of
the natural aristocracy of the French people was identical to
Mille's, and both agreed that it was threatened by democratic
ideas. Like Mille, Barrès believed that the intellectual's task was
to recall the nation to its essential basis, race, and to
counterbalance the proletarianization of the unemployed petty-
bourgeois graduates, of whom Mille's Louise is an obvious example.

Mille was far from alone in proposing imperialist solutions
to the problem of the 'intellectual proletariat' in France. Leblond

had contributed to discussions of this problem(5), while Hugues Le Roux also tried to sketch a way in which colonial experience would actas a corrective to the damaging influence on French youth of modern education and recent history. 'We have not managed to preserve our territorial integrity,' he wrote bitterly in 1898, reflecting on the loss of Alsace and Lorraine, 'let us save the race'. His imperialism aimed to combat degenerative qualities in French life. The sentence with which his work opens - 'Il faut créer une France au dehors'(6)(we must create an overseas France) - illustrates both Arendt's thesis and Mannoni's model of colonial society. It highlights the ideological function of imperialism, expressed in literature, as a corrective to ills of the metropolis.

Kipling too, after his return from India, gradually directed his attention from the colonies to domestic topics. In due course his 'democratic' ideas placed him firmly among those right-wing radicals whose activities had such an impact on British conservatism. Already in 1899 the outbreak of the Boer War had produced a strong resurgence of Kipling's 'democratic' beliefs. He had placed his faith in 'the common people - the third-class carriages' and had turned away from faith in the traditional leaders of Britain. His wife noted in her diary that Kipling 'feels he has joined up all his ideas with the others of many years ago'(7). The culmination of this colonial legacy was expressed in the story 'The Army of a Dream', published in Traffics and Discoveries (1904). It describes an elite professional army, where all classes enjoy complete social equality, while maintaining strict military efficiency. The army is a symbol of that harnessing of democratic forces to national ends which had been demonstrated by the colonies.

Yet the story is only a dream: perhaps this army can never exist in reality, and so the story is prefaced by a verse in praise of the Old Guard. Kipling dreamt of change and of equality harnessed to traditional ends. He represented a position which, as Cole and Postgate have suggested, was typical of much of the social thinking at the height of New Imperialism: a domestic Radicalism combined with an unquestioning acceptance of imperialism(8). But Kipling's radicalism was limited not merely by his assent to imperialism: it was hedged in also by existential fears, in particular by his dependence on society for security and protection in a threatening universe. He is ready to dream of equality for the sons of earls and Lambeth publicans, but the dream must never shake the foundations of the world, for these are at best fragile.

The dilemma is illustrated by the two stories 'Below the Mill Dam' (1902) and 'The Mother Hive' (1908)(9). The first is an allegory attacking the staid conservatism of an England which will not be harnessed to the new energies of the day: an example of the radical nature of Kipling's view of the domestic class-system; the second an attack on the destructivenss of radical ideas. Without changing his terms of reference, therefore, Kipling had turned an

149

apparent full circle from colonial days. Talking of equality he had come to accept the status quo and to reject those who tried to change it. Preaching the equality which membership of one race confers, his works gradually come to show the inviolability of the established social order.

His life too, even as it emerges from official biographies, illustrated this contradiction. We see him campaigning for the peasantry, but falling out with his tenant-farmers, praising the people in the third-class carriages but moving to Bateman's in order to escape from them, criticizing the aristocracies of the world but delighted to become 'one of the gentry' himself(10). This effortless dichotomy between radical ideology and highly conservative practice was a major contribution of colonial authors to the radical right. It was not nationalism which they brought to Europe - indeed many of them put nationalism well behind racism in their scale of values(11) - but a particular combination of social radicalism, race-thinking and hostility to socialism.

Ernest Psichari also dreamed of national revival on the basis of a classless army. Like Kipling he quickly disclosed his political intentions. L'Appel aux armes (1912) unites the domestic and the colonial worlds in a classless vision of the French race, perfectly symbolized by the 'proud and violent' colonial army. Captain Nangès wooes Maurice Vincent, a petty-bourgeois intellectual, into joining the army, breaking down his class prejudices in order that he may discover at a deeper level a national and racial identity. After a few months of Vincent's service, Nangès looks proudly at 'this little soldier who had become France herself', and reflects:

> Maurice was a perfect work of art, and - what Nanges found more moving still - made from the same clay as himself.(...)He felt that a secret fraternity linked them.(12)

(Leblond also describes one character as 'a work of art of France'(13), although he avoids the eroticism which pervades Psichari's book, and many Nazi books on race, with their often questionable mixture of eugenics and sexuality in the worship of the 'racially pure' body.) Psichari's arguments mirror those of the totalitarian movements. Having 'discovered' an irreducible core within man, which he chose to identify as that of race, he planned the rebuilding of France on the basis of that discovery. Once again, his outspokenly right-wing opinions are much less significant than the fact that his whole approach to the problems of France was based on the healing of social divisions by race.

We need to be careful of terminology here. It was common, for instance, at the beginning of the century to speak of 'race-regeneration'(14). Although this concept did not exclude eugenic considerations, it often implied nothing more sinister than a concern for public health, and the word 'race' was sometimes merely a synonym of 'nation'. A modern reader has to be careful not to overreact to this now discredited language. Nevertheless, Psichari like the majority of the writers with colonial experience stressed both the distinctiveness of racial strains (within France as well as in discussions of inter-racial conflict) and the superiority of the white over other races. In addition his mysticism and cult of the soil took Psichari far beyond the neutral parlance of his day and led him to a view of race to which the age of the dictators would give greater resonance but hardly greater definition. Finally, the usefulness of colonial literature to Fascism was augmented by its constant demonstration that colonial experience contained the answer to the problems confronted by the urban working-classes, and to the form of social unrest posed by them. The distinctive form of the anti-socialist trend of colonial literature also helped to bring its authors into sympathy with the right-wing movements in Europe.

From the first the German colonial movement had been associated with campaigns for improving the lot of the working-classes. Friedrich Fabri, founder of the Colonial Union, had been an inspector of the Rhenish Mission particularly concerned (as the title of his first book in 1862 ran) with The housing shortage and its alleviation for workers in the factory towns. The study portrayed the consequences of the living conditions of the urban working-classes as representing a serious threat to moral and political stability. A combination of self-help and state action, Fabri argued, would restore self-respect to the working-classes and ensure their otherwise questionable loyalty to the state: 'You should consider what it would mean to have tied our working-classes to property, so that at times of political and social upheaval they protect rather than threaten property'(15). The same anxiety led him to campaign for German colonial settlement in the 1870s and 1880s. Determined to preserve emigration as 'a kind of safety valve'(16) for the social pressure otherwise leading to socialism, Fabri tried to show that in the colonies the white proletarians would be transformed by the enjoyment of property and status. Fabri was rapidly overtaken as a spokesman for imperialism by more aggressive groups, who saw urban overpopulation as constituting a divine right to a place in the sun rather than as a problem. Fabri and his friends were attacked as 'political Buddhists' for the defensive, insecure orientation of their imperialism(17). Nevertheless, even at the height of New Imperialism, this domestic angle was never forgotten, as our study of the colonial novelists has shown. Behind much of the social commentary of the colonial novel was a preoccupation with the spectre of socialism at home. One novelist remarked, for instance, about the socialist deputies in the 'Reichstag':

> 'If we had got a small plantation in Africa for each of these trouble-makers, they would have fallen on our necks and kissed us gratefully in brotherly love.'(18)

The suggestion is not merely to buy off the socialists by giving them colonial estates. Writers believed that socialism was artificial and over-intellectual, and that when the socialists found themselves in the colonies the wide open spaces would destroy their sectarian ideology and give them 'healthy' national ideas instead.

Opinions of this kind were hardly challenged by the confused patriotic revisionism prevalent within the Social Democrat parties. It had been Bernstein who had expressed most pragmatically the attraction of imperialism for the working classes and who had dismissed as irrelevant to such discussions any 'romantic sentimentalities about the weak'(19). Typically Hans Grimm included in Volk ohne Raum a lengthy account of the pro-imperialist position put forward at an SPD congress by Karl Hildenbrand, and presented it as evidence that the working classes (as distinct from their leaders) might indeed be prepared to go over to the imperialist cause.

French colonial writers also emphasized the appeal which the colonies held for the proletariat, and there was in France too a tradition of attempting to use the colonies (notably Algeria) as resettlement territory for the urban poor.(20) It was for these reasons writers stressed the classlessness of the new colonial society. Leblond too was obviously trying to portray colonial society as a solution to the problems of the French proletariat, when he referred with sympathy to those settlers in Algeria who had 'no lasting reason to look back affectionately on the poverty and toil reserved for the proletariat in France'.(21) Bertrand also explained Algerian developments, particularly its tendency towards separatism, as a repudiation of working-class conditions in Europe by those who had found a better life in the colony.(22)

Sympathy for the working classes, like sympathy for the colonized peoples, concealed little more than a sense of superiority. The only effect which the colonial writers wished colonial life to have on the proletarian settlers was that they should turn into solid members of the bourgeoisie. A prominent theorist of the German colonial movement had made this very clear, in arguing that emigration should concentrate on the urban working class:

> for the working man may find in the exertions which colonization brings with it a good educational experience, 'which is capable of repairing the many damages of civilization and of making good many proletarian sins'(23).

We saw that the colonies were often thought of as schools. Really they were finishing schools in bourgeois etiquette.

Similar attitudes lay behind colonial fiction's frequent attacks on urban and industrial society. Although colonial writers usually portrayed their dislike in terms of a feeling for nature, their inspiration was much more political. When Mrs. Perrin, for instance, wrote of an Indian prince's depression at the experience of living in London ('the damp piles of brick and mortar, the glimpse of sullen sky and the vulgar little birds that cared nothing for green fields and fragrant woods') her sentimentality was only part of a more specific attack on urban society; with its degradation of women, its inefficiency, and its restless masses -that 'crowd of unwholesome-looking men in dirty clothes' which so offends the Fleetwood family on their return(24). Kipling too attacked London as a symbol of all that was wrong with western civilization, both in his letters ('a vile place,' he called it, 'strange and disconcerting') and in his stories(25). 'One View of the Question' took the form of a letter from a high-ranking Indian diplomat, recording his impressions of a stay in London. The writer is horrified at the difference between the nobility of the Sahibs and their domestic life at home. London, he says is

> accursèd, being dark and unclear, devoid of sun, and
> full of low-born, who are perpetually drunk, and howl
> in the streets like jackals, men and women together.

'The Record of Badalia Herodsfoot' takes the reader still deeper into the slums of London, and into the world of drunkenness, brutality and vice, enlightened (and perhaps only here Kipling's hope for the future is expressed) by the practical sense and readiness to help of Badalia herself. Mr. Keating, in a rewarding essay(26), sees the story as a major step forward for fiction, in that Kipling communicates the language and the mentality of the slum characters without obtrusive narrative interventions; but this impartiality (if such it was) soon faded, and as the years passed Kipling's dismay at conditions of life in the cities turned increasingly to attacks on those 'remittance men and loafers' in whom Kipling saw a natural breeding-ground for socialism.

It was this fear of socialism which led him to take such a great interest in the various schemes advanced by his close friend Rider Haggard to combat rural depopulation and to ship out the urban poor to the colonies.

These schemes reveal both the range of prejudices inspiring Kipling and Haggard and also the criteria which colonial experience had made appear relevant to social planning. Very early in the 1900s, Haggard managed to make Kipling worried about rural depopulation in England.(27) While Kipling responded to these fears by burying himself in the English countryside, Haggard devoted his energies to public campaigns and investigated two possible areas for the resettlement of the urban population: the Garden Cities and the colonies.

Haggard saw the Garden City movement as a way of providing land, and thus moral and political stability for the urban population. He regretted the passing of 'that admirable old yeoman class which has been squeezed out by the pressure of circumstances of late years', and claimed that the nation needed 'strong, steady, equal-minded men, who can only be bred on the land'(28). It is hardly fanciful to see in these remarks both a racial-cum-political cult of the peasantry and a view of the soil as the spiritual reservoir of the nation. Similar attitudes informed his writings on the overseas settlements intended for the rehabilitation of the urban poor. He believed that the 'healthful plenty' of colonial land would solve 'the wretchedness of our overcrowded cities', and counteract the 'desperate, ominous shapes of Misery and Want, and in their hands the swords of Socialism'(29). No less impressive than these ideological positions is the way in which Haggard (who always claimed that he was too radical on questions of land reform to have been a 'real Tory'(30)) advocated right-wing solutions, with state planning in order to solve structural social problems. It was this decisive break with laissez-faire economic liberalism which put Haggard so far outside the ranks of traditional Conservatives and brought his views close to the radical European conservatism of the 1930's.

Kipling took a great interest in Haggard's travels and ideas. There can be no doubt that he agreed with his suggestions. But his own personal response to these problems was to bury himself in the English countryside and to elevate it to mystical, ultimately to racial, significance. There was nothing particularly unusual about his views, which were shared by many who did not have his colonial background. Not every aspect of his political thinking had necessarily to come from his colonial past, and there were other factors which linked him with his fellow colonial novelists in their reaction to the political developments of the twentieth century. Yet it is striking how closely their views run parallel, and how consistently certain assumptions from colonial life were followed. Not only the class and race arguments, but the primitive and irrational view of man, the willingness to mix ideology and social planning, and an impatience with other opinions than those which worked overseas - all these habits of mind proved lasting and influential.

Kipling's return to the soil of England was notable not simply as a continuation of his belief in the primitive, natural man. It was in one rather dramatic sense a complete reversal of certain of his previous attitudes. This is in no sense to say that he abandoned his colonial attitudes: rather it suggests the truth of the thesis that I am engaged in arguing - namely that the colonial attitude was never autonomous of the European situation, that its rebellion against Europe was at a deeper level conditioned by Europe, and that its protest at the class attitudes of Europe was radical only in appearance. Gone was Kipling's contempt for the 'little Englanders'(31) content with their knowledge and love of England. Small-mindedness was now a higher virtue:

> God gave all men all earth to love,
>   But, since our hearts are small,
> Ordained for each one spot should prove
>   Belovèd over all...('Sussex')

In a series of poems and stories he shows the powers of the English soil to remake and heal broken lives and unbalanced characters

> Take of English earth as much
>   As either hand may rightly clutch(...)
> It shall sweeten and make whole
>   Fevered breath and festered soul. ('A Charm')

The story 'My Son's Wife' shows that socialist ideas are part of
the 'fevered breath' which the English countryside makes whole,
in this instance by the marriage of a former socialist into the
local aristocracy. The most ambiguous lines which Kipling wrote
- ambiguous, that is, to the close reader - come in the poem
'Sussex':

> So to the land our hearts we give
>   Till the sure magic strike,
> And Memory, Use, and Love make live
>   Us and our fields alike -
> That deeper than our speech and thought,
>   Beyond our reason's sway,
> Clay of the pit whence we were wrought
>   Yearns to its fellow-clay.

There is a serious problem of terminology. These lines openly
celebrate the links between the soil of the homeland and the spirit
and mind of man. We are 'fellow-clay' of the soil. The lines,
therefore, go beyond a merely sentimental parochialism, and suggest
a position close to that of Psichari. The National Socialists too
would have recognized the poem's affinities with the Blood and
Soil literature which they officially encouraged. They would also
rightly have seen Kipling's cult of the peasantry and his adoption
of a country life-style as a repudiation of intellectual and avant-
garde culture, just as the would have been convinced that the
opening pages of Lawrence's <u>Rainbow</u> (describing the early
generation of the Brangwens feeling in their blood 'the pulse and
body of the soil') belonged in their anthologies.* 'Heimatkunst',
as the Germans called the literary cult of the homeland, is an
universal phenomenon and literature did not need to be pernicious
to qualify for the Nazis' approval. Nevertheless, it must be asked
whether Kipling's cult of the Sussex soil is racist in any useful
sense of that word. Kipling certainly had used the word 'race'
frequently(32). Like most colonial writers, he extended the tribal

---

*Somerset Maugham described Lucy Allerton (the only person
who understands MacKenzie in his search for the greatness of
Britain in the colonies), in terms no less close to those which the
Nazi were to canonize. It is by way of an explanation of this
understanding that Maugham speaks of her hereditary debt to 'the
peculiar lie of the land on which they were born and bred' and of
her 'cult' of her ancestors: shades of Maurice Barrès (<u>The Explorer</u>,
Heinemann, 1908, p.11).

classification of the colonized peoples into classifications of his own nation: hence his Irish, Cockney and Yorkshire stock types. His race-thinking is active in Europe, therefore, but aggressive only within the colonies, and on the level of the discussion of world politics where, like many other nineteenth century commentators, he found it convenient to describe international relations in terms of race-relations. The ideology was there, with its political equivalent - the opposition to socialism - and, despite its genteel expression in poems such as 'Sussex', Kipling's race-thinking was very very close to an attitude which would need only external circumstances to transform into aggressive racism.

The racist cult of the soil was a common feature of French right-wing literature both before and after 1914. Ernest Psichari summarized his view of race in a cult of the soil of France. We saw in chapter four that his relationship to nature was intense, and that the simplicity of African landscape offered him a purification of the heart far removed 'from the rottenness of modern civilization'. How much more should the soil of France seem the final purification of the race. Psichari speaks of

> the harmonious countryside in which he seemed once more to take root, feeling his strength being renewed by the millions of ancestral forces which still lived in the soil, by these pleasant streams which shared their secrets with him.

The soil of France adds its voice to the scene, all too messianically:

> 'I am your native soil, full of youth and hope. Cease complaining. I am coming to you and you will know me. I am Strength and Virtue. Believe in me.'(33)

Albeit at a different level, Kipling's poems and stories had made much the same point. It is perhaps only the expression which make us unhesitatingly identify Psichari's text as the very essence of racist nationalism, and it is worth remembering that, in the years preceding 1914, France was suffering from precisely that shock which, we suggested, might push Kipling into explicit racism.

It is hardly surprising that Hans Grimm should embrace a similarly parochial cult of the German countryside and peasantry. Like Kipling, he self-consciously struck his roots into a rural community, demonstrating his conviction that writers depended for their literary inspiration on 'a proper relationship to their native soil': an honour which, as Julian Benda remarked, 'they shared with the slugs and grasshoppers'(34). No less important was his feeling that the intensity of life which he had discovered in Africa, the closeness to what was most real in himself and in the world, could be sustained in the simple life of the German countryside. He was, as he said,

> once more, as in Africa, brought tangibly close to the

realities of life: this time they were the realities of German life, and the spirits of my ancestors' home were constantly around me.(35)

It was while Grimm was installed in his country home, working at the novel Volk ohne Raum, that the Nazi party first began to make headway in Germany, and in due course drew him into its orbit. We have tried to show how typical Grimm was of many of the aspirations and attitudes of the colonial mind, in the hope that his entanglement in totalitarianism might illustrate the potential attitudes of other colonial writers, more fortunate than Grimm in that they lived in countries preserved from the particular manifestations of organised Fascism.

There was, after all, little reason why Kipling should have become directly involved in any of the minor political movements of the extreme right in England, even if his ideas were often very close to theirs. His hatred for Germany prevented his being attracted to those movements apeing German models. Although Moseley, like Kipling, was a characteristic figure of the radical right(36), his East End antisemitism would have been abhorrent to Kipling, and in any case the relative social stability of the1920s and 1930s made it unthinkable that Kipling would betray his class in political action as he had betrayed it in words at the turn of the century and take openly to populist radicalism. Nevertheless, he remained close to the radical right position which was first clearly defined during New Imperialism.

The situation of the French writers was different in this respect. Many of them were close to the militant right-wing organizations in France, and many of their attitudes were expressed in terms identical to the tenets of National Socialism: one thinks, for instance, of Leblond's attack on the 'semitic' elements in Marxism and his conjuration of 'a French socialism which will rise up en masse against the anti-Latin religion of Marxism'.(37) Yet Louis Bertrand was one of the few to cross the barrier of Franco-German hostility and openly praise Hitler's Germany(38) (admiration for Mussolini's Italy was more widespread), and, although one could collect evidence of colonial writers' collaboration with the Germans under Vichy and find more echoes of their ideas in Pétain's programme(39), there is little chance to assess their real potential as supporters of totalitarianism in Europe.

We examine Grimm's experience the more eagerly, therefore, for the light which it may shed on the imponderable 'if only' which lies behind British history, both public and individual, in the 1930s.

It was above all the democratic nature of the Nazi party which impressed Grimm, as he attended its meetings and met its leaders during the early 1930s. He felt that Hitler and Goebbels were shaping a truly classless society on the basis of race, and that the Party was proving able to educate the middle-classes (shaken by inflation and the spectre of revolution) into an 'aristocratic' outlook. He was impressed by Hitler's 'constant insistence on the need to cultivate the German personality, and on the dangers of the values of personality being swamped by the masses'(40). Those reactions clearly had their origin in colonial experience, and when Grimm went on to call Hitler's movement 'the only authentically democratic movement of the German nation' it was clear that the words could have only a colonial sense. (In 1935 Bertrand was to say that the spirit of Hitler's Germany was 'democratic', in both foreign and domestic policy.(41)) Another telling legacy from colonial days was his emphasis on Hitler's determination to preserve private property and to control the working classes. Grimm's only worry about the Nazi movement was that it might actually take seriously the socialist-sounding policies in its programme, and thus the one act of violence which might have opened his eyes to the Party's real nature (the Roehm Putsch of 1934) actually reassured him.

Grimm's reactions to Hitler make it clear that the important legacy of his colonial days was class- and race-thinking rather than any kind of imperialism. This can be seen in Grimm's attitude to Nazi foreign policy. Grimm, always campaigning for a restoration of Germany's colonies by tearing up the Treaty of Versailles, was bitterly disappointed that Hitler had no interest whatsoever in colonial expansion. He treated Grimm's suggestions for colonial activity with open contempt, and regarded his serious-minded views on a racially correct foreign policy as an embarrassment.(42) He remarked that the best thing about Grimm's novel on colonial living-space was its title, which he used in propaganda for expansion in the East. Yet, as a colonial, Grimm saw no reason to alter his support for Hitler merely because he totally rejected all ideas of colonial expansion. What did matter to Grimm was the experience of a classless society which defended the middle-classes under the banner of race.

Grimm's colonial experience prepared him well for life in the Third Reich. He liked the sense of order and organization which prevailed in Germany, the sense, too, of moral regeneration through discipline and action. Persecution took place at a convenient distance, and when he encountered violence towards individuals he protested against it, not because he disagreed with Hitler's view that the Jews were a threat to Germany but because it was 'unnecessary' that Jews should be ill-treated in public. In just the same way he and other colonial writers had looked down contemptuously on the inexperienced settlers who ill-treated the 'Natives' rather than using the less obvious forms of dominance. In almost every way, and certainly in the respectable good conscience of the oppressor, Grimm's colonial days had equipped him for life under Hitler.

We began by suggesting that the victims of imperial rule would not speak loudly through the pages of this book. Colonial fiction would not hear their voice. It does not seem appropriate to follow any further that machinery of still more ruthless oppression in which so many colonials themselves were caught.

Colonial theory and domestic practice

1. Quoted in B.Parry, Delusions and Discoveries (Allen Lane, 1972), p.131.
2. H.Grimm, Volk ohne Raum (Munich, 1926), vol.2, p.603.
3. P.Mille, Louise et Barnavaux (Paris, 1912), pp.138/39, 143.
4. P.Mille, Barnavaux et quelques femmes (Paris, 1908), pp.49/50.
5. M.A.Leblond,'Le prolétariat français aux colonies' in H.Béranger (ed.), Les Prolétaires Intellectuels en France (Paris, 1901), pp.275/335.
6. H.Le Roux, Nos filles - qu'en ferons-nous? (Paris, 1898) pp.1,211.
7. C.Carrington, R.Kipling (Penguin Books, 1970). pp. 374f, 321.
8. G.D.H.Cole & R.Postgate, The Common People (Methuen, 1971), p.411.
9. Both reprinted in R.Kipling, Short stories, vol. 1 (Penguin Books, 1971).
10. Carrington, pp.433,386,445.
11. Two blatant examples of the disregard for nationalism: J.Boissière, Fumeurs d'Opium (Paris, 1896), pp.228,300 & H. Grimm, Der Gang durch den Sand (Munich, 1923), pp.9/32.
12. E.Psichari, L'Appel des Armes (Paris, 1912), p.101. The earlier quotations on pp. 29,107.
13. M.A.Leblond, En France (Paris, 1910), pp.383/84.
14. Cf. R.F.Horton, National ideals and race regeneration (Cassell, 1912); Havelock Ellis, The problem of race-regeneration (Cassels, 1911), etc. A review of Haggard's ideas in The Times praised him for counteracting the 'tendency to race-ruin' (quoted in H.R.Haggard, The Poor and the Land, Longmans, 1905, p. 145f).
15. F.Fabri, Die Wohnungsnoth der Arbeiter in Fabrik-städten (Eberfeld, 1862), pp.59/60.
16. F.Fabri, Bedarf Deutschland der Kolonien? (Gotha,1879) p.85. Cf. als Renan's remarks to the same effect, quoted by R. Maunier, The sociology of colonies, vol. 1 (Routledge & Kegan Paul, 1949), p.162.
17. W.Hübbe-Schleiden, Deutsche Colonisation (Hamburg, 1881), p.21 etc.
18. G.Bolle, Unsere Kolonien (Berlin, 1890), p.6.
19. Maunier, p.371.
20. Ibid., p.225f.
21. M.A.Leblond,'L'esprit algérien' in Revue Bleue, 4th series vol. 19 (1905), p.508.
22. L.Bertrand, Le sang des races (Paris, 1899), pp.245/80.
23. K.T.Eheberg,'Die deutsche Auswanderung' in W.Frommel & F.Pfaff (ed.s),Sammlung von Vorträgen, vol.14 (Heidelberg, 1885), p.178. The quotation is from Roscher.
24. A.Perrin , The Anglo-Indians (Methuen, 1912), pp. 282, 148/49.

25. M.Cohen (ed.), R.Kipling to R.Haggard (Hutchinson, 1965), p.30f. See also Carrington, pp.184,187.
26. P.J.Keating, The working-classes in Victorian fiction (Routledge & Kegan Paul, 1971), p.150f. H.E.Bates, however, calls Kipling's working-class characters 'as real as a ventriloquist's doll' (The Modern Short Story, Nelson, 1941, p.115).
27. Cohen, p.43.
28. H.R.Haggard, introduction to T.Adams, The Garden City and Agriculture (Garden City Press, 1904), p.9.
29. H.R.Haggard, The Poor and the Land (Longmans, 1905), pp.29,xxix,xxii. See also H.R.Haggard, The After-War Settlement and Employment of Ex.Servicemen in the Overseas Dominions (Royal Colonial Institutde, 1916), p.8.
30. Quoted by P.B.Ellis, H.Rider Haggard (Routledge & Kegan Paul, 1979), p.148f.
31. E.Salmon's official history distinguishes Kipling absolutely from 'the support of little Englandism and kindred parochialisms' (The Literature of the Empire, Collins, 1924, p.159).
32. R.Escarpit argues convincingly that Kipling subscribed to specific race-theories (R.Kipling, Servitudes et Grandeurs Impériales, (Paris, 1955), pp.79/84).
33. E.Psichari, L'Appel des Armes (Paris, 1912), pp.83.101.
34. J.Benda, The great betrayal, translated R.Aldington (Routledge & Kegan Paul, 1928), p.48 (quoting Antisthenes).
35. H.Grimm, Der Schriftsteller und die Zeit (Munich, 1931) p.15.
36. Cf. J.R.Jones,'England' in H.Rogger and E.Weber (ed.s), The European Right (Berkeley, 1974), p.65. Jones also discusses the influence of the radical right in England on army reform and state intervention. Also cf. A.Wilson, The strange ride of R.Kipling (Granada, 1979),pp. 289, 319/21. These approaches are more promising than any simple identification of political tendeny and voting pattern.
37. M.A.Leblond, La France devant l'Europe (Paris, 1913), p.63.
38. L.Bertrand, Hitler (Paris, 1936); L'Internationale - Ennemie des Nations (Zurich, 1936); L'Afrique Latine (Rome, 1938).
39. See Rogger & Weber, pp.108, 113 etc.
40. H.Grimm, Von der bürgerlichen Ehre (Munich, 1932), passim, esp. p.15.
41. L.Bertrand, Hitler, pp. 55,84.
42. See for instance the efforts Grimm made to develop his own contacts with the British government in the late 1930s, trying to outflank Ribbentrop's Embassy. Cf. H.Grimm, Englische Rede (Gütersloh, 1938).

BIBLIOGRAPHIES

This is not a complete bibliography of all the
colonial fiction written in England, France and
Germany before 1914 and of its attendant secondary
literature. Such a list would be longer than the
book itself, and I have therefore confined this
bibliography to those works found directly relevant
to my theme and (in the case of primary texts)
directly referred to in the chapters and their
notes. The works are listed according to the
separate countries, except for the first two chapter
chapters, in which the differentiation is between
primary and secondary material.

The organisation of the bibliography is therefore as follows:

1   Works relating to <u>Robinson Crusoe</u> and its
    successors
2   Exotic literature as a precursor of
    colonial literature:
        Primary literature
        Secondary literature
3   The adventure story as a precursor of
    colonial literature:
        Primary literature
        Secondary literature
4   America in the mirror of European fiction
        Primary literature
        Secondary literature
5   Colonial literature
        Secondary literature:England
        Primary literature: England
        Secondary literature: France
        Primary literature: France
        Secondary literature: Germany
        Primary literature: Germany
6   Works discussing the general and
    historical background to New Imperialism

Where a later edition of a work has been consulted,
the date of the original publication has been added
in brackets.

The only translations of French and German
colonial fiction into English which I can trace are
as follows:

P.Mille, <u>Under the tricolour</u>, tr. B.Drillien
(John Lane,1915) (=<u>Barnavaux et quelques femmes</u>)

P.Mille, <u>Louise and Barnavaux</u>, tr. B.Drillen
(John Lane,1916).

G.Frenssen, <u>Peter Moor's Journey to South-West</u>
(Constable, 1908)

162

SHORT BIOGRAPHIES OF LEADING COLONIAL WRITERS

ENGLAND

ARNOLD,WILLAM DELAFIELD. 1828-1859. Younger son of Arnold of Rugby. Went as ensign to India. Asst.Commissioner of Punjab and director of public instruction in 1856. One work.

CANDLER,EDMUND. 1874-1926.Went to India 1896. Teacher and traveller; Many works.

DIVER,MAUD. 1867-1945. Born into a military family in India. Married a subaltern, subsequent Lt.Col. in Indian Army. Settled in England 1896. *(I must stress my debt to B.Parry's work for certain of the biographical details on this page.Her work contains much greater detail on the Anglo-Indian novelists.)*

HAGGARD, HENRY RIDER. 1856-1925.In many ways an exotic rather than strictly colonial writer, his experience in the Transvaal 1876/77 and in South Africa 1881/82 tended his works into colonial attitudes. Returned to England in 1881.

HENTY, GOERGE ALBERT. 1857-1909. Miliary service in the Crimea, journalist to Abyssinia 1867, to Ashanti 1873, to India 1875. Prolific writer.

KIPLING, RUDYARD. 1865-1936. Journalist, initially in India, 1882/89. Returned to London 1889, then travel and fame.

MAUGHAM,WILLIAM SOMERSET. 1874-1965. Celebrated novelist and short-story writer. Visits to the Far East after 1916,but no record of African travel before The Explorer.

PERRIN,ALICE. 1867-1934. Born into Anglo-Indian military family, married into a family associated with Indian Public Works.

TREVELYAN, GEORGE OTTO. 1838-1928. Worked with father, C.E.Trevelyan, in India, being influenced by new liberal movement of the 1960s. Member of the Governor General's Council in 1863.

FRANCE

BERTRAND, LOUIS. 1866-1941. Trained as a teacher, and sent to Algeria in 1891 as a punishment for praising the works of Zola. Elected to Académie française in 1925.

BOISSIÈRE,JULES. 1863-1897. Vice-Resident of France in Tonkin and Annam, returned to France in 1891 between postings.

DAGUERCHES,HENRI (=Charles Valat). No dates. Worked in French administration in Indo-China for the majority of his life, writing many non-fiction works on the area.

EBERHARDT,ISABELLE. 1877-1904. Lived in Algeria, married to a Mohammedan, whose faith she had adopted. Killed in an earthquake.

FARRERE,CLAUDE. 1876-1957. Naval officer and author of numerous mil i tary and naval works. Awarded Prix Goncourt in 1905 for Les Civilisés.

FRESCALY, M. No dates. Pseudonym of Justin-Marcel Palat, officer of the Spahis, i.e. the colonial troops in North Africa.

LEBLOND,MARIUS-ARY (=Georges Athénas (1877-1953) and Aimé Merlo (1880- ?)). Both born in La Réunion, working after 1900 in Paris as political and literary journalists and writers. Awarded the Prix Goncourt in 1909.

LE ROUX, HUGUES.1860-1925. Popular and voluminous novelist. No details of overseas experience.

LOTI,PIERRE (=Julien Viaud).1850-1923. Celebrated novelist. Member of the Académie française in 1892. Author of numerous works of travel and exotic adventure. Cf. C.Wake, The novels of P.Loti (The H ague,1976).

MILLE, PIERRE.1864-1941. Legal training, worked as journalist in France,1894/97 in Madagascar, subsequently in the Far East. Chief colonial correspondent of Le Temps. President of the association of colonial writers. Translator of Kipling. Awarded Prix Lasserre in 1916, Prix Flaubert 1923. Cf.W.J. Everts, The Life and Works of P.Mille (Columbia U.P.,1938).

POUVOURVILLE,ALBERT de. ?-?. Highly placed colonial civil servant in the French administration in Tonkin. Author of numerous works on French Cochin-China, some under the pseudonym Mat Gioi. Acquaintance of Maurice Barrès.

PSICHARI, ERNEST. 1883-1914. Grandson of Renan. Served in the Colonial artillery in French Congo in 1903, and in Mauretania in 1908. Killed in the First World War.

VIGNÉ D'OCTON,PAUL. 1859-1943. Naturalist novelist. No details on life.

VILLEMAGNE, ALIX de. No details. Hors de sa race her only novel. Pouvourville supported this work and thus established its limited validity in the genre.

164

BÜLOW, FRIEDA von. 1857-1909. Born into a Mecklenburg aristocratic family. Went to East Africa as a nurse in 1887 and took over the running of her brother's estates there after his death. Returned to Berlin in 1895. Novels and short stories appeared from 1891 onwards.

FRENSSEN, GUSTAV. 1863-1945. A well-regarded author of realistic peasant novels, notably <u>Jörn Uhl</u> (1901). Soergel refers to <u>Peter Moors Fahrt</u> as his 'most sympathetic work' but many would regard this as a harsh judgement on the others.

GRIMM, HANS. 1875-1960. Prolific and, in his day, widely read author. Best known for <u>Volk ohne Raum</u> (1926), and briefly after the war for a number of works which read like attempted justifications of the Third Reich, in its aspirations if not its achievements. Cf.I.C.Knopf,<u>The English Background to the works of Hans Grimm</u>, Diss. M.A. London, 1938).

PUTTKAMER, JESCO von. 1858-1916. Journalist, based in Berlin.

The obscurity of the other German novelists has proved too profound to be cracked. This is a practical consequence of the especially rapid shift of taste and political judgement in German literary historical writing, especially on this type of theme.

1 Works relating to 'Robinson Crusoe' and its successors

Primary literature

J.H.Campe, Robinson, der Jüngere in Sämmtliche Kinder-
und Jugendschriften, Braunschweig, 1981 (1795)
D.Defoe, Robinson Crusoe, Penguin Books, 1970 (1715)
F.Marryat, Masterman Ready, or the Wreck of the Pacific,
Macmillan, 1897 (1841)
J. Schnabel, Die Insel Felsenburg oder wunderliche Fata
einiger Seefahrer, introduced by L.Tieck, Breslau, 1828
(1731-43)
J.C.Wezel, Robinson Krusoe, Neu Bearbeitet, Leipzig,1779
J.D.Wyss, The Swiss Family Robinson: or adventure of a
shipwrecked family on a desolate island, Nelson n.d.(1841)

Secondary literature

F.Brüggemann, Utopie und Robinsonade.Untersuchungen zu
Schnabels 'Insel Felsenburg', Weimar, 1914
P.B.Gore, The Imaginary Voyage in Prose Fiction, Holland
Press, 1961 (1941)
A.Kippenberg, Robinson in Deutschland bis zur 'Insel
Felsenburg', Hannover, 1892
E.Liebs, Die pädagogische Insel. Studien zur Rezeption
des 'Robinson Crusoe' in deutschen Jugendbearbeitungen,
Stuttgart, 1977
O.Mannoni, Prospero and Caliban. The psychology of col-
onisation, transl. Pamela Powesland, New York, 1964
I.Watt, 'Robinson Crusoe: Individualism and the Novel'
in The Rise of the Novel, Chatto & Windus, 1957

2 Exotic literature as a precursor of colonial literature

Primary literature

J.H. Bernardin de Saint-Pierre, Paul et Virginie, Paris,
1964 (1786)
F.-R. de Chateaubriand, Atala (1801) & René (1802) in
Oeuvres Romanesques et Voyages, Paris, 1969
G.Flaubert, Oeuvres complètes, vol.12,Paris,1974
Th.Gautier, La Préface de Madame de Maupin,Paris,1946
(1836)
F.Gerstäcker, Die Missionare, rev. ed.,Berlin,1908(1868
F.Gerstäcker, Tahiti. Roman aus der Südsee, Jena,n.d.
(1854)
(P.Loti (=LMJ. Viaud) Aziyadé, Paris, 1879
P.Loti, Lettres à Mme Juliette Adam, Paris,1924
P.Loti, Madame Chrysanthème, Paris, 1887

C.Sealsfield (=K.Postl), Morton oder die große Tour
Stuttgart, 1846 (1835)
R.L.Stevenson, In the South Seas. Being an account of
Experiences in the Marquesas, Panmotus, & Gilbert Islands,
Chatto & Windus, 1900

Secondary literature

F.Brie, 'Exotismus der Sinne. Eine Studie zur Psychologie
der Romantik' in: Sitzungsberichte der Heidelberger Aka-
demie der Wissenschaften, 1920, Abhandlung 3.
G.Chinard, L'Amérique et le rêve exotique dans la litt-
érature française au xviie et au xviiie siècle,Paris,1934
Eva B.Dykes, The Negro in English Romantic Thought,
Washington, 1942
P.B.Ellis, H.Rider Haggard. A voice from the infinite,
Routledge & Kegan Paul, 1978
H.N.Fairchild, The Noble Savage. A study in Romantic
Naturalism, New York, 1955 (1928)
P.Jourdha, L'Exotisme dans la littérature française depuis
Chateaubriand, vol.1 Paris 1938, vol.2 Paris 1956
M.G.Lerner, Pierre Loti, New York, 1974
A.Maler, Der exotische Roman. Bürgerliche Gesellschafts-
flucht und Gesellschaftskritik zwischen Romantik und
Realismus, Stuttgart, 1975
M.Praz, The Romantic Agony, rev. ed. OUP, 1970
G.Schaeffer, Le voyage en Orient de Nerval. Etude de
structure, Neuchatel, 1967
I.Schuster, China und Japan in der deutschen Literatur
1880-1925, Bern, 1977
C.Wake, The novels of Pierre Loti, The Hague, 1976

3 The adventure story as a precursor of colonial
literature

Primary literature

G.Aimard, L'Araucan, Paris, 1864
G.Aimard, Curumilla, Paris, 1860
G.Aimard, The Trail Hunter, Ward & Lock, 1861
K.May, Der Pfahlmann. Ein Abenteuer aus dem wilden Westen,
Vienna & Berlin, n.d.
K.May, Winnetou: Reiseerzählung, 244-265 Thousand,
Radebeul, 1932 (1892)
E.J.Trelawny, Adventures of a Younger Son, ed. W.St.Clair,
OUP, 1974
J.Verne, Around the World in 80 Days, Sampson Low, 1873
J.Verne, Aventures de trois Russes et trois Anglais
dans l'Afrique australe, Paris, n.d. (1871)
J.Verne, Nord contre Sud, Paris, 1887

Secondary literature

E.Bloch, Erbschaft dieser Zeit, Frankfurt/Main, 1977
(1935), esp. pp.168/86 'Über Märchen, Kolportage und
Sage'.
J.Chesneaux, Une lecture politique de Jules Verne,
Paris, 1971
Amy Cruse, The Victorians and their Books, Allen & Unwin,
1935
Margaret Dalziel, Popular Fiction 100 Years Ago. An
unexplored tract of literary history, Cohen & West, 1957
M.Green, Dreams of Adventure, Deeds of Empire, Routledge
& Kegan Paul, 1980
L.James, Fiction for the Working Man 1830-1850, rev. ed.
Penguin Books, 1973
V.Klotz, Abenteuer-Romane. Sue - Dumas - Ferry -
Ratcliffe - May - Verne, Munich, 1979
H.Plischke, Von Cooper bis Karl May. Eine Geschichte des
völkerkundlichen Reise- und Abenteuerromans, Düsseldorf,
1951
A.P.Thornton, For the File on Empire. Essays and Reviews,
Macmillan, 1968
G.Ueding, Glanzvolles Elend: Versuch über Kitsch und
Kolportage, Frankfurt/Main, 1973
H.Wollschläger, Karl May in Selbstzeugnissen und Bild-
dokumenten, Reinbek, 1965

4 America in the mirror of European fiction

Primary literature

Atlantische Studien. Von Deutschen in Amerika, Göttingen,
1848
H.Börnstein, Die Geheimnisse von Saint Louis, Cassel,1851
P.Chasles,'Les Américains en Europe et les Européens
aux Etats Unis', Revue des deux mondes, N.S. vol. 1
(Feb. 1843), pp.446/76.
S.P.Hyatt, The little brown brother, London, 1911(1908)
J.Fröbel, Die deutsche Auswanderung und ihre culturhisto-
rische Bedeutung. 15 Briefe an den Herausgeber der 'All-
gemeine Auswanderungs-Zeitung', Leipzig, 1858
F.Gerstäcker, Achtzehn Monate in Süd-Amerika und dessen
deutschen Colonien, Leipzig, 1863
F.Gerstäcker, Der deutschen Auswanderer Fahrten und
Schicksale, Leipzig, 1847
F.Kapp, Über Auswanderung (Speech), Berlin, 1871
F.Kürnberger, Der Amerika-Müde. Amerikanisches
Kulturbild, Frankfurt/Main, 1855
F.Münch, Die Zukunft von Nordamerika. Blicke aus der
neuen Welt in die alte, Bremen, 1860

J.H. St. John Crèvecoeur, Letters from an American Farmer,
Chatto & Windus, 1908 (1782)
L. Schefer, Die Probefahrt nach Amerika, Bunzlau, 1837
C.Sealsfield (=Karl Postl), Das Kajütenbuch oder Nationale
Charakteristiken, Munich, 1963 (1841) (cf. recent edition
ed. Alexander Ritter, Stuttgart, 1982)
C.Sealsfield, Süden und Norden, Stuttgart, 1842
R.Solger, Anton in Amerika. Seitenstück zu Freytags 'Soll
und Haben' aus dem deutsch-amerikanischen Leben,Berlin 1862
G.Struve, Kurzgefaßter Wegweiser für Auswanderer mit be-
sonderer Rücksicht auf NORDAMERIKA, die britischen Colonien,
Mexiko, die südamerikanischen Republiken, Brasilien und
Australien, Bamberg, 1867
E.Sue, Atar-Gull, Paris, 1845

Secondary literature

S.Bauschinger, H.Denkler & W.Malsch, Amerika in der
deutschen Literatur. Neue Welt - Nordamerika - USA,
Stuttgart, 1975
H.Blumenthal, American and French Culture, 1800-1900.,
Interchanges in Art, Science, Literature and Society,
Baton Rouge, 1976
E.C.D.Crossley,'Quelques aspects de l'Américanisme
romantique', Nineteenth Century French Studies, vol.6 no.
1 & 2 (1977/78), pp.446-76.
M.Djordjewitsch, Charles Sealsfields Auffassung des
Amerikanertums und seine literaturhistorische Stellung,
Weimar, 1931
E.W.Dobert, Deutsche Demokraten in Amerika. Die Achtund-
vierziger und ihre Schriften, Göttingen, 1958
D.Echeverria, Mirage in the West. A History of the French
Image of American Society to 1815, Princeton, 1968
A.B.Faust,'Charles Sealsfield's place in literature'
Americana Germanica, vol.1 (New York, 1897),pp.1-18.
L.A.Fiedler, The Return of the Vanishing American,
Palladin, 1972
M.Green, A Mirror for Anglo-Saxons, Longmans, 1961
T.M.Hammond, American Paradise. German travel literature
from Duden to Kisch, Heidelberg, 1980 (Not consulted for
this study)
J.T.Hatfield & E.Hochbaum,'The influence of the American
Revolution upon German literature', Americana Germanica,
vol.3 (New York, 1899), pp.338-85.
C.Hentschel,'Campe and the discovery of America', German
Life & Letters, vol. 26 (Oct.1972), pp.1-13.
H.Jantz,'Amerika im deutschen Dichten u.Denken' in Stammler
W. (ed.) Deutsche Philologie im Aufriß,vol.3,Berlin, 1962
W.F.Kamman, Socialism in German-American Literature,
Philadelphia, 1917

A.N.Kaul, The American Vision. Actual and Ideal Society in Nineteenth Century Fiction, Yale U.P., 1963

D.H.Lawrence, Studies in Classic American Literature, Penguin Books,1971 (1924)

E.Lucas, La littérature anti-esclaviste au 19e siècle.Etude sur Mme Beecher-Stowe et son influence en France,Paris,1930

G.E.Maclean, 'Uncle Tom's Cabin' in Germany, Pennsylvania U.P., 1910

F.Monaghan, French travellers in the United States, New York, 1933

G.A.Mulfinger,'Lenau in Amerika' in Americana Germanica, vol.2 (New York, 1898), pp.7/61.

H.Mumford Jones, O strange new world. American culture: the formative years, New York, 1965 (1952)

A.Nevins (ed.), America through British eyes, OUP,1948

R.L.Rapson, Britons view America. Travel commentary, 1860-1935, University of Washington P., 1971

R.Slotkin, Regeneration through violence, Middletown, 1973

H.Zimpel, Karl Postls Romane im Rahmen ihrer Zeit, Frankfurt a. Main, 1941

5 Colonial fiction

ENGLAND: Secondary literature

C.A.Bodelsen, Studies in mid-Victorian Imperialism, Copenhagen, 1960 (1924)

F.Brie, Imperialistische Strömungen in der englischen Literatur, Halle, 1916

P.D.Curtin, The Image of Africa. British Ideas and Action 1780-1850, Macmillan, 1965

D.C.R.A. Goonetilleke, Developing countries in British fiction, Macmillan, 1977

A.J.Greenberger, The British Image of India. A study in the literature of imperialism 1880-1960, OUP, 1969

A.Haslam (ed.), Anthology of Empire, Grayson & Grayson,1932

W.Hill, The overseas empire in fiction. An annotated bibliography, OUP, 1930

S.Howe, Novels of Empire, New York, 1949

G.D.Killam, Africa in English Fiction 1874-1939, Ibadan UP, 1968

J.Meyers, Fiction and the colonial experience, Boydell Press 1973

B.Parry, Delusions and Discoveries. Studies on India in the British Imagination 1880-1930, Allen Lane, 1972

E.Salmon, The literature of the Empire, Collins, 1924

A.Sandison, The Wheel of Empire. A study of the Imperial Idea in some late 19th and early 20th century fiction, Macmillan, 1967

Bhūpāl Singh,A survey of Anglo-Indian fiction, OUP, 1934

B.V.Street, The Savage in Literature. Representations of 'primitive' society in English fiction 1858-1920, Routledge & Kegan Paul, 1975

ENGLAND:Primary literature consulted

E.Candler, The general plan, Blackwood, 1911
H.Cunningham, Chronicles of Dustypoore. A tale of modern Anglo-Indian society, Smith, Elder & Co, 1875
Maud Diver, Desmond's Daughter, Blackwood, 1916
Maud Diver, The Hero of Herat. A frontier biography in Romantic form, Constable, 1912
Maud Diver, Lilamani - A study in possibilities, Hutchinson, 1911
H.Rider Haggard, The After-War Settlement and Employment of Ex-Servicemen in the Overseas Dominions, Royal Colonial Institute, 1916
H.Rider Haggard,Black Heart and White Heart and other stories, Longmans, 1900
H.Rider Haggard, 'Introductory Address' in T.Adams, The Garden City and Agriculture. How to solve the problems of rural depopulation, Garden City Press, 1904
H.Rider Haggard, Nada the Lily, Longmans, 1892
H.Rider Haggard, The Poor and the Land. Being a report on the Salvation Army Colonies in the United States and at Hadleigh, England, Longmans, 1905
H.Rider Haggard, Works in one volume,New York, 1928
G.A.Henty, The Dash for Khartoum: a tale of the Nile Expedition, Blackie, 1892
C.J.Cutcliffe Hyne, Atoms of Empire, Methuen, 1923
R.Kipling, Complete Works (Uniform Edition),Macmillan,1899f
W.S.Maugham, The Explorer, Heinemann, 1908
Alice Perrin, The Anglo-Indians, Methuen, 1912
Alice Perrin, The Spell of the Jungle, A.Treherne & Co,1902
Punjabee (=W.D.Arnold), Oakfield, or Fellowship in the East, Longman,Brown,Green and Longmans, 1854
Flora A.Steel, On the Face of the Waters, Nelson,1907 (1896)
Flora A.Steel, From the five rivers, Heinemann, 1893
G.O.Trevelyan, The Competition Wallah, Macmillan, 1864
W.Westrupp, The Land of Tomorrow, Alston Rivers Ltd.,1912
J.M.S.Young, Merely a Negress. A West African Story,J.Long, 1904
J.M.S. Young, Passion's Peril: A romance, Hermes Press, 1906

FRANCE: Secondary literature

H.Brunschwig, French Colonialism 1871-1914. Myths and Realities, transl. W.G.Brown, Pall Mall Press, 1964
L.Fanoudh-Siefer, Le mythe du nègre et de l'Afrique noire dans la littérature française (de 1800 à la guerre mondiale), Paris, 1968

A.R.Lebel, L'Afrique occidentale dans la littérature française, Paris, 1925

A.R.Lebel, Les établissements français d'outre-mer et leur reflet dans la littérature, Paris, 1952

A.R.Lebel, Histoire de la littérature coloniale en France, Paris, 1931

Martine A.Loutfi, Littérature et Colonialisme. L'expansion coloniale vue dans la littérature romanesque française 1871-1914, The Hague & Paris, 1971

Agnes Murphy, The ideology of French Imperialism 1871-1881, Washington, 1948

E.Pujarniscle, Philoxène, ou de la littérature coloniale, Paris, 1931

FRANCE: Primary literature consulted

L.Bertrand, D'Alger la romantique à Fez la mystérieuse, Paris, 1930

L.Bertrand, Le sang des races, Paris, 1899

J.Boissière, Fumeurs d'Opium, Paris, 1896

H.Daguerches, Le Kilomètre 83, Paris, 1913

M.Delafosse, Les états d'âme d'un colonial, Paris, 1909

I.Eberhardt, Pages d'Islam, ed. V.Barrucand, Paris,1920

C.Farrère, Les Civilisés, Paris, 1905

C.Farrère, La Bataille, Paris, 1921

C.Farrère, Les hommes nouveaux, Paris, 1922

M.Frescaly, Mariage d'Afrique, Paris, 1886

E.Fromentin, Sahara et Sahel, Paris, 1879

M.A.Leblond (= Georges Athénas & Aimé Merlo)

M.A.Leblond,En France, Paris, 1910

M.A.Leblond,La France devant l'Europe, Paris, 1913

M.A.Leblond,L'Idéal du xixe siècle, Paris, 1909

M.A.Leblond,Le miracle de la race, Paris, 1914

M.A.Leblond,Les Sortilèges, Paris,1905

H.Le Roux, Nos filles - Qu'en ferons-nous?, Paris, 1895

H.Le Roux, Je deviens colon. Moeurs algériens, Paris, 1895

P.Loti, Le roman d'un spahi, 3rd ed. Paris, 1881

P.Mille, Barnavaux et quelques femmes, Paris, 1908

P.Mille, Louise et Barnavaux, Paris, 1912

P.Mille, L'Illustre Partonneau, Paris, 1924

P.Mille, Sur la vaste terre, Paris, 1905

P.Mille, La femme et l'homme nu, Paris, 1924 (with André Demaison)

A. de Pouvoirville, L'Annam sanglant, Paris, 1912 (1890)

A. de Pouvoirville, Deux années de lutte, 1890-91, Paris, 1892 (Pseudonym: Mat Gioi)

E.Psichari, L'Appel des Armes, Paris, 1912

E.Psichari, Terres de Soleil et de Sommeil, 2nd ed. Paris, 1908

R.Randau, Les algérianistes. Roman de la patrie algérienne, 3rd ed. Paris, 1911

R.Randau, Les Explorateurs. Roman de la Grande Brousse,
Paris, 1909
P.Vigné d'Octon, Fauves Amours, Paris, 1892
P.Vigné d'Octon, Chair noire, Paris, 1889
P.Vigné d'Octon, La gloire du sabre, 3rd ed. Paris, 1900
(1899)
Alix de Villemagne, Hors de sa race, Paris, 1912

GERMANY:Secondary literature

F.Marass, Der deutsche Kolonialroman, Vienna, 1935
G.Patzlaff, Die Kolonien und der Kolonialgedanke in der
erzählenden Literatur, Diss. Greifswald, 1938
E.Sembritzki (ed.), Der Kolonialfreund. Kritischer Führer
durch die volkstümliche deutsche Kolonial-Literatur,
Berlin, 1919
J.Trümpelmann,'Das deutsche schöngeistige Schrifttum über
Südwestafrika', Veröffentlichungen der wissenschaftlichen
Gesellschaft für Südwestafrika, Swakopmund, 1934, pp.101-
152.

GERMANY: Primary literature consulted

G.Bolle, Unsere Kolonie, Berlin, 1890
F. von Bülow, Im Lande der Verheißung. Ein deutscher
Kolonialroman, Berlin, 1892
F. von Bülow, Ludwig von Rosen. Eine Erzählung aus zwei
Welten, Leipzig & Dresden, 1899
F. von Bülow, Tropenkoller. Episode aus dem deutschen
Kolonialleben, Berlin, 1896
J.Dose, Ein alter Afrikaner, Erzählung, Wismar, 1913
K.Dove, Die Kobra, Südafrikanische Erzählung, Berlin,1911
C.Falkenhorst, Jung-Deutschland in Afrika, Dresden, n.d.
G.Frenssen, Peter Moors Fahrt nach Südwest. Ein Feldzugs-
bericht, 239-253 Thousand Berlin, 1936 (1907)
A.Funke, Afrikanischer Lorbeer. Kolonialroman, Berlin,1907
H.Grimm, Der Gang durch den Sand und andere Geschichten
aus Südafrika, Munich, 1923
H.Grimm, Lüderitzland, Sieben Begebenheiten, Munich, 1934
H.Grimm,Südafrikanische Novellen, Frankfrut/Main, 1913
H.Grimm, Der Richter in der Karu, Munich, 1930
H.Grimm, Volk ohne Raum, Munich, 1926
F.Kraze, Heim Neuland. Ein Roman von der Wasserkante und
aus Deutsch-Südwest, Stuttgart & Leipzig, 1909
R.Küas, Vom Baum der Erkenntnis. Deutscher Kolonialroman,
Leipzig, 1911
J.von Puttkamer, Das Duallamädchen, Leipzig, 1908
H.Rohrmann, Kulturfirnis. Koloniales Zeitbild, Leipzig,
1909

6 General background works on New Imperialism

H.Arendt, The origins of totalitarianism, rev. ed. Allen
& Unwin, 1967

D.Bald, Deutsch-Ostafrika, 1900-1914, Munich, 1970

K.Ballhatchet, Race, Sex and Class under the Raj. Imperial
Attitudes and their critics, 1793-1905, Weidenfeld &
Nicolson, 1980

G.D.Bearce, British attitudes towards India 1784-1858,
OUP, 1961

M.D.Biddiss (ed.), Gobineau: Selected political writings,
Jonathan Cape, 1970

H.Bley, South-West Africa under German rule, translated
H.Ridley, Heinemann, 1971

C.A.Bodelsen, Studies in mid-Victorian Imperialism,
Copenhagen, 1960 (1924)

Christine Bolt, Victorian attitudes to Race, Routledge &
Kegan Paul, 1971

H.A.C.Cairns, Prelude to Imperialism. British Reactions to
Central African Society 1840-90, Routledge & Kegan Paul,
1965

P.D.Curtin, The Image of Africa. British Ideas and Action
1780-1850, Macmillans, 1965

H.Drechsler, Südwestafrika unter deutscher Kolonialherrschaft, E.Berlin, 1966

K.T.Eheberg, Die deutsche Auswanderung, Heidelberg, 1885

K.Fabri, Bedarf Deutschland der Kolonien? Eine politisch-
ökonomische Betrachtung, Gotha, 1879

L.H.Gann & P.Duignan,The Rulers of British Africa 1870-1914,
Croom Helm, 1978

L.H.Gann & P.Duignan,The Rulers of German Africa, Stanford,
1977

J.Hammerton, Emigrant Gentlewomen: Genteel Poverty and
Female Emigration, New Jersey, 1979

G.Hardy, Histoire de la colonisation française,Paris,1928

R.Heussler, Yesterday's rulers. The making of the British
Colonial Service, Syracuse, 1963

R.Hyam, Britain's Imperial Century 1815-1914. A study of
Empire and expansion, Batsford, 1976

W.D.Jordan, White over Black. American Attitudes towards
the Negro, 1550-1812, Chapel Hill, 1968

V.G.Kiernan, The Lords of Human Kind. European attitudes
towards the outside world in the Imperial Age, Weidenfeld
& Nicolson, 1969

V.G.Kiernan, Marxism and Imperialism, Edward Arnold, 1974

P.Mason, Prospero's Magic. Some thoughts on class and
race, OUP, 1962

R.Maunier, The sociology of colonies. An introduction to
the study of race-conflict,translated by E.O. Lorimer,
Routledge & Kegan Paul, 1949

A.Memmi, Portrait du colonisé, rev. ed. Quebec, 1972

Jan Morris, Heaven's Command, Penguin Books, 1979

S.Neill, Colonialism and Christian Mission,Lutterworth Press, 1966

P.Rohrbach, Der detusche Gedanke in der Welt, Düsseldorf & Leipzig, 1912

P.van den Berghe , Race and racism. A comparative perspective, New York, 1967

INDEX

'B' indicates that a short biography of the writer is included on pages 163/65.